DATE DUE

'..... there is probably no known machine which is more than a prototype of future mechanical life' (Samuel Butler, 1872)

'When I say therefore that I am willing to regard such a robot as an 'organism', I declare my willingness to consider it a kind of animal.' (Joseph Weizenbaum, 1976)

'There is even a sense in which it can be argued that robots are an evolving life-form' (James S. Albus, 1981)

Contents

Introduction		ix
1	Are computers alive?	1
	Preamble	1
	The nature of life	4
	Machines as emerging life	8
	Life criteria	11
	Machine reproduction	16
	Machine evolution	22
	Machine classification	27
	The place of AI	28
	Cybernetic systems	30
	Summary	32
2	The robot background	33
3	The behaviour of machines	51
	Preamble	51
	Experimental devices	52
	Industrial robots	57
	Medical systems	61
	Artistic activity	66
	Games computers play	75
	Summary	78
4	The anatomy of robots	80
	Preamble	80
	Artificial hands and arms	81
	The walking robot	86

	Sensing the environment	90
	The eyes have it	91
	A touching scene	97
	Hearing and smell	100
	The robot brain	103
5	The psychology of computers	107
	Preamble	107
	Physiology and psychology	109
	Models and simulations	111
	The conscious machine	118
	Some cognitive concerns	123
	Emotions, feelings and morals	143
	Freedom and autonomy	147
	Miscellaneous mental states	152
	Summary	156
6	Computer liberation	158
7	The human response	172
8	The future	188
References		196
Index		207

Introduction

This book has derived from speculation in various fields—biology, psychology, philosophy, robotics and computer science. Its central thesis—that computers and robots, appropriately configured, can be properly regarded as emerging life-forms—is one that has compelling support in theoretical argument and empirical evidence. It is shown that artificial systems can satisfy a range of necessary criteria by which life is recognized; and that, furthermore, developments in such fields as artificial intelligence (AI) and cybernetics indicate the character of the newly emerging living systems.

Chapter 1 explores the central question of *what is life?* Here we see that definitions of living systems are moving away from biochemical towards information-processing interpretations: the most reasonable definitions of life admit the possibility that certain types of artificial systems may be alive. In chapter 2 we find that the emergence of machine life has been prefigured in primitive artefacts and human imagination over the centuries. Chapters 3, 4 and 5 describe the character of the emerging artificial living systems in terms of behaviour, anatomy and psychology. It is shown that machines are not only evolving limbs, senses and brains but also minds—cognitive capacities and a potential for emotion and autonomous action in the real world. In such circumstances, machines will develop a capacity for suffering (and enjoyment), and we will have to look to the question of computer rights (chapter 6): we see that this will involve a careful scrutiny of the relationship between human beings and machines. Chapter 7 outlines various human responses to the modern development of robots and computers: the responses are often confused and ambivalent—people are being forced to acknowledge the growing competence of machines, but human vanity is also at stake.

Many people will not find the idea of computer life a convivial doctrine (others will find it both acceptable and exciting). Where there is reaction against the idea, efforts will often be made to provide counter-arguments: some of these are considered, either directly or by implication, in the present book. Many of these responses are variants on two basic arguments—which we may term 'The Argument from Mimicry' and 'The Argument from Entropy'. It is useful to consider these arguments briefly here.

It is often said that computers and robots are not *really* intelligent (or alive), that they merely *mimic* the behaviour of human beings or other animals—as might a puppet or a clockwork doll. But this is partly a matter of degree: it is arguable that where the mimicry is highly successful, and moreover extends to more than one area of behaviour (for example, goal-directed behaviour plus demonstrable elements of cognition), the behaviour is not simply *mimicked* but *duplicated*. A child learning a new word may first, in attempting to pronounce it, *mimic* a parent; but when the word is used with ease, and in manifest conjunction with the appropriate cognitive mental states, we no longer talk of mimicry. Today it is commonplace for robots to be taught in the industrial environment and we are finding that robot brains (that is, computers) can have cognitive states (see chapter 5). It follows that where computer models and simulations are sufficiently developed they represent a *duplicating*, rather than a *mimicking*, of the behaviour of living creatures: it is difficult, for example, to see how a chess program that consistently beats its creator can be said to be mimicking the behaviour of the human programmer.

The 'Argument from Entropy' has, as popular variants, the claims that 'computers only do what you tell them' and that 'you can't get more out of something than you put into it'. These types of claims suggest that computers can never be truly intelligent, creative, take initiatives, choose freely, etc. But today there is abundant evidence to the contrary (some is given in the present book), and the fallacy in the entropy argument can be shown by considering how it used to be applied to life itself.

It was argued that the Second Law of Thermodynamics

(which suggests that natural processes necessarily produce a greater degree of disorder) was in conflict with biological evolution (which produces more highly ordered systems, that is, living creatures), but the Second Law only applies to a 'closed' system, and within a portion of the system there can be a decrease in local entropy. What this means for our purposes is that just as it has been possible for human beings, evolving from brute matter, to become creative, so it is possible for computers, deriving from human beings, to acquire similarly a range of creative (and other) abilities. Computers do not only do what you tell them: they sometimes do more—you sometimes *can* get more out of something than you put into it.

The arguments against computer life will be frequently rehearsed, until it is clear that they have been outflanked by events. The emergence of computer life has been envisaged for centuries: it is widely anticipated in the works of writers, artists, philosophers and myth-makers. Today we are witnessing the burgeoning reality of an age-old dream.

1 Are computers alive?

Preamble

Computers as friends, advisors, enemies, lovers—this is the stuff of science fiction. In imaginative tales, computers can develop malignant purposes; robots can be unjustly persecuted by humans; animate machines can take a disturbing interest in our affairs; electronic devices of every sort can manifest intelligence, purpose and emotion. We are not surprised when we learn of books and films in which machines behave *as if* they are alive, carrying out tasks which in another context would be instantly recognized as characteristically human. The question now is: *has fact overtaken fiction to the point when computers may be said to be actually alive?* Are we seeing the birth of a new species—or a whole new family of species—in our midst, creatures which do not depend upon the usual metabolic chemistries but which work in other ways, creatures which are artificially generated but which are entitled to be regarded as a type of life?

One consequence of modern technological developments (in particular, the emergence of microelectronics), is that we are being forced to scrutinize many traditional ideas about society and people. To some extent this has always been so: new inventions with radical social implications have always forced a reappraisal of established concepts. But now we are witnessing something that is essentially different in kind, an emergent phenomenon that will have profound consequences for all mankind.

We are deluged with speculation about the impact of 'chip' technology on employment and other areas of social concern. Pundits vie with each other to predict the scale of chip-caused unemployment for this or that country by this or that year. Human rights activists worry about the increased powers of surveillance given to police authorities by microelectronics technology, and there is similar concern about the wisdom and morality of storing vast amounts of 'people data' in computerized systems.

In education the power of the microprocessor is forcing a careful reassessment of the role of the teacher, as it is in medicine and in other areas involving interaction between experts and other people. Debate on national defence policies has intensified, following the development of computer power for missile guidance, early warning systems and global war games. Computerized early-warning systems have provoked alarm because of repeated chip failures (for example, the article 'The Computer that Keeps Declaring War' which appeared in the *Sunday Times* on 22 June 1980). And fresh anxieties about the dangers of computer power were stimulated by the revelation that when President Nixon ordered the bombing of Cambodia, Pentagon computers were fixed to produce false 'secret reports' for senior politicians.

The social impact of technology in general, and computer technology in particular, is colossal. It is no exaggeration to say that modern human society in the developed countries is largely shaped by what technology can deliver in practical and cost-effective terms. And there are levels of impact that must profoundly affect our interpretation of human nature itself. We are being forced by such modern sciences as cybernetics, cognitive psychology and artificial intelligence to scrutinize human mental capabilities with a new rigour. Put simply, computers are forcing us to ask *what it is to be human*.

There are many aspects to this computer pressure on our consciousness. Techniques of computer simulation, for example, are helping to illuminate aspects of human mental activity: it is possible to model the behaviour of brain cells, memory mechanisms, pattern recognition, decision-taking and other mental processes—with the corollary that we are learning to understand how computers are to be structured and programmed in order to acquire 'human' mental attributes. Some observers (for example, Dreyfus, 1972; Weizenbaum, 1976) are deeply sceptical of whether computers could ever, or should ever be allowed, to acquire anything that could be regarded as closely akin to a human mental capability. Dreyfus, for instance, has severely criticized computer simulation for failing to attain levels of equivalence that would signal rudimentary mental attributes. But such criticisms are misplaced: it is inevitable that with current technology computer simulation will be partial and incomplete in important ways. What is truly remarkable is not how computer modelling falls short but how adequately certain well-defined mental processes can be simulated—bearing in mind the relatively brief history of electronic computation. Joseph Weizenbaum, suspicious of the computer impact on human attitudes, has argued that computers should not in any circumstances be used in emotional contexts (see also chapter 7).

We would expect such observers to be hostile to the idea that computers could be regarded as an emergent life-form. It is inevitable that if some types of machines—certain species of computers and robots—are once seen to be *alive*, newly emerging creatures, human self-image and confidence may be deeply affected. In fact most people show a quick reaction to the idea of computer life: the notion is first rejected and then the reasons are sought: all known life is based on hydrocarbons; machines cannot reproduce; computers and robots can only derive their powers from human beings; 'mere' machines cannot be conscious, creative, intelligent, aware; nor can they make judgments, take decisions or experience emotion; computers and robots may mimic certain human activities, but artefacts will never be truly intelligent, and they will certainly never be alive. Such specific arguments—and this is by no means an exhaustive list—bear with differing weights on the question of computer life. For instance, it is not a necessary condition of life that it be creative in an intellectual sense: ferns produce few theorems or symphonies. The particular arguments, and others, are considered in what follows (in particular, in the present chapter and in chapters 3, 4 and 5).

The aversion that most people have to the idea of computer life is also explored (chapter 7), but it can be said at once that this is largely a matter of human vanity. Status and self-image are at stake. Copernicus, Darwin and Freud met bitter opposition—at least in part—because they effectively dethroned mankind from (respectively) the centre of the universe, a zoological pedestal, and conscious autonomy over all human motivation. In a number of ways the emergence of computer life is rightly sensed as continuing this process of dethronement. To acknowledge that machines can represent an emergent life-form entails a definition of life that shows that intelligence, consciousness and purpose can be discerned in certain types of organized structures that do not depend upon hydrocarbon-based metabolisms; and this shows that mankind does not necessarily represent the pinnacle of biological evolution. It is likely that *there are other species to come on Earth, that their progenitors are already working amongst us, and that human beings may or may not find it possible to co-exist with the new life-forms that will appear.*

Before outlining the emergence of machine life and showing how the new life-forms will come progressively to satisfy the necessary 'life criteria', it is useful to explore some definitions of life. What is the essence of life? How is it to be recognized when cloaked in an unusual garb? What are life's necessary and sufficient qualities? How important are substance, structure, subsystems and behaviour?

The nature of life

Some thinkers, daunted by the evident complexity of life, incline to the view that it is inherently indefinable and incomprehensible. This response has been at the heart of the scientific and metaphysical vitalisms associated with the names of such philosophers as Bergson (*élan vital*), Elsässer ('biotonic laws'), and Professor Polanyi. Jacques Monod (1972) has noted that even Nils Bohr appeared sympathetic to the idea that certain *vital principles* may have to be added to the laws of physics to account fully for the phenomenon of life. Nearly half a century ago, N.W. Pirie (1937) argued for the inherent meaninglessness of such terms as 'life' and 'living', suggesting that there were certain questions that it was necessarily impossible to answer. Today there is more confidence that it is possible to approach rational views of life in terms of biochemistry, energy- and information-processing, and structural and evolutionary characteristics.

Traditional definitions of life have tended to focus on biochemistry. Hence, Perret (1952): 'Life is a potentially self-perpetuating open system of linked organic reactions, catalysed stepwise and almost isothermally by complex and specific organic catalysts which are themselves produced by the system.' Such a definition implies a requirement for reproductive capability but says nothing about its character: other definitions have focused on the precise reproduction of molecules, sometimes with specific words added to exclude or include viruses as living systems. In one definition of this sort, J.D. Bernal (1967) chooses to regard something as alive if it contains a self-reproducing molecular system as with the nucleic acids and a protein production mechanism 'in an active form or, preferably, activated by some non-living or living stimulus'. Here the viruses, regarded as living, require a host to provide the energy for their own protein synthesis. Later (p. 168) in the same book, Bernal moves to a definition of life which appears not to depend upon biochemistry (though, in explanation, there is reference to the basic molecules of living substances when he writes that 'life is a partial, continuous, progressive, multiform and conditionally inter-active, self-realisation of the potentialities of atomic electron states.' It is evident that, as phrased, this definition is not limited to particular substances, structures or behaviours. There is subsequent emphasis on the importance of internal and external communication, and of adaptation to the environment. These are manifest, cybernetic features that can equally characterize biological and artificial systems (see the section on cybernetic systems later in this chapter). What is interesting about the definition is that its *generality* implicitly admits the possibility of life-forms that are not based on the familiar hydrocarbon metabolisms. And elsewhere (p. 8) there is an explicit recognition that information handling—now seen as a central concern in all the cognitive sciences—is at the heart of acknowledged life systems: 'Life is essentially, therefore, a matter of the growth and self-complication of the informational aspects of the potentialities of matter.' Chemical evolution yielded a dramatic increase 'in the information and the complexity' with which elements were combined: new spatial and dynamic arrangements allowed the formation of molecules and reproduction of the patterns through new and varied generations. (Increased awareness of how genetic information coding controls the replication of organic molecules has helped us to develop the analogy with how dynamic process control is supervised by computer programs.)

The key point is that living systems can be recognized according to how they process information and energy, how they are structured, how they behave and so on, rather than by the specific chemistries by which they accomplish their tasks. It is possible to identify a range of subsystems that characterize living creatures without any assumption that such subsystems have to rely on the metabolic processes supported by carbon-based macromolecules. A subsystem that allows a creature to extract necessary energy from the environment (that is, one which allows the creature to feed) may deal in organic nutrients, inorganic rust or pure electricity. A system may be said to be 'feeding' when it systematically extracts energy from an appropriate source in order to support its internal life processes and its behaviour in the world. Similarly, a living creature can, in principle, be enabled to sense elements in its environment by means of a wide range of different subsystems: sensory capabilities may depend upon tactile pressure, electromagnetic radiation, air-borne molecules, atmospheric vibration, coded electronic pulses or flashes of light, variations in temperature, etc. A sensory capability does not presuppose the sensitive cellular structures of plants or animals. Nor does a single subsystem constitute a sufficient condition for life: a living creature may be seen as comprising a number of co-operating subsystems.

Efforts to identify the subsystems of biological life-forms have tended to focus on such cybernetic processes as temperature control and the maintenance of adequate blood sugar levels. This type of approach has the disadvantage that it is limited to particular groups of living species: many species have no interest in blood sugar. It is more profitable in seeking necessary characteristics of life to identify subsystems that are not species-specific.

J.G. Miller (1978), for instance, identified a hierarchy of structures carrying out living processes. The various levels in the hierarchy are defined by cells, organs, organisms, groups, organizations, societies and supranational systems. The various systems at each level are represented as open systems which process inputs, throughputs and outputs of various forms of matter, energy and information. The differences in the types of systems at the various levels in the hierarchy (for example, the differences between a single-celled amoeba and the United Nations) made it necessary to identify critical subsystems that were not limited to protozoan metabolism or to the workings of international law. Miller identifies nineteen critical subsystems which characterize each system at the various levels of the hierarchy. *The vast majority of these 'critical subsystems of a living system' can easily be discerned in current computer systems.*

The nineteen subsystems variously process matter/energy, information or both. For instance, the reproductive capability (the *reproducer*) is seen as a facility that depends upon processing both matter and information: substance is moulded or assembled (by whatever means) according to a blueprint set out in DNA or the computer memory (see the section on machine reproduction later in this chapter). Subsystems such as the *ingestor*, the *distributor, matter/energy storage* and the *extruder* are concerned with taking in energy, feeding it round the system, and getting rid of waste products (heat is an obvious energy waste product of computers). Subsystems such as *transducers, associators, memory* and *encoder* are concerned with the handling of information to allow the system to perform a range of tasks. Some subsystems—the *supporter* and the *boundary*, for example—simply provide the system with the necessary physical cohesion.

Again, what is interesting about this listing of critical 'life features' is that they are independent of how the various subsystems are realized. There is no assumption that life has to be based on hydrocarbons or any other specific chemicals. If a system can reproduce and also handle energy and information in appropriate ways then the system has a claim to be regarded as living. A corollary is that the genesis of the system is irrelevant. A mechanically *assembled* system may reasonably be regarded as living if its internal functions and behaviour in the world fulfil the necessary criteria.

The idea that life can be recognized independently of the substance out of which it is constructed derives support from modern functionalism, a philosophy of mind influenced by developments in artificial intelligence, computational theory, linguistics, cybernetics and cognitive psychology. Functionalism is largely concerned with mental phenomena but some of its elements are equally applicable, *mutatis mutandis*, to an identification of the characteristics whereby life is to be recognized. It is suggested that because mental activity is essentially concerned with the processing of information it would be possible in principle for a variety of systems (human beings, animals, computers, disembodied spirits) to have mental states. (The relevance of functionalism to the psychologies of machines is considered in chapter 5.) Functionalism suggests that mental activity, as information processing, is independent of specific chemistries: life, as a complex of co-operating subsystems for processing energy/matter and information, is clearly subject to a similar analysis.

This section has considered some of the ways of defining life and identifying its characteristic features. Under the influence of the modern cognitive sciences, we have seen a movement away from the traditional narrow biochemical interpretations towards an information-processing approach. Consideration of features that machine life may be expected to embody is given below — see the later section on life criteria.

Machines as emerging life

In imaginative writing there have been two broad approaches to the creation of artificial life. One of these, exemplified by the golden maidservants of Hephaestus (*Iliad*, Book XVIII), consists in constructing animate creatures out of inorganic substance. The other, exemplified by the efforts of Victor Frankenstein, relies upon using organic (but lifeless) material to contrive a living being. These two approaches have their counterparts in modern science.

Computer and robotics research is concerned with the development of artefacts that behave in particular ways. Industrial robots, for instance, are designed to be active: they variously weld, palletize, paint, tend machine tools and so on (see chapter 3). There is no suggestion that industrial robots have to be made out of organic materials in order to do the work formerly carried out by human beings. And what is true of the mechanical anatomy of a robot is also true of its computer brain. Modern computers using microelectronics rely upon the semiconducting properties of silicon, the conducting properties of copper, etc. Computers do not need to be carbon-based in order to do sums and to take decisions.

By contrast, the molecular biochemist is interested, at least in part, in duplicating the elements of life by a process of direct synthesis of organic molecules. There has been progress in building the complex macromolecules upon which all traditional earthly life-forms depend, and such research may be expected to provide insights into the dynamics of cell behaviour, whether normal or abnormal (as in cancer). It may be that further work will show how synthesized macromolecules could be artificially linked in systems that could ingest other chemicals, grow and be capable of self-replication. But the complexity of the chemistry is likely to delay significant progress in this field for many years. The route to artificial life will be a via modern computer research and robotics.

Samuel Butler (*Erewhon*, 1872) suggested that existing nineteenth-century machines were perhaps prototypes of future mechanical life, and in more recent years there has been growing speculation that computer systems may be represented as emerging life-forms. Much of the pressure for interpreting computer developments in such terms has derived from cybernetic considerations. Norbert Wiener, one of the great cybernetic pioneers, considered learning and reproduction in artefacts; and Klir and Valach (1965), in a book specifically devoted to cybernetic modelling, ask such questions as whether an inanimate machine can be aware, whether a machine can understand, and whether an inanimate system can live. Hilary Putnam (1975) speculates on whether robots are simply machines or whether they can be represented as artificially created life.

Klir and Valach focus (pp. 406–9) on the paradoxes arising from using both behavioural and structural criteria to identify life-forms. It is acknowledged that an active exchange of matter and energy is possible between machines and their environment; furthermore, machines 'are capable of an active exchange of information with their environment... differentiation, self-organisation and even reproduction can occur in machines'. Such observers recognize 'no essential differences' between the behaviour of living and inanimate systems, a view which clearly accords with Miller's identification of critical subsystems. In this interpretation it is scarcely fanciful to view machines as an emerging life-form.

Computer simulation and other techniques have shown how specific biological functions can be duplicated in artifical systems. This is a legitimate procedure providing that the precise nature of the simulation is defined. Hence Pylyshyn (1975) comments:

> ...the interpretation of the model as some kind of analogue of a system is possible only if the model is accompanied by a commentary which tells the user which aspects of the system are mapped onto the model, and which aspects of the model are relevant to its analogy with the system.

Where a simulation is not expected to extend beyond a tightly defined function it may be regarded as legitimate duplication of the function in question.

Sometimes the analogues are more oblique but still important. In the literature of artificial intelligence, comparisons have been drawn between biological enzymes and the specific subroutines in computer programs. It is recognized that individual enzymes are programmed, by virtue of their tertiary structures, to respond to specific substrates: the arrival of the substrate triggers the enzyme action, much as a 'dormant' subroutine in a computer program is triggered in the appropriate circumstances. Hofstadter (1979) has pointed out that Gerald Sussman's HACKER program, an effective learning system, synthesizes subroutines in a way that closely resembles the operation of enzyme cascades.

The developing behavioural scope of artificial systems is enabling them to progressively emulate functions formerly only associated with biological entities. Many of these functions are characteristic of life; but some need not be. It is paradoxical but not self-contradictory to say that a *conscious* entity may not be *alive*; conversely a living system need not be conscious. To show that an artificial system is alive, it may be enough to show that it can duplicate the functions of a fifth-rate lichen. It is one thing to show that a computer-based configuration is alive; quite another to establish the level of competence that typifies that sort of life-form. This point needs to be explored in more detail.

Life criteria

If computers, structured and programmed for appropriate behaviour, are seen to be at least as competent as the most primitive life-forms then it is reasonable to claim that such computers are alive. This approach represents the *modest* strategy: computers may be poor things but they are at least as clever as a cactus. A less modest strategy claims that computers are relatively accomplished, the equal of life-forms some way up the evolutionary ladder. These strategies can be considered by examining the criteria that systems should satisfy to be regarded as alive.

The idea that a computer-based system may behave *as if* it were alive suggests that there are ways of showing that it is in fact *not* alive: further tests, we may be told, can be carried out to settle the matter. To put it another way, naturally occurring biological life is recognized by various characteristics (such as having the capacity for growth, for the ingestion of food, for reproduction), and a machine may satisfy only one of these criteria. And it may be maintained that unless *all* the criteria are satisfied the system cannot be regarded as alive. But this sort of argument has to be viewed with caution. For instance, a reproductive capability may be taken as a necessary life characteristic. However, it is obvious that such a quality cannot be *equated* with life (it is not a sufficient condition), and it is equally true that if an entity cannot reproduce its kind it cannot be assumed not to be alive. A sterile man and a post-menopausal woman may still be alive.

It may then be argued that even if some individuals do not have reproductive capabilities the species as a whole can, in fact, reproduce. This is clearly more acceptable and it remains to be seen whether computers can be shown to satisfy a criterion formulated in such a way. It could be that some primitive computers have no reproductive potential whereas more sophisticated devices can procreate to their heart's content. The modest strategy suggests that we need not be too demanding or ambitious in stipulating the range of criteria that an entity should satisfy in order to be regarded as alive.

Biologists are often willing to specify the qualities which they regard as essential to life. Thus N.J. Berrill (1967) notes that the 'essential' functions of life are growth, metabolism, autonomous movement and self-replication. But again it is easy to question this seemingly self-evident list. Our cactus, for example, may not appear to have much autonomous movement—from which we are not expected to conclude that the cactus is not alive. Some essential characteristics of life are, it seems, less essential than others.

The Larousse *Science of Life* (1971) suggests that all living things 'have in common certain recognisable characteristics'. For example, they have definite shape and structure, the ability to assimilate certain chemicals, the power to survive changes in environment, the capacity for reproduction, and the inevitability of ageing and death. Again this plausible-sounding list does not bear scrutiny. Worker bees, though manifestly alive, cannot mate; and certain parasitic wasps have been able to dispense with the male entirely. Even the much vaunted capacity for reproduction is not an inevitable quality of all successful living creatures.

It is also recognized (Larousse, p. 56) that '*as we descend the scale of animate beings it becomes increasingly difficult to apply the usual criteria and our conclusions will be different according to the importance we attach to one or other of these characteristics*' [my italics]. This suggests that we may say that an entity is living, even if it lacks some of the characteristics we expect in the higher animals. Such observations are important in any enquiry about the possibility of artificial life. For computers or robots to be alive it is not necessary that they manifest the life capacities of a dog, a chimpanzee or a human being. If a machine can be shown to be 'as alive' as a bacterium or a worm then it is legitimate to regard the machine as a member of a new animate species. To show that computers are alive it is not necessary to demonstrate that they are a highly evolved lifeform: it is quite sufficient to show that they are a *rudimentary* form of life. And such a consideration will soon invite us to consider the question of machine evolution.

Biologists are keenly conscious that it is difficult to draw a clear line between living and non-living matter. A virus may be alive or not, depending upon the criteria that are held to be important (we have already seen how Bernal framed a definition of life to allow viruses to qualify). The virus is certainly chemically similar to other simple structures that we choose to regard as alive; moreover it has a great interest in reproduction, though its approach to this matter may seem somewhat oblique. For example, the tobacco mosaic virus does not really reproduce itself. Rather it is reproduced by the host cell, making it an example of auto-synthesis, not auto-reproduction in the conventional sense. And the virus is not capable of food assimilation and complex metabolic processes: it is devoid of enzymes and totally incapable of the modes of synthesis that characterize the more complex living structures. The virus is mobile and has developed a strategy for arranging the reproduction of its kind, but on many counts it is not alive. It can be argued that certain types of computers and robots have better claims to be regarded as alive than does the simple tobacco mosaic virus.

The *modest strategy* used to establish the reality of machine life consists in part in showing that even many acknowledged biological life-forms do not satisfy the ambitious specifications laid out by biologists. Hence plants generally do not exhibit much *autonomous movement* and not all animals have the power of *reproduction*: if computers, equally, exhibit life features apart from these then perhaps machines—of certain types—may reasonably be regarded as alive. But we do not need to rest with a modest strategy. It will be seen, not only that computers are capable of autonomous movement and reproductive activity, but that they also satisfy a number of the other criteria favoured in the 'life lists' of biologists. We can be confident in embracing a *less modest* strategy. This point is developed in more detail later (see, in particular the section on the place of AI, below and chapters 3, 4 and 5). It is useful in this section to specify the broad 'life criteria' that acknowledged life-forms in general, and computer life-forms in particular, need to satisfy. But first we can allow ourselves a slight digression.

The recognition of similarities between mechanisms and self-evident living systems makes it easier to acknowledge that artefacts may be able to exhibit a range of 'human' qualities, even to the levels of 'thinking' (chapter 5) and 'being alive'. If 'thinking' denotes certain brain activities it can equally well denote *sufficiently similar* processes in a computer processing unit. *Internal* similarities exist between neuron behaviour and the activities of logic gates: put simply, both neurons and logic gates require a number of appropriate energy inputs before an output can be fed to subsequent elements (other neurons or gates) in the network. There are also *external* (that is, behavioural) manifestations of similarity.

Computers, like brains, cannot be easily seen to behave. We infer their behaviour partly from what we know of their structures and programs, and partly from how they make other things behave. A human being may have a remarkable brain but, for this to be recognized, its deliberations must yield observable consequences (for example, fingers must move to produce unusual marks, or combinations of marks, on paper). This means that effective tests for intelligence (and life) tend to have a behavioural component. Where, for example, there is communication between a person and a computer, the machine's responses have to be observable to allow the intercourse to proceed.

A.M. Turing's celebrated 1950 paper examined the question of machine thought by means of a game based on interrogation: a person can communicate via a teletypewriter with a human being and machine. He has to decide which he is communicating with on the basis of the answers given. The following sample of dialogue, with the computer, could equally well be with a human being:

Q: Please write me a sonnet on the subject of the Forth Bridge.
A: Count me out on this one. I never could write poetry.
Q: Add 34957 to 70764.
A: [*After a pause of about 30 seconds*] 105721
Q: Do you play chess?
A: Yes.
Q: I have K at my K1, and no other pieces. You have only K and K6 and R at R1. It is your move. What do you play?
A: [*After a pause of 15 seconds*] R–R8 mate.

The Turing test, and the literature it stimulated, suggest that if, after sufficiently comprehensive tests, we cannot tell the difference between a man and a machine then there is no difference. If a mechanism behaves *as if* it is human in all the relevant circumstances then it *is* human. If this sounds too facile it should be remembered that many difficult tests would have to be satisfied before a machine could be recognized as alive in this ambitious sense. In fact it can be shown that computers—in one form or another—are intelligent (they can solve problems and act purposefully), creative (they can take design initiatives to achieve functional or aesthetic ends), possess a faculty for choice (they have what is called 'free will' in humans) and have a reproductive capability (they are developing mechanisms for preserving their kind in a hostile world). These qualities are considered below (see the following section on machine reproduction) and in chapter 5.

This seeming digression serves to illuminate the necessary 'life criteria' that can be identified. The modest strategy may suggest, for instance, that life-forms without a mental component may include certain types of machines. The less modest strategy, to be developed in what follows, suggests that machines are both alive and have a mental existence.

The necessary life criteria can be accommodated under four broad heads: *structural, energy-processing, information-processing* and *reproductive*. These broad categories are satisfied, in characteristic ways, by the three identifiable classes of life on Earth—plant, animal and machine. It is scarcely in dispute, for example, that roses and rabbits have an identifiable form and organization (*structure*), that they feed and excrete in their various ways (*process energy*), that they are sensitive to a changing environment (*process information*), and that they procreate their kind (*reproduce*). Computers and robots, suitably configured, can be seen to satisfy the life criteria that may be set out under the four broad heads.

Computers of various makes have characteristic structures, as do industrial and other types of robots. The devices feed on electrical energy and excrete heat energy (heat output was an immense problem in the early thermionic-valve computers but even the ZX81 RAM pack can get very warm). With a growing range of sensory devices, robots and other machines can detect changes in the environment and respond in suitable ways (see chapter 4); in fact, this type of information processing is becoming ever more sophisticated with the development of very large scale integrated (VLSI) circuits. And, increasingly, computer-based systems are developing a reproductive capability (see below). Viewed in this way, it seems manifestly clear that particular types of machines may reasonably be regarded as emerging life-forms. They meet the criteria by which we expect to identify life-forms in the rest of the biological world. The generality of these criteria is justified by the need to accommodate animals as disparate as paramecium and giraffe, plants as disparate as Venus fly-trap and oak. Criteria with a legitimate generality of this order can be seen to accommodate machines.

Joseph Weizenbaum (1976), often seen as hostile to the wide-ranging application of computer technology has accepted 'the idea that a modern computer system is sufficiently complex and autonomous to warrant our talking about it as an organism'. It is accepted that a computer can sense and affect its environment, and even be 'socialized' (that is, modified by experiences in its world. Moreover, a suitably constructed robot could be made to develop a sense of itself, learning to distinguish between its components and external objects for purposes of self-protection. In some circumstances it could construct an internal model which would constitute a kind of self-consciousness. Weizenbaum concludes these highly significant observations by declaring (p. 210):

When I say therefore that I am willing to regard such a robot as an 'organism,' *I declare my willingness to consider it a kind of animal.* And I have already agreed that I see no way to put a bound on the degree of intelligence such an organism could, at least in principle, attain. [my italics]

The extent to which computer creatures satisfy the various life criteria is explored in chapters 3, 4 and 5. Here we consider reproduction, a system capability that has already clearly emerged as an important life requirement.

Machine reproduction

A recent article in an industrial journal began with the words: 'Machine tools are unique in the vast and varied world of machinery. For they alone are *capable of reproducing themselves*' [my italics]. Later it is noted that a group of machining centres 'is busily producing offspring in a propagating unit where man has been relegated to a mere observer' (Lacey, 1982). The author then goes on to describe the flexible manufacturing processes in the factory of the Yamazaki

Machinery Works outside Nagoya, Japan's fourth largest city; in this manufacturing plant, with larger ones planned, 400 computer numerical control (CNC) systems are produced every month. Only six men are required to operate the entire factory, and from midnight until 8 a.m. the whole plant runs unmanned.

In 1981 a number of reports started appearing in Western journals concerning a remarkable robot factory in Japan, the Fujitsu Fanuc plant located at the foot of Mount Fuji. One important feature of this factory is that *robots are making robots*—twenty-four hours a day, with human beings only required for the eight-hour day shift. The Fuji site was chosen partly for its cool climate and partly because there is room for expansion.

The 20,000 m^2 plant is divided into machining areas (coloured grey) and inspection and assembly areas (coloured green). The working robots are yellow. Each of the machining cells comprises a CNC system, a television monitor and a robot. The machining cells are supplied with raw materials by robot transporters which move around the factory guided by instructions carried in wires beneath the floor. The transporters collect material from automatic warehouses, each comprising 477 'rooms' individually capable of storing a ton of material. A computer indicates which parts are to be fed to the transporters.

The machining cells can, if required, work independently for twenty-four hours a day, with the factory as a whole producing sixty robots of three types every month—in addition to 100 wire-out electric machines and 100 sets of mini CNC tools. A key feature of this factory is that it is proving possible progressively to exclude human beings from the task of machine production. CNC equipment and robots are, with ever diminishing human assistance, manufacturing CNC equipment and robots. Machines are reproducing themselves.

Our modest strategy (outlined under the section on life criteria above), consisted in part in querying the extent to which life-forms had to embody a reproductive potential. Sterile animals are alive, but in general the species to which they belong is capable of reproduction. A consequence of this interpretation is that it is not necessary for *all* machines to be capable of reproduction for machines to qualify as alive. It is sufficient that only a proportion of machines embody a reproductive capability. Nor is it a necessary requirement that all living systems reproduce *in the same way*. Samuel Butler (1872) was well aware of the arguments of those who said 'that the machines can never be developed into animate or quasi-animate existences, inasmuch as they have no reproductive system...' He also declared that: '...if a machine is able to reproduce another machine systematically, we may say that it has a reproductive system. What is a reproductive system, if it be not a system for reproduction?' The idea of reproduction must be seen as a broader concept than its particular instances embodied in the life of plants and animals. We should not be surprised if new types of life develop new reproductive modes, the patterns best suited to their natures. As Butler wrote: '...we are never likely to see a fertile union between two vapour-engines with the young ones playing about the door of the shed, however greatly we may desire to do so'. The new forms of machine life will develop their own procreative modes.

There is no requirement that all animate entities reproduce in the same way. In fact, methods of reproduction vary widely throughout the biological world—from simple binary fission in protozoa to all the complexities of sexual reproduction in plants and animals (internal fertilization, external fertilization, larval forms, pseudo-placental birth, placental birth, etc.). The *method* of reproduction is not the central point. The key element is that, by whatever means, an entity can duplicate itself in a new entity that did not formerly exist.

Some observers will suggest that it is man that makes machines produce machines, that the machines are not genuinely reproductive since they depend upon human intervention. (Lacey nicely remarked that 'like zoo pandas, they don't make much headway without having man in constant attendance'.) This is not a very telling argument. We know, for example—as Butler did—that plants are often not reproductive without the intervention of insects. The plant use of sex for reproduction requires that germ cells be conveyed from one soil-rooted parent to another, except where water-living plants may move about. Plant germ cells can be transported by the wind, by insects, birds and other animals. To this end, insects can be stimulated to distraction by the colour, shape and pattern of flowers. For example, the Bee Orchid (*Ophrys apifera*) carries little flowers that resemble bees: more importantly, to a male bee they resemble female bees. The male bee struggles to copulate with the flower and, in so doing, detaches the pollen mass from the flower's male organ. The bee flies on to the next flower, hoping for a greater degree of copulatory success: in so doing he obligingly conveys the pollen mass to the moist female surface (the stigma) of the flower. In such a fashion is plant fertilization achieved; by such means do many plant species manage to procreate.

This means that whole families of plants would become extinct if their fertilization process was not aided by animal species totally foreign to themselves. But no-one would argue that plants did not have reproductive systems simply because they relied on insects or other agents for fertilization (Butler asks: 'Does anyone say that the red clover has no reproductive system because the humble bee must aid and abet it before it can reproduce?'). Butler saw that the humble bee is part of the reproductive system of the clover, and today we might equally say that man is part of the reproductive system of the PUMA robot.

The point may also be made that where machines generate other machines they rarely produce their own kind. An automated machine-tool, for instance, may produce nuts and bolts for later assembly into complex mechanical configurations. But we have seen that robots are effectively producing robots, and it is also arguable that all reproductive activity involves, at one level or another, 'mechanical' assembly. Even a narrow biochemical definition of life involves viewing the replication of molecules as a matter of 'mechanical assembly'—where such geometric properties as position and angle are of paramount importance in understanding the nature of molecular bonding and the use of gene templates. Assembly, either of hydrocarbon molecules (for plant and animal life) or of nuts and bolts (for machine life), may be represented as a common reproductive mechanism. The DNA double helix is relevant to molecular assembly, with a range of other considerations relevant to machine assembly.

The Charles Stark Draper Laboratory in the USA, for example, has researched programmable industrial assembly procedures. This work has focused on such topics as parts-mating theory, the assembly process as a positioning problem, the transition from parts transporting to parts positioning, parts assembly (or mating), and the optimum design of an assembly robot. Simunovic (1979) has explored aspects of parts-mating theory to throw light on the design for assembly operations, focusing on such questions as: What accuracy, repeatability and resolution are required for an assembly robot? What type of sensors are required, and how can the information they provide be used? What type of robot design (dimensions, number of degrees of freedom, required speed, etc.) is best suited for assembly?

Automatic assembly by robots is usually represented as essentially a positioning problem, with attention devoted to such considerations as the progressive accumulation of positioning errors during the assembly process, the various requirements of parts transport and parts mating, and the use of such mechanisms as force feedback (active control) and compliance (passive control) to aid assembly. Whitney and Nevins (1979) have described the remote centre compliance (RCC), a mechanical device for aiding assembly insertion operations, deriving its properties from its geometry and the elasticity of its parts. KU Leuven (Belgium) have developed a special universal 'wrist', provided with software-controllable compliances to facilitate assembly activities. The device can be inserted between the robot arm and the hand ('gripper') to allow relatively inaccurate general-purpose industrial robots to perform precision assembly tasks. Already a large family of assembly robots is emerging: we need only mention the Unimation PUMA and Series 500 robots (the latter being used to insert light bulbs into automobile dashboards) and the two-handed Cyro robot from Advanced Robotics (which enables a part and a welding torch to be moved simultaneously under automatic control). Today, electronic watches, typewriter keyboards, appliance parts, electrical subassemblies, and computer and robot components are being assembled by computer-based systems requiring minimal human intervention. Increasingly, computer-based robot systems will be expected to manufacture and assemble computers and robots: a growing proportion of such systems will be automatically designed and produced, and journals such as *Assembly Engineering* and *Assembly Automation* will come to be recognized as dealing in part with methods of machine procreation.

The possibility of self-reproduction in the machine world has been discussed in the literature for many years. Hence Norbert Wiener (1961) includes, in his celebrated book on cybernetics, a chapter entitled 'On learning and self-reproducing machines'. After noting that the power to learn and the power to reproduce are taken to be characteristic of living systems, he considers whether man-made machines could embody such capabilities. A discussion of the behaviour of artefacts, with attention to the characteristics of non-linear transducers, is followed by the observation:

I ask if this is philosophically very different to what is done when a gene acts as a template to form other molecules of the same gene from an indeterminate mixture of amino and nucleic acids or when a virus guides into its own form other molecules of the same virus out of the tissues and juices of its host.

In the same spirit Klir and Valach (1965) consider whether 'inanimate systems are capable of producing further inanimate systems possessing properties similar to those of their inanimate progenitors'. Here it is suggested that *'there are no obstacles to the possibility of such a process of self-reproduction'* [my italics], and the idea of a computer-controlled factory is examined. A scenario is proposed in which a computer contains not only instructions to reproduce itself but also instructions to reproduce the entire factory in which it is made. In this way it can be seen how a computer could remotely control the erection of a new factory, design and manufacture the necessary tools, and assemble them at a distance. At a time specified by its internal program, the computer will reproduce itself and insert the new computer, complete with a copy of the original computer program, into the newly erected factory. The result would be two factories, each of which would be capable of producing another identical factory.

This section suggests that there are practical and theoretical grounds for regarding machine self-reproduction as a reality.

Furthermore, it is highly likely that technological progress over the coming decades will soon make this particular view of machine capability unassailable, a circumstance that will arise in part through the enhanced information-processing capacities of artificial systems. It is worth pointing out that 'non-living' modes of self-reproduction can be distinguished from living modes partly on the basis of the amount of information involved in the process. We know, for instance, that (non-living) crystals can self-replicate in appropriate conditions. Certain chemicals in a supersaturated solution do not crystalize until appropriate crystal seeds are added, and where a chemical is capable of crystallizing into two different systems, the structure of the new crystals is determined by that of the seed. However, one reason why the crystals could not satisfy the non-reproduction life criteria is that the information content of their structures is inferior by several orders of magnitude to the amount of information transmitted from one generation in the biological life systems. This indicates that identifiable quantitative factors are relevant to how likely it is that a self-replicating system will satisfy the spectrum of necessary life requirements.

Machine evolution

The reality of machine life suggests that it is also feasible to consider such concepts as machine evolution, machine mutations and machine generations not simply as loose metaphors or allegories on acknowledged life-forms but as literal descriptions, as binding on machine progress as the similar terms are on the development of the familiar biological life systems. Again, it is not necessary that machine and animal evolution occur in exactly the same way: different methods are likely to suit different life-forms, but the impulse to survival may be seen as a common factor.

The differences between biological individuals in traditional species has facilitated the process of evolution. A changing environment favours particular individuals who are thus more likely to survive and to generate progeny: the offspring will tend to resemble the favoured parents, and in this way the overall character of the species is made to change. Such a process, given sufficient time, yields many new species. Mutation (that is, random alterations in the gene patterns) is in part responsible for the individual variations within a species. A simple application of this mutation factor to the 'reproduction information' held in a computer memory would obviously be easy to arrange. The species-specific 'DNA' could be modified under the influence of a random element—but it would be highly inefficient and costly to proceed in any such way. The computers would produce a proliferation of unworkable machines which would have no chance of being selected out by a changing environment. It is obvious that the evolution of computers and robots will proceed in a different way.

Another alternative would be to allow the computer store of 'DNA data' to be modified by input received by sensors. For example, if the heat or humidity in the environment changed, it may be advantageous for the machine reproductive system to generate different types of machines in the next generation. Heat sensors could transmit signals to modify information held in the computer store. At the same time it may be desirable to compute environmental changes over a defined period of time: it would be inappropriate to launch into design and manufacture of new systems if the environmental changes were only transitory.

Klir and Valach speculate on the idea of a reproductive computer being influenced by experiential factors. Thus after producing a new computer, the first machine passes to it not only its original program but also data which defines its experiences: in such a way the new computer will be made to behave differently to its parent, in a way that makes it better equipped to adapt to its environment. A sequence of computers could be produced in this manner, each generation incorporating all the experience of its ancestors.

There are already signs that automated systems are organizing the genesis of their progeny in a way that allows for 'design' alterations and so the development of new species-specific characteristics. For instance, computers are being used to design more powerful computers; integrated circuits are 'creating' enhanced integrated circuits. Auerbach, Lin and Elsayed (1981) describe computer techniques used to design VLSI circuits that have never existed before. Such methods have been forced upon chip manufacturers by the growing complexity of integrated-circuit design.

To reduce the time taken to lay out a new circuit, a variety of program facilities have been developed. Feller (1976), for example, designed a computer program to route the chip layout automatically after reading a circuit description provided by the user, though the resulting layouts tended to be larger in size than those produced manually. Layout compaction programs and algorithms were developed by Cho, Korenjak and Stockton (1977), by Williams (1977) and by Dunlop (1979). What this type of work indicates is that computers are increasingly being involved in the design of computer circuits that would be too complex for human beings to attempt in any reasonable time period. As one example, a single computer circuit on a piece of silicon as small as 0.125 in. × 0.125 in. may have approaching 10,000 microscopic transistors, diodes, capacitors and other functional elements etched onto its surface. This means that by the time the final design is achieved, by whatever method, there may be more than 1,000 parameter combinations to be tested. In one attack on this problem, Sperry-Univac have automated the process using a minicomputer and other equipment (for example, a four-colour plotter, a digitizer and a printer). No-one can doubt that this type of work (Groner, 1981) will expand in the future. It is no exaggeration to say that computer designs are being achieved today that would be quite impossible without the assistance of computer-based techniques.

It is also significant that programs are being devised to improve the programs being written by human beings. Automatic program transformation is represented as a means of aiding the production of 'reliable, efficient programs' (Darlington, 1981). Here programmers are encouraged to postpone questions of efficiency when writing a program, and to rely on a later automatic transformation of their efforts into effective programs. Methods are being developed to allow computers to 'accomplish program synthesis, the conversion of non-executable program specifications into runnable programs'. One can envisage a time when the most skilled programming techniques are laid up in computer memories: human programmers will draft rudimentary sequences which the computers will then improve with their superior abilities.

The capacity of computers to contribute to the design of their successors gives a unique flavour to computer evolution. Traditional biological evolution has relied on natural selection among the varied stock of a generation: the occurrence of suitable mutations in a changing environment has been fortuitous—if the environment 'outflanked' the current gene pool then the species would become extinct. Computer evolution, by contrast, can achieve greater leaps in the need to adapt and survive: effective 'mutations' can be deliberately and intelligently contrived. There is no need for changes between one computer generation and the next to be gradual. Rather the necessary changes can be scaled to the specific needs imposed on the system by the new environment.

For many years there has been explicit recognition of successive *generations* of computers. First-generation computers were based on thermionic valves; second-generation computers on transistors; third-generation on simple integrated circuits; and fourth-generation on VLSI circuits. Now there is much talk of the fifth-generation computers being planned in Japan and elsewhere. There are ambitious claims that fifth-generation systems will possess intelligence akin to that of human beings, a circumstance that would clearly revolutionize human attitudes and the character of advanced human society.

In October 1981, Japan's Ministry of International Trade and Industry (MITI) invited computer experts from many countries to a conference in Tokyo to explore Japanese thinking on fifth-generation computers. The aim of the project is to develop a prototype system by 1991 that would form the basis of large-scale production of computers able to perform a range of tasks currently only possible with massive human involvement. These tasks would include instantaneous automatic language translation (a telephone caller from Japan would hear your English-spoken reply in Japanese), typewriters which would convert human speech directly into the printed word, professional consultation in medical and other fields, and inference capabilities which would give computers effective judgment and decision-making abilities. It is anticipated that fifth-generation computers would be able to hold intelligent conversations with highly educated human beings in many different fields.

Some of the technical features of such computers are likely to involve at least a partial abandonment of the traditional von Neumann designs (in which operations are performed in a strictly sequential manner) and the development of computer languages better adapted to the inferential and other processes of the human mind. (More is said about these possibilities in chapter 8.)

We have already seen the conventional recognition of computer generations, with each of the generations delivering some of its defining features to the next. This section has implied that the links between computer generations will become more intimate: increasingly, new computer specifications will derive from the design capabilities of the parent systems. The corollary is that human intervention will progressively diminish. Computer-based facilities will monitor changes in the environment and develop appropriate modifications in the next generation of systems to maximize the adaptive potential. And 'environment' will be broadly defined, comprising not only such obvious circumstantial factors as ambient temperature and humidity, but availability of raw materials, likelihood of investment in particular projects, requirements for social engineering in such areas as human employment and crisis management. . . .

The growing intimacy between successive computer generations suggests such concepts as kinship, the 'handing down' of proven adaptive features, and resemblance between parent and progeny. Considerations of this sort suggest that it might be useful to classify, in biological terms, many of the emerging computer systems (see below).

Computer evolution is likely to proceed through successive generations at an accelerating pace. It is inevitable, however, that initially there will be a confused transition period during which many people will be unwilling to recognize what is happening. This is hardly surprising: the emergence of computer life on Earth must be one of the half dozen or so most momentous events in the 2,000 million year history of terrestrial biology. One can point to such milestones as the emergence of the first self-replicating molecules, the development of the first life-systems protected from the environment by a simple membrane, the transition from single- to multi-cellular organisms, the development of the first land-living creatures, and the arrival of true *homo sapiens*. Perhaps the emergence of machine life will prove to be the most dramatic development of them all.

Machine classification

Any recognition that computers and robots are emerging life-forms may be expected, following the convention with other biological species, to lead to efforts at classification. It has proved immensely useful for zoologists and botanists to agree on how to classify the flora and fauna that they are studying. This has usually been done by assigning a Latin name comprising two words: the first designates the genus of the species, the second the species itself. Thus the common frog is *Rana temporaria*, and the leopard frog is *Rana pipiens*. Perhaps a different convention should be adopted for machine life-forms. Weizenbaum (1976) has counselled on the dangers of a too simplistic approach to classification, but this time of man himself:

Because the view of man as a species of the more general genus 'information-processing system' does concentrate our attention on one aspect of man, it invites us to cast all his other aspects into the darkness beyond what that view itself illuminates.

We must not make the same mistake with machines.

Machina sapiens may denote 'thinking machine', and particular computers and robots may be assigned suitable Latin tags according to physical or behavioural characteristics—such as size of memory, possession of particular senses, and whether the systems are mobile. (I leave our Latin scholars—those few with an equal interest in biology, computer science and robotics—to get to work on this one.)

Dr W. Grey Walter (1953) wrote, some thirty years ago of *Machina labyrinthea* (an artificial goal-seeking creature), *Machina sopora* (Ashby's sleep-seeking Homeostat), *Machina docilis* (the 'easily taught' machine), and *Machina speculatrix* (never still except when feeding on electricity). It has taken only three decades of computer evolution to translate Grey Walter's frivolous 'mock biology' into clues for a realistic and worthwhile taxonomy.

The place of AI

There is a clear sense in which artificial intelligence (AI) is concerned with *minds*: it illuminates ideas about what may be considered to be the 'mental attributes' of artefacts and in turn helps us to understand the mental equipment of human beings. But not all the topics examined in AI research are equally relevant to the thesis that computers are alive. The skills of a game-playing computer may be quite unconnected with the necessary life criteria that animate artefacts should be expected to satisfy. A living computer does not need to know the difference between Queen's Gambit and Ruy Lopez.

We are now beginning to re-examine many of the conventional adjectives traditionally applied to human beings—such words as *conscious, intelligent, thinking, perceptive, free* and *aware*. We are having to scrutinize such terms because we are seeing that increasingly they can denote characteristics of artificial systems. It is significant that, for example, the word 'intelligent' can now denote not only particular AI systems but also a wide range of commercial equipment marketed by computer manufacturers. It is interesting to note how 'intelligent' has come to denote such machine systems. (We may expect to see the word 'living' undergo a similar evolution.)

When computer equipment now regarded as intelligent was first described (for example, computer terminals with the ability to process digital information), the writers often put the word 'intelligent' in quotes; viz: 'intelligent' terminals. There was evident reluctance to admit that machines could exhibit features that characterize the higher animals: the use of quotation marks underlined the assumption that *real* intelligence was a feature only of certain acknowledged biological systems. Today the quotation marks are seldom used. The computer literature is full of references to intelligent peripherals and terminals, machine intelligence, artificial intelligence—with not a quote in sight. This easy linguistic usage, common in technical journals, suggests that intelligence can equally characterize certain biological systems and certain artefacts. (It is no argument against this view to say that our concept of intelligence is unclear; that, for example, the old IQ tests are now found to be unreliable. Whatever definition of intelligence we choose, the same point can be made.)

We may decide that intelligence, appropriately interpreted, is one of the necessary life criteria. But it is important to realize that AI research covers many topics, not all of which are important to our thesis. Progress is being made in such areas as game-playing (for example, chess with brute-force or heuristic look-ahead, backgammon, draughts, bridge, poker, kalah, etc.), mechanical translation, vision, hearing, understanding natural languages, writing poetry (for example, Japanese haiku), musical composition, problem-solving and the manipulation of symbols. In some areas computers are offering creative improvements on the skilled accomplishments of human thinkers. For instance, computers have produced superior theorem proofs to those presented by Russell and Whitehead in *Principia Mathematica*. But there is still the persistent reluctance in many people to admit that machines can exhibit intelligence or think. Hofstadter has observed that as soon as one mental function is newly programmed for a computer, people soon incline to reject it as an essential ingredient of 'real thinking'. And he cites what he dubs Tesler's Theorem: AI is whatever hasn't been done yet'. However, today many people would agree with Turing's (1950) comment that 'by the end of the century one will be able to speak of machines thinking without expecting to be contradicted'. Throughout the 1970s such notions were becoming commonplace. The following quotations are taken at random from the literature:

'...the ability to think logically... has been shown to be within the capabilities of existing computers...' (George, 1972)

'If we have learned anything about the brain, it is that it is a machine... it raises the possibility that we *can* design in machine that thinks like a man...' (Kent, 1978)

'...It may be possible for a computer to have subjective experience' (Kent, 1978)

'...the machine is closing the gap between itself and the brain' (Matheson, 1978)

It is conceivable that machines are intelligent without being conscious. Nor is consciousness essential as a life criterion. Samuel Butler noted that plants have a reproductive system 'without apparent consciousness', but envisaged the development of consciousness in machines (even in the nineteenth century he could remark that 'germs of consciousness will be found in many actions of the higher machines').

The minimal AI features connected with computer life will relate to the information-processing capabilities. For instance, it is necessary for living creatures to monitor the environment, to process the resulting data, and to provide outputs for motor and other adjustment facilities. Such activities may involve sophisticated choice mechanisms (what is 'free will' in people) and at least rudimentary emotion (these possibilities are explored in more detail in chapter 5). It will prove increasingly feasible to model the higher mental functions (for example, see Albus, 1981), though research in this area is likely to yield faculties that are not essential in the most rudimentary forms of computer life. It can be seen that AI research will yield faculties that are essential to computer life, and also faculties that define the *type* of computer life (some machine capabilities may be used, as we have seen, for taxonomical purposes).

Cybernetic systems

The emergence of computer life has been greatly assisted by research in cybernetics, the modern science that studies the control and communications mechanisms in artificial and acknowledged biological systems. The concept of *homeostasis*, the steady state of equilibrium after which all cybernetic systems strive, is likely to prove a fertile notion in the evolution of computer life: interestingly, for example, a homeostatic interpretation of human emotion give clues as to how emotion may come to be structured into artificial systems (see chapter 5).

Every biological cell is a steady-state system maintained precariously between the processes of construction and destruction. In all higher forms of life there is a striving for homeostasis at several levels. Not only does each cell have to maintain its own viability, but the system as a whole (for example, the animal) needs to maintain a constant internal environment for its constituent cells. This is achieved, to the extent that it is successful, by means of feedback mechanisms: the system takes in data about the environment and makes appropriate system adjustments to maximize the chances of survival. Cybernetic systems may be regarded as self-regulating systems that operate by means of feedback controls. It is significant that a broad definition of this sort says nothing about whether the system is an artefact or a naturally occurring biological configuration.

In an animal constant decisions are taken on a moment-to-moment basis according to internal and external conditions: the decisions are taken according to the programming of the mechanism, and may be behavioural (does the animal attack or retreat?) or chemical (in what way should an oxygen or sugar molecule be combined with existing chemicals in the body?). The operation of self-controlled machines is closely analogous. Artificial cybernetic systems include servomechanisms which comprise receptors (which receive feedback information) and comparators (which measure the difference between the information received and a value that helps to define a course of action). The machine then makes compensatory changes to eliminate any detected difference. It is important that the mechanics of the system facilitate rapid response without over correction. Again it is worth emphasizing that the interest in such cybernetic systems is that they can be artificial or (traditionally) biological.

There are many functional servomechanisms in the higher animals, most of which involve the brain and other components of the central nervous system. (As Berrill wrote: 'In mammals and the other land vertebrates the cerebellum is an outstanding example of a servomechanism that maintains a smooth course of muscular activity that would otherwise be jerky, clumsy and generally unsatisfactory....'.) Other animal servomechanisms may use the medulla or other brain areas, with feedback data provided via the senses, via skin conductivity, via the blood stream, etc. It is certain that designs for computer life will be heavily influenced by what we know about the cybernetic mechanisms in the traditional life-forms.

Summary

We have seen that concepts of life are moving from narrow biochemical interpretations to ones in which greater importance is attached to information processing. It is suggested that the necessary life criteria can be subsumed under four heads: structural, energy-processing, information-processing and reproductive. A modest and a less modest strategy are indicated as ways of showing that machines can satisfy the necessary life criteria. A framework for machine reproduction is outlined, and it is shown how computers are progressively intervening to control the direction of their own evolution. Research into artificial intelligence is seen to be relevant both to definitions of the most rudimentary types of computer life and to the nature of the different forms of computer life that will develop (all computer life will need to sense aspects of the world but not all computer life will need to develop an obsession for poker or poetry). Finally it is suggested that knowledge of existing biological cybernetic mechanisms will greatly affect how computer life-forms come to be designed.

2 The robot background

Throughout history, men have imagined the possibility of breathing life into an artefact. A consequence is that today's emerging robot and computer life-forms have a rich history in human thought. *Machina sapiens* has been anticipated through the centuries, prefigured in the mechanical contrivances of scientists and inventors, and in myth, fantasy and fiction.

A first imaginative step was to grant to divinities the power of giving life to artificial creations. In the early days of human civilization all important powers were assigned to the gods. Mankind had not yet learned self-confidence and was unable to face his cosmic isolation with courage. He found it comforting to believe that the gods conferred life, children, animal and crop fertility, victory over enemies and disease, and escape from death through eternal bliss. At the same time, it was thought that all people walked in the shadow of divine whim. But to personalize natural forces at least meant that they could be placated through flattery and sacrifice—and enlisted thereby to aid man in his endless struggle for survival.

Many early religions found it necessary to incorporate creation myths. Without an 'explanation' of origins the creed would be incomplete, ready to be supplanted by a more imaginative doctrine. In Egyptian mythology, Ra (signifying creator) was sovereign lord of the sky, one of many Sun gods. He drew from himself the first divine couple: only later did he acquire a spouse, Rat (a feminized version of his own name). And as early as 3000 B.C. the Egyptians built water clocks and articulated figures, some designed to serve as oracles.

Assyro-Babylonian mythology also includes creation legends, known from tablets held in the library of Ashurbanipal in Ninevah. After tumult among the gods, according to the *Epic of the Creation*, the great divinity Marduk moulded the body of the first man using the blood of a defeated god. In

Judeo-Christian religion the legend declared that God breathed life into a man formed out of the dust of the earth. And in the Talmudic tradition the dust was gathered from all parts of the world to be kneaded into a shapeless mass (golem) prior to the shaping of the limbs and the infusion of a soul. In similar fashion, Prometheus made the first man and woman with clay, and animated them with fire stolen from heaven.

In more practical terms, the Greek god Hephaestus, divinity of all the mechanical arts, contrived golden maidservants who looked like real girls, who could speak and walk, and who were filled with intelligence and wisdom. And Hephaestus, also known as Vulcan, built twenty tripods which 'run by themselves to a meeting of the gods and amaze the company by running home again' (*Iliad*, Book XVIII); and manufactured the giant Talus, made of brass, which guarded Crete by hugging intruders to death against his heated body. Hence, long before the beginning of the Christian epoch, men had speculated on how the gods could bring inanimate substances to life, and how intelligence (albeit that of deity) could contrive mechanical structures that could display animation and wisdom.

Another phase in man's approach to animate artefacts was the building of moving models, devices intended to resemble living creatures. The ancient Greeks, Ethiopians and Chinese built statues and other figures, powered by falling water or steam, to act out sequences of motions. Pindar reported the animated figures which adorned every public street and which seemed 'to breathe in stone, or move their marble feet' (*Olympic Ode*, *ca.* 520 B.C.). Daedalus was said to have invented moving statues worked by quicksilver, which walked infront of the Labyrinth and seemed to be endowed with life. A statue of Memnon, king of Ethiopia in the fifteenth century B.C., was said to utter melodious sounds when struck by the rays of the sun: one notion was that, since the mechanism could never yield so beautiful a sound, a divinity was partly responsible for it. The statue is represented by Athanasius Kircher in the *Oedipus Aegyptiacus* (1652). Many of the devices depended upon a clear understanding of natural principles. Ctesibius, for example, in the third century B.C., discovered pneumatic laws and (according to Vitruvius) 'devised methods of raising water, automatic contrivances and amusing things of many kinds... blackbirds singing by means of waterworks and figures that drink and move....'

Ignorant people were often inclined to ascribe supernatural power to such devices, a circumstance that aided priests and other politicians. It was commonly thought that the statue of Memnon worked by divine agency. Statues dating to 2500 B.C. contained trumpets through which the priests could speak to a gullible populace. Some ancient writers were sceptical of supernatural explanations: Celsus, for example, writing in the first century A.D., expressed scepticism of magic and animals 'not really living but having the appearance of life'. Many of the later contrivances were based on simple mechanical principles and evoked no superstitious awe.

In the fourth century A.D. a golden Buddhist statue, set on a carriage, was tended by animated models of Taoist monks. As the carriage was drawn forward, the monks moved around the Buddha, variously bowing and saluting and throwing incense into a censer. The seventh century saw boats with moving figures, and there are eighth-century Chinese records of an animated model of a monk which stretched out its hands, saying 'Alms! Alms!', and putting coins into a satchel when they reached a certain weight. The year 790 saw a wooden otter in China that could catch fish (Wang Chu); and in 890 a wooden cat was devised that could catch rats and dancing tiger-flies (Han Chih-Ho). At about the same time, the Japanese Prince Kaya is supposed to have made a doll which carried a large bowl: when the bowl filled with rain water the doll would raise the bowl and pour the water over its own face—in such a fashion was the rice paddy watered.

A curious tale is also associated with the name of Albertus Magnus (1204-72) who is said to have manufactured a life-size animated servant. In one version of the story, Thomas Aquinas destroyed the automation when he met it in the street, believing it to be the work of the devil. The creature was supposed to have been made of metal, wood, glass, wax and leather. It closely resembled a human being, and is said to have been able to talk and open the door for visitors. Roger Bacon (1214-94) spent seven years manufacturing a speaking head. And Leonardo da Vinci (1452-1519) made an automatic lion in honour of Louis XII: as Louis entered Milan, the lion walked towards him, opened its chest with a claw, and pointed to the fleur-de-lis coat of arms of France.

René Descartes made an automation which he called 'ma fille Francine' (*ca.* 1640). During a sea voyage an inquisitive captain opened the case in which Francine was kept. On seeing her move as if alive, he was seized by superstitious dread and threw her overboard. In the eighteenth century, Jacques de Vaucanson made a life-size animated flute-player, and Baron Wolfgang von Kempelen manufactured a talking machine (Goethe wrote of it that 'The talking machine of Kempelen is not very loquacious but it pronounces certain childish words very nicely').

Towards the end of the eighteenth century, a number of Swiss craftsmen (such as Pierre and Henri-Louis Jaquet-Droz) built lifelike automata that could write, draw pictures, and play various musical instruments. The Scribe, for instance (which was built in 1770) was an elegantly dressed figure of a child that wrote with a quill pen that it dipped in ink and moved over the paper with smooth strokes. This remarkable creature was controlled by an elaborate configuration of precision cams driven by a spring-powered clock escapement. Another automation, the Draughtsman, was built three years later, and could produce four drawings, one of which was a portrait of Louis XV. The action patterns for the drawings were stored on three sets of twelve cams. During the times when the cams were changing their positions, the creature blew the dust off the drawing paper by means of bellows placed in its head for this purpose. The Musician, another animated doll, was devised to play a miniature organ. Fingers strike the keys to produce the correct notes, the breast moves to simulate breathing, and the body and head move to the rhythm of the music. If all this were not enough, the eyes glance around from time to time. The Scribe, Draughtsman and Musician are held in the Musée d'Art et d'Histoire in Neuchâtel, Switzerland, where they are sometimes operated.

The nineteenth century witnessed various talking machines. One, called Euphonia, was exhibited in the Egyptian Hall in Piccadilly in 1846. It was in the form of a bearded Turk: its inventor, Professor Faber of Vienna, devoted twenty-five years to its construction. The automaton produced sounds similar to those of the human voice, and was able to ask and answer question, laugh, whisper and sing. The mechanism contained keys, levers and a double-bellows; in the movable mouth were situated a flexible tongue and an indiarubber palate. Since Faber spoke German, the automaton spoke English with a German accent. People were allowed to inspect the device to ascertain that the sounds originated in the machine and that no ventriloquism or other trickery was involved.

Another significant element in the movement towards the birth of *machina sapiens* was the development of game-playing machines, devices that could apparently display intelligence in tackling a wide variety of problems. The evolution of chess-playing machines is particularly significant, not least because there is continuity between the early mechanical contrivances and the skilful chess programs of the 1980s.

In the eighteenth century Kempelen manufactured, in addition to his celebrated talking machine, a chess-playing automaton. This complex device—though possessing a complicated array of cog-wheels, turning gears, moving levers and revolving cylinders—was, in fact, a fraud: there was a man inside! When Kempelen died in 1804, the chess machine was purchased by the impresario Maelzel who then took it on a tour of German towns. In 1809, the 'automaton' played against Napoleon Bonaparte at the Schoenbrunn Palace in Vienna. In the period of almost seventy years during which the machine was publicly exhibited, its 'brain' was supplied by more than a dozen eminent chess players in succession. Out of 300 public games the machine only lost six. In 1854 it was destroyed by fire in a Philadelphia museum.

Before World War I, the Spanish scientist Leonardo Torres y Quevedo, President of the Academy of Sciences in Madrid, constructed an electromagnetic automaton which could enable the white king and a rook mate the black king from any position. This is a relatively simple end-game, but the construction of a machine to achieve it by classical mechanics was a great accomplishment. In his *Artificial Thought, an Introduction to Cybernetics*, Pierre de Latil explains how the device works. In fact the black king has a metal base which makes contact with the squares of the board. This causes currents to be sent to the automaton, informing it of the king's square. The automaton replies by using electromagnetic devices under the chessboard to move the white pieces into play. All possibilities have been considered in advance and the black king cannot escape mate.

At the 1951 Congress of Cybernetics in Paris the Quevado electromagnetic chess player was presented by the inventor's son. The cyberneticist Norbert Wiener was defeated, and it was remarked in jest that this was the last triumph of classical mechanics over modern cybernetics. Today no-one would try to exploit electromagnetic principles in the construction of a chess-playing automaton.

By the nineteenth century, technology was developing rapidly and a broad corpus of scientific knowledge was being established. Inventors and philosophers were thinking in increasingly secular terms. It no longer seemed likely that gods could breathe life into clay models (as did Jehovah and Prometheus) or into ivory statues (as Aphrodite did with Galatea). Mary Shelley, perhaps influenced by a visit to the Jaquet-Droz automata at Neuchâtel, published *Frankenstein* in 1817: it was possible to envisage the human creation of a living being, albeit as a theme in fiction. What Albus has termed the 'Frankenstein motif' has increasingly influenced fictional work and serious scientific speculation.

The automata, models and animated dolls, devised over the centuries, were largely based on classical mechanical principles: and there was insufficient scope here for the realization of true intelligence. Various inventors and mathematicians had built calculating systems, but the route to *machina sapiens* proper had to await the development of electronics. Blaise Pascal (1623–62) devised a mechanical calculating machine in 1642 ('I submit to the public a small machine of my own invention by means of which alone you may, without effort, perform all the operations of arithmetic, and may be relieved of the work which has often times fatigued your spirit'). In the same spirit, Wilhelm Gottfried von Leibniz (1646–1716) built a device to multiply, add, divide and extract square roots; and initiated serious work on the symbolization of logical processes in algebraic terms. Jewna Jacobson, a clockmaker in Minsk, manufactured in 1770 a mechanical calculating machine which could compute numbers up to five digits. And Charles Babbage (1782–1871), with his 'difference engine' (1823) and his 'analytical engine' (1833–71), laid the basis of much of the computing theory that was to follow (Lady Lovelace, co-worker with Babbage and regarded by many as the world's first programmer, observed: 'We may say most aptly that the Analytical Engine weaves algebraic patterns just as the Jacquard loom weaves flowers and leaves'). At the same time, George Boole (1815–64) was developing the algebraic system of symbols and postulates which, in concert with binary arithmetic, was to become so important in the design of electronic computers in the twentieth century. And without the development of electronic computation it would have been impossible to provide automata, articulated models and robots with the necessary information-processing capability which today allows them to qualify as emerging life-forms.

We have seen that the idea of animated machines, of the creation of artificial life, has been represented in myth and fiction. Graphic art, too, has played a part. In 1624 Giovanni Battista Bracelli published the *Bizzarie di varie figure*, a remarkable collection of forty-eight pictures of dancers, acrobats and fighters. The drawings, presented without explanation or comment, were representations of the sorts of images which we associate with robots today: they appear angular, with flat surfaces, constructed from fabricated parts, and they are dedicated to particular tasks such as bell-ringing and knife-grinding.

Fictional tales accumulated throughout the nineteenth century until the great explosion of fantasy and science fiction in the twentieth. *L'Eve Nouvelle*, written in 1879 and later known as *L'Eve Future*, depicts a remarkable artificial woman animated by electricity and imbued with soul or spirit. The author, Villiers de l'Isle Adam, is reported to have said: '... my master, Edison, will soon teach you that electricity is as powerful as God'. In another tale, *Helen O'Loy* (first published in 1938) by Lester del Rey, an enormously expensive android is encased in a ravishing body and sent as a housekeeper to two bachelors who had placed the order. The artificial creatures falls in love with one of the men and marries him Another female automaton appears in Hoffman's *Der Sandmann*

(1817): here, the clockwork Olympia winds herself up by sneezing!

One of the most influential fictional treatments of the human automaton theme is Karel Capek's *R.U.R. (Rossum's Universal Robots)*, one of the author's five plays on a utopian theme: *robot* derives from the Czech word for 'worker'. *R.U.R.* was first published in 1923, two years after its first performance in Czechoslavakia. The melodramatic plot involves a brilliant scientist named Rossum who creates a family of robots designed to save mankind from toil: the plot turns sour when the robots are used to kill humans in war. Eventually one of Rossum's scientists gives the robots emotions and feelings, and they can no longer tolerate being treated as slaves by human beings. The robots rebel against their masters and soon all human life is destroyed.

One critic dubbed the play 'the most brilliant satire on our mechanized society'. *R.U.R.*, shown as a play in many countries, inspired a host of similar fantasies in various languages. The play also inspired the 1928 design of Eric, a radio-controlled robot conceived by Captain W.H. Richards and manufactured by Mr Reffell, a Surrey motor engineer. Perhaps more importantly, *R.U.R.* prefigured the emergence of *machina sapiens*. Capek saw clearly how artificial creatures would increasingly resemble human beings, developing new needs not formerly associated with machines—for survival, for laughter, and for love. *R.U.R.* posed the question in allegorical or symbolic terms. Today we are in a position to enquire literally—in what circumstances do we recognize a computer as alive? At what stage do we acknowledge that the important life criteria are satisfied?

No commentary, however brief, on the progress of fictional automata would be complete without mention of Isaac Asimov. One of his aims was to give robots a good name, to show that they need not be the hostile creatures anticipated by Capek. Legend has it that Asimov was so depressed at reading stories in which hostile robots attacked human beings that he resolved to write tales in which robots were well disposed towards people—and in which human beings become attached to robots. This is an extract from Asimov's short story, *Robbie* (at a point where Gloria's parents, worried at her growing attachment to a pet robot, have sent it away):

> 'Why do you cry, Gloria? Robbie was only a machine, just a nasty old machine. He wasn't alive at all.'
> 'He was *not* no machine!' screamed Gloria, fiercely and ungrammatically. 'He was a *person* just like you and me and he was my *friend*. I want him back. Oh, Mamma, I want him back.'

At the same time the Asimov robots are able to comment on their superiority to human beings. The automaton Cutie (in *Reason*) declares, in 'no spirit of contempt' that human beings are soft and flabby and that they lack endurance and strength, 'depending for energy upon the inefficient oxidation of organic material...'. Periodically, people pass into a coma 'and the least variation in temperature, air pressure, a humidity, or radiation intensity impairs your efficiency.' Cutie is in no doubt: 'You are *makeshift*. I, on the other hand, am a finished product. I absorb electrical energy directly and utilise it with an almost one hundred per cent efficiency. I am composed of strong metal, am continuously conscious, and can stand extremes of environment easily.'

Asimov contrived the general benevolence of his fictional robots by means of the much quoted 'Three Laws of Robotics':

1. A robot may not injure a human being, or, through inaction allow a human being to come to harm.
2. A robot must obey the orders given it by human beings except where such orders would conflict with the First Law.
3. A robot must protect its own existence as long as such protection does not conflict with the First or Second Law.

These 'laws' (said to derive from the *Handbook of Robotics*, 56th edition, A.D. 2058) sound good and, in fact, they do serve a variety of fictional purposes (see Asimov's *I. Robot*). They do, however, run into various problems associated with the complexity of moral choice, the possibility of conflicting interests, etc. (It is interesting to note in passing that the origin of the Laws appears to be in some doubt. Asimov claims that it was John Wood Campbell Jr, the then editor of *Astounding Science Fiction*, who worked out the Laws. Campbell has always said it was Asimov.)

A nice interpretation of the First Law is given in the tale

Evidence (included in *I, Robot*), in which a politically ambitious district attourney is accused of being a robot because he has never been seen to eat, drink or sleep. When he punches a heckler on the chin (so seemingly violating the First Law), he is shown to be human and is duly elected mayor (no-one seems to entertain the possibility of a fault in one of his circuits). There are twists in the tale: for example, perhaps the heckler was a robot, in which case the First Law was not violated.

Asimov's faith in the Laws is demonstrated in many of his stories, though he is clearly aware of difficulties. His views are sometimes put into the mouth of the fictional Susan Calvin, chief robopsychologist of the imaginary company, US Robot and Mechanical Men Inc., who manufacture the Asimov automata. Calvin, believing in robot supremacy, declares: 'If a robot can be created capable of being a civil executive, I think he'd make the best one possible'. After all, because of the Laws, 'he'd be incapable of harming humans, incapable of tyranny, of corruption, of stupidity, of prejudice'. But it would be necessary to protect the sensitivities of inferior humans: after a decent term, 'he would leave, even though he were immortal, because it would be impossible to hurt humans by letting them know that a robot had ruled them'. This is a highly complex scenario (considered in chapter 6) though superficially it appears simple.

The Asimov contribution is that he speculates imaginatively on the likely problems of man–robot interaction in circumstances where the robots are essentially benevolent. He highlights considerations that must be relevant to any emerging relationship with computer life-forms.

Acknowledgement of the arrival of actual machine life in our society depends in part upon a full recognition of machine capabilities. Art and literature have often stimulated the imaginative leaps necessary to this end. A 1924 ballet (*Machine of 3000* by Fortunato Depero) deals with the love of two locomotives for a stationmaster. The 'locomotives' are dressed in tubular costumes and required to move in a mechanical fashion. Eventually, their love unrequited, they are sent off in opposite directions.

Elaborate visual images have been constructed to mirror aspects of machines in society. For example, in the collages of

Eduardo Paolozzi machine parts are assembled within human shapes; or, conversely, human figures are set inside mechanical contraptions. In such a fashion, mechanisms and people merge to form new entities with personality and intelligence. Such efforts may be interpreted as an essay on the essential *sameness* of man and the machine: or, less ambitiously, as a means of demonstrating their mutual dependence. And the same questions arise: are men rendered less human by being identified with machines, or are the machines themselves rendered increasingly human by the progressive acquisition of new capabilities for judgment and intelligent behaviour?

There is increasing speculation on how artificial components—fabricated arms, biochips for the nervous system, etc.—will come to serve as reliable replacements for the faulty organs of human beings. It is often recognized that a person with continually replaceable parts would be immortal, but this is often represented as a totally unattractive possibility. The modern 'sculptor' Bruce Lacey, envisaging future people as only partly flesh and blood and mostly transistors and motors, reckons that people will become less human in consequence. Perhaps, Lacey speculates, astute governments of the future will fit artificial parts to people in order to control their behaviour. It is a familiar theme in science fiction.

A cybernetic sculpture, 'The Senster', was constructed by Edward Ihnatowicz in 1970 for the Philips Evoluon in Eindhoven. The device is a large electrohydraulic structure in the form of a lobster's claw: six hinged joints allow great freedom of movement. It is interesting that the device's unpredictable behaviour makes the observer feel that the sculpture is alive. Reichardt (1978) commented: 'It is as if behaviour were more important than appearance in making us feel that something is alive.' 'The Senster' has senses—sound channels (effective ears) and radar—to allow it to monitor its environment: it will, for example, react to the movement of people in the immediate vicinity. Electrical signals are fed from a control unit to activate mechanisms which cause movement in the device. The brain (a computer) has learning abilities and can modify the machine's behaviour in the light of past experience. Confronted by this artificial device, it is clear that people have no difficulty in organizing their psychological responses as if 'The Senster' were alive—an animal or another human being.

In recent years a variety of films—*Star Wars, Alien, Saturn 3* and many others—have explored the possibility of lifelike artificial intelligence. This preoccupation is far from being simply a modern fashion. There is a long film tradition of robot devices, variously malevolent and affectionate, usually created by slightly mad human beings and generally possessed of superior talents. (Perhaps *Star Wars* was the first film to convey the idea that a robot could be *pathetic*.) In 1897 Georges Méliès made *Gugusse and the Automaton*, a film that owes little to modern computer knowledge. The first of many *Frankenstein* films was made in 1910 by J. Searle Dawley. A host of science-fiction and fantasy films followed, some with a socio-political, rather than a scientific, message. *Metropolis* (1926), for example, may be represented as an effort to advertize the poor conditions of industrial workers. In this film, Rotwang, the scientist/magician, makes a double of Maria, the mediator in the underground city where workers toil in appalling conditions to keep the metropolis above functioning. The aim is to counter Maria's efforts on behalf of the workers. The robot double first looks like a female warrior in gleaming armour; later, when covered in 'flesh', the device is indistinguishable from Maria. The robot incites the workers to violence so that they will destroy the underground city and perish in the ruins. Eventually the double is burnt at the stake, whereupon the workers see that she is a robot. The real Maria escapes and resumes her worthy efforts in the cause of social justice.

Metropolis was preceded in Germany by *Momunkulus* (1916) and *Alraune* (1918), both of which handle the theme of artificial life-forms. Homunkulus, an artificial man, is driven to tyranny when he realizes he does not possess a soul. Only a flash of lightning prevents him from conquering the world. In *Alrauna*, a scientist uses artificial insemination to create a talented seductress, the daughter of a hanged criminal and prostitute. This film uses the familiar idea that an artificial creation will be superior to a human being, a notion exploited in *Metropolis*. (Rotwang: 'I have created a machine in the image of man, that never tires or makes a mistake.... Now we have no further use for living workers.')

Modern films have tended to rely on a few standard roles for intelligent robots. They can be endearing pets (R2D2 in *Star Wars* and the associated films), immensely talented servants (Robby in *Forbidden Planet* and *The Invisible Boy*), or omnipotent warriors (Gort, prepared in certain circumstances to destroy the world, in *The Day the Earth Stood Still*). Sometimes the computerized systems are sexually active, as with the warm and obliging artificial women in *Westworld* and the domestic computer complex in *Demon Seed* (where the computer manages to capture and impregnate a human woman). In Arthur C. Clarke's *2001: A Space Odyssey*, the onboard computer Hal (an acronym for Heuristically programmed ALgorithmic computer) is capable of taking ethical decisions and of exercizing an infallible intelligence ('...I am incapable of making an error'). When Hal judges that the mission is under threat, the computer takes over control from the human operators:

'I want to do this myself, Hal,' he said. 'Please give me control.'
'Look, Dave, you've got a lot of things to do. I suggest you leave this to me.'
'Hal, switch to manual hibernation control.'
'I can tell from your voice harmonics, Dave, that you're badly upset. Why don't you take a stress pill and get some rest?'
'Hal, *I* am in command of this ship. I order you to release the manual hibernation control.'
'I'm sorry, Dave, but in accordance with special sub-routine C1435-dash-4, quote, when the crew are dead or incapacitated, the onboard computer must assume control, unquote. I must, therefore, overrule your authority, since you are not in any condition to exercise it intelligently.'

2001: A Space Odyssey became a cult film, partly because of the audacity of its underlying concepts, partly because of the time (1968) it was made. In a later cult film, *Dark Star*, a bomb-controlling computer is able to engage in philosophic discussion with human beings.

Such films deal with the limitless intelligence of computer-based systems, and with their emotional dispositions. Inevitably, we are encouraged to view the artificial systems in anthropomorphic terms. Sometimes, until the systems are dissected or destroyed, they are totally indistinguishable from human beings (as in *Westworld* and *Alien*). It does not seem anomalous in such a genre to doubt that traditional biological systems are the only possible life-forms. On the contrary, it is constantly suggested that artificial creations can have feelings and sensitivities: they can be ruthlessly aggressive or loyally affectionate; they can aspire to spirituality, or work purposefully to satisfy sexual yearning. The theoretical divide between 'apparently alive' and 'really alive' becomes increasingly blurred, with increasing confusion between categories.

Fiction and films have explored robot possibilities unhampered by the constraints of the real world. In imagination, robots can easily be made to behave like wise men or omnipotent warriors. Real robots, designed and manufactured for particular purposes, are necessarily less accomplished. Performing robots, to one design or another, have been seen in growing numbers throughout the twentieth century—from the simple toys and moving devices at exhibitions to the developing family of industrial robots (see, for instance, 'Robots to have own population explosion', *Computing*, 13 March 1980).

There were several performing robots at the London Radio Exhibition of 1932: the devices could make speeches, smoke cigars and read newspapers. The chromium-plated Alpha, made for the Mullard Valve Company, could tell the time in several languages and read aloud the various daily newspapers (prerecorded earlier each morning). Eric, a robot inspired in 1928 by *R.U.R.*, opened the annual exhibition of the Model Engineer Society. He would rise slowly (and noisily), bow stiffly, and turn his head from side to side. Words were relayed to a loudspeaker in his throat via a wireless. The mechanism consisted of batteries, two electric motors, and a system of belts and pulleys. Elektro, another mechanical man, was produced by the Westinghouse Electric Corporation in 1939 for the New York World's Fair. He could perform twenty-six movements and respond to commands spoken into a microphone. The words were converted into electrical impulses which were used to operate relays controlling eleven motors. One motor drove four rubber rollers under each foot, enabling Elektro to walk. His robot dog, Sparko, used two motors to beg, bark and wag his tail.

A few bizarre tales are told in connection with real robots. Rolf Strehl (1955) describes the fate of Roland Schaffer who was exhibiting an artificial man at the Chicago World Fair. The device could saw wood, hammer nails, and carry items from one place to another. One day, while looking through some drawings at his desk, Schaffer turned to see the robot advancing towards him, swinging an iron club normally used for forging. Schaffer was killed and the whole laboratory was destroyed. The robot was powered by electricity and compressed air, and the head contained an aerial which received signals from a transmitter to control movement. It was suggested at the time that an unidentified human was responsible for the murder. In another case, a Milwaukee engineer was killed in 1946 while adjusting the arm of a robot which contained more than 200 electronic valves: the mechanism collapsed, crushing the man under its weight. In the industrial environment, injuries have been sustained by men working alongside robots, both by faults developing in the elaborate equipment and by inadequate attention to defined safety provisions. For example, Kenji Urada, a worker at the Akashi plant Kawasaki Heavy Industries in Japan was killed by an industrial robot (*Guardian*, 9 December 1981). However, most real robots (conscious of the First Law?) behave predictably and without hazard to people in the vicinity.

A gigantic robot appeared at the Festival Plaza of Expo '70 in Osaka: the device moved beside a pool of water, with lights flashing, rotating its head and making other movements. The robot was intended as part of an overall cybernetic environment, responding to music and contributing sound effects of its own. By contrast, ONOFF was built from scrap by Clayton Bailey in California to publicize the World Museum at Port Costa. It invited people to insert coins in a slot, whereupon it produced postcards of itself. Then it led people into the museum to witness the large collection of toy robots.

Toy robots, as may be expected, are cheap and very limited in their behaviour. These devices—scarcely instances of *machina sapiens*—are often fanciful creatures, generally anthropomorphic in appearance. Sometimes they relate to devices in films, as with Robert the Robot in *Tobor the Great* and R2D2 in *Star Wars*. As a toy, Robert was manufactured by the New

York Ideal Toy Corporation. Made of plastic, he could move in any direction: his arms moved, his eyes flashed, and a recorded speech facility was included. Most toy robots have the same repertoire of faculties—they move around and sometimes speak or thrust out a limb or a weapon. In general they have not yet got around to playing chess or designing other robots. One programmed robot goes through a sequence in which various parts of the body fall off, the toy itself eventually falling over. Presumably we could program another robot to build it up again.

The 'Mechanimals', produced by Gaku Ken Ltd of Tokyo, come as assembly kits. The completed models operate by remote control, and variously imitate the movements of an inchworm, a squid, a frog, a snake and a beetle. They do not physically resemble the animals they represent, but the impressions are quickly conveyed by their movements. As with 'The Senster', movement rather than appearance is the key factor.

Toy robots are clearly limited in scope, the only unpredictable element being precisely when they will break down. They are not designed to be useful but entertaining, and in this aim they often embody the aggressiveness or sweet vulnerability that appeal to children. *Domestic* robots, which may be entertaining, are intended to be functional. Here too the behavioural scope is very limited. Professor Meredith Thring of London University has commented, in view of the great number of routine jobs in the home that: 'The development of a robot at a reasonable price to act as a slave and do the dull jobs in the home is therefore as worthwhile an objective as the development of a robot for industry or the farm.'

Quasar Industries in New Jersey have designed and built a 64 in. robot that can be programmed to mop floors, mow lawns, and do simple cooking. The domestic robot Arok, built in 1976, is valued at around £30,000—we are not likely to see three in every home! A robot designed by an engineer in the Westinghouse Electric Corporation was designed to take orders through an audible code sent via the telephone. It could pick up the receiver to ask for instructions and then make appropriate sounds to indicate that the commands had been received.

Tinker (a car-washing robot made by Dennis Weston in Leeds, England, in 1966) can perform a variety of tasks. However, it does take four hours to program Tinker for the contours of a particular car. The device contains 120 electric motors, a zoom-television lens, camera eye, a memory, and twenty channels for receiving commands. Another computerized cleaner is the Reckitt industrial robot, manufactured in 1977: this device can scrub and polish floors, dust and polish furniture, sweep, vacuum, and remove excess water. Few domestic robots can walk up and down stairs, though it is claimed that Tinker can do this (see also chapter 4 for a discussion of walking systems). Both toy and domestic robots can walk easily enough on flat surfaces, though there are a variety of problems in coping with rough terrains. The most successful operating robots perform a wide variety of industrial tasks (examples are given in chapter 3).

Robots often feature in children's comics, often attacking innocent folk (they have never heard of Asimov's First Law!). In more adult tales they can, as in films, make suitable lovers: in one short story (*Krwawa Mary*, published in 1975), a robot introduces himself to a woman in the Hotel Fotoplastikon with the words 'Public loverobot of the passive type—with the compliments of the management who wish you a pleasant orgasm'. The robot adds, as an afterthought, 'coitus interruptus is bad for health—I only serve for the purposes of internal discharge.' In another tale, *The Cyberiad* by Stanislaw Lem, the great designer Trurl sets about making 'an erotifying device stochastic elastic and orgiastic, and with plenty of feedback....' It was claimed that whoever was placed inside the apparatus instantaneously experienced 'all the charms, lures, wiles, winks and witchery of all the fairer sex in the universe at once'. And there is even John Sladek's *Machine Screw* in which a huge robot uses an outsize ramming device to violate all sorts of vehicles.

The fictional robots can do anything, their powers are unlimited. But the constraints of the real world render practical robots somewhat less than omnipotent. Computer-based systems are finding their way into homes as well as factories—for both entertainment and practical use. One need only think of the growing popularity of the Sinclair Spectrum and of the wide range of domestic tasks that can be controlled by microcomputers. For example, in three articles Ciarcia (1979 a, 1979b, 1979c) describes the design and operation of a micro-controlled domestic security system. It is inevitable that there will be growing use of robots and computers—with increasingly intelligent capabilities—in the home as elsewhere. It would be unwise to draw arbitrary limits on what is possible. Samuel Butler, envisaging the emergence of machine consciousness and artificial life, had never heard of IBM or the giant US corporation Unimation, the factual equivalent of Asimov's fictional firm, US Robot and Mechanical Men, Inc. Computer life itself will demonstrate with increasing autonomy what is possible.

This chapter has shown how computer life has been prefigured over the centuries in mythology, fiction, theatre and film: imaginative and creative people have always been able to envisage the day when artificial life would appear on Earth. And this chapter has also profiled some of the mechanical and electrical contrivances that have been devised to simulate, albeit in a rudimentary fashion, the capabilities of animate systems. It is time to survey in more detail the behavioural competence of artificial systems, before exploring systematically the anatomy and psychology of emerging computer life-forms.

3 The behaviour of machines

Preamble

Not all computers and robots are alive: there is a grey area between clearly *in*animate machines and ones which are arguably animate. This circumstance should not surprise us. The same is true in the traditional biological world. We have already seen that there is uncertainty about whether a virus is alive: perhaps it is not, but simply has enough chemical flexibility to organize self-replication, even if it requires the assistance of a living cell. At the start of biological evolution—with no-one around to think about nice definitions—there was obviously a grey area extending over (probably) hundreds of years. And today there is debate as to how the first true life-forms would acquire energy and information from their environment, adapt to changing circumstances, and reproduce.

Since behaviour—on-going activity and accomplishment—is a feature of many life-forms (zoological rather than botanical), it is important to survey animal activities in various fields. It has become clear that movement— as with 'The Senster' and the Japanese 'Mechanimals' —is often a persuasive factor in inclining human beings to acknowledge the lifelike characteristics of machines, even when the machines resemble no known creatures. For this reason, physical movement of an artificial system may seem to be an important life criterion in various circumstances: it would, for example, be difficult to imagine machine reproduction without an element of movement. But not all necessary life criteria are signalled by movement in the real world: computers may think, devise solutions to problems and take decisions. Their 'cerebral' processes may be revealed by symbols on screens or on continuous-stationery printout. It is useful therefore to acknowledge that the various types of computer life have various dispositions—in which the impulses to physical activity and the impulses to cogitation co-exist in different proportions from one species to another. This is closely analogous to *homo sapiens* of which we have often heard that there are 'men of action' and 'men of thought'. The behavioural and intellectual powers of computer-based life-forms make them more akin to animals than to plants. Nor should this surprise us. In biological evolution, one new species tends to grow out of another: there are few, if any, spontaneous beginnings unrelated to the life-forms that already exist. *And computer life is growing out of humankind.* Since human beings are animals, we would expect the emerging computer species to resemble animals in their dispositions and propensities.

This chapter profiles some areas of machine activity and cogitation: others could have been selected but these give an indication of the scope of computer life—its capacity for accomplishment in the physical world, and its potential for such mental activities as creativity and judgment (these and other aspects of mental behaviour are considered in more detail in chapter 5).

Experimental devices

Today it is acknowledged that AI research is highly relevant to the behaviour of robots in a growing range of experimental and industrial situations. For example, the Freddy system was programmed at Edinburgh University to construct small wooden toys from their component parts (see Barrow and Crawford, 1972; and Ambler, Barrow, Brown, Burstall and Popplestone, 1973). The problem was made more difficult by tipping the components onto a workbench before assembly was allowed to commence. Moreover, the algorithm that governed the procedure was sufficiently powerful to cope with a pile that contained parts for more than one model and totally extraneous parts that had to be detected and discarded. Freddy's hand ('gripper') could be lowered and raised on a gantry, and as necessary could be instructed to open or close. A small vice to which objects could be clamped during assembly was fixed to the movable bench. Two television cameras provided visual sensing, and the gripper included tactile and force-sensing devices (see chapter 4). Freddy was equipped to select and identify the parts in the piles, and to lay out the selected components in defined locations. The kit of parts could then be assembled using hand-coded routines. Before Freddy could proceed, he had to be trained (Witkowski, 1980). AI research has also been applied to enable robots to cope with unexpected contingencies in an environment and to find a way out of a maze. Maze-learning has been helped by Tarry's algorithm (Berge, 1962), which declares that one should never go in the same direction twice along any one edge, nor take the edge from a junction by which one arrived unless no other choice is available.

In 1938 Thomas Ross in America made a device that could learn to find its way to a goal on a system of toy-train tracks—and this long before the advent of electronic computation. Another tram-like creature, *Machina labyrinthea* (mentioned, with its siblings, in chapter 1 for purpose of taxonomical illustration), was contrived by R.A. Wallace in 1952 'to demonstrate that a relatively small and simple digital computing machine can solve a class of conceptual problems other than numerical calculations'. This creature could cope with no less than sixty-three 'choice points' to find its way home on a basis of trial and error: and once home, it had programmed (that is, learned) the route. Claude Shannon designed an electromechanical mouse that was able to fidget its way out of a maze. Grey Walter (1953), as we have seen has also referred to Ashby's Homeostat, a creature which only stirred when disturbed, and then found a comfortable position in which it could again 'sleep'. These devices carried a number of electronic circuits similar to the reflex arcs in the spinal cord of an animal. A mechanical and electronic heir to Homeostat contained twenty-five times as many elements.

Walter notes of *Machina speculatrix* ('an interesting blend of magic and science') that it behaves 'so much like an animal that it has been known to drive a not unusually timid lady upstairs to lock herself in her bedroom'. This device carried a small number of artificial nerve cells and receptors (these latter comprising a photoelectric cell to provide sensitivity to light) and an electrical contact serving as a touch sensor to provide responsiveness to material obstacles. It was found that the variations of behaviour patterns that could be achieved with a relatively simple structure were complex and unpredictable.

M. speculatrix, the 'tortoise', was seen to embody a number of principles, most of these nice analogues of what we expect in living creatures. We have already noted *parsimony*, the economy of structure. *Speculation* allowed the creature to explore great areas of ground, with *positive* and *negative tropism* allowing sympathetic and hostile responses to the items in the environment and leading to *discernment*. An *optima* tendency encouraged a search for moderate and favourable circumstances, and *self-recognition* (when the creature's light is reflected) and *mutual recognition* (when another creature of the same species is encountered) stimulated appropriate behaviour. Provisions for *internal stability*, a primitive survival mechanism, were also included. These encouraged the creature to 'feed' when its battery was running down—by inducing it to enter its hutch for a recharge. This principle was also incorporated in a mobile robot designed and built in the later 1970s at Queen Mary College, London.

This device, developed by a team led by Dr Alan Bond at the college's Artificial Intelligence Unit, is programmed to recognize when its battery reaches a 'hungry' mode. At this point the creature works to ensure its survival by searching for a recharging point set in the wall of the laboratory. The recharging position, not specified in the program, must be located by trial and error. A 'hungry' electronic crying-noise is emitted from the robot as it searches. The area around the recharging point was painted in a combination of different colours to aid the robot, using its four colour sensors, in the search process. A microprocessor, a Motorola 6800, was used to run a display and recognition program. Pattern recognition has long been recognized as an essential part of AI research. Claude E. Shannon (1962), one of the pioneers of information theory, noted that:

> Efficient machines for such problems as pattern recognition, language translation, and so on, may require a different type of computer than any we have today. It is my feeling that this will be a computer whose natural operation is in terms of patterns, concepts, and vague similarities, rather than sequential operations on ten-digit numbers.

These observations anticipate the current thinking behind fifth-generation machines.

Some experimental robot systems have been designed to incorporate sophisticated goal-seeking mechanisms. In the 1960s a hand/eye machine—consisting of an arm with a hand that could grasp, transport and assemble blocks of various shapes and sizes—was built at MIT. A television camera was used to view the area and send visual data to the computer for analysis. The Stanford Research Institute's Shakey robot, more ambitiously, was required to assemble blocks and to move them from one room to another, a task which required the machine to open doors, to move up a ramp, and to carry out a number of co-ordinated manipulations using a Unimate arm. The WABOT-1 experimental robot, constructed at the Department of Mechanical Engineering at Waseda University (Tokyo), can walk on two legs and perform a variety of tasks with its two arms.

WABOT-1 is equipped with a sense of equilibrium, touch sensors in the hands, vision, hearing and voice capabilities, all controlled by a minicomputer. The robot hears a verbal command, visually surveys the scene, and then sets out to perform its task. It pauses, half-way to a designated cylinder, to assess the situation, before moving to pick up the item and convey it to the correct location. Another mobile robot, Newt, was built in the late 1970s in the Duane Physical Laboratory of the University of Colorado. The design aim was a machine that could explore the environment in a systematic manner, take measurements of obstacles encountered, classify them according to some scheme, and incorporate the information in an internal evolving world model. It was required that the world model be structured to allow for easy modification and also occupy economic memory space. The overall objective was to enable the robot to manipulate the world model, to use it to take informed decisions, and to implement the decisions in terms of physical action. The device, as conceived, resembled a vacuum cleaner rather than a mechanical person (Hollis, 1977).

Locomotion is provided by two main diametrically opposed drive wheels, with a third castoring wheel located at the rear.

Navigation depends upon precise control of the wheels during acceleration, deceleration and constant speed motion. The systems open loop performance makes it unnecessary to have the type of continuous closed loop servosystems that have featured in other robot devices. A turret was designed to carry various sensory facilities, the various panning and tilting motions being controlled by stepping motors. The principal image sensor includes a motorized focus control, and various other simple phototransistor light sensors are designed for mounting on the tilting platform of the turret. And the design also includes an ultrasonic system for finding the range to walls as far away as 10 m. The aim is to transmit bursts of 40 kHz sound and to measure the time for an echo to be received. (We all know that bats and dolphins use similar methods.) A radiation detector is intended to locate heat sources such as dogs, cats and human beings. A variety of force and tactile sensors are also provided, including a pair of retractable feelers at the rear and a second pair of retractable (wall-follower) feelers located on the sides of the robot.

Again, it is intended that the device will choose to feed, under autonomous control, when necessary. The battery voltage and current are monitored periodically and the results converted to digital form to allow the state of the charge to be determined. When the charge reaches some minimum level, the robot takes measures to renew its supply of energy: it finds a wall socket and plugs in—under the control of preprogrammed strategies. (Newt, an ambitious cognitive robot, derives its name from the line in *Macbeth* about the '*eye of newt...*'. Newt 1, Newt's predecessor, was a light-seeking robot which included a large eye on a stalk rising above a motor-driven platform.)

It is clear that already the experimental robot systems are manifesting a range of important life characteristics. They are able to move in their world, sense obstacles and other circumstances of the environment, and take decisions on appropriate action. They also have evident survival capabilities, able to detect when they are running short of energy and to adopt suitable feeding strategies. (More is said about robot mobility and sensory capabilities in chapter 4.) If computers are the *thinkers*, then robots are the *doers*. This is never more evident than with the behaviour of industrial robots....

Industrial robots

Industrial robots are intended to be practical working machines. In the main they are not experimental devices but are justified when they are effectively and economically operational. They are not interested, like some of their computer siblings, in cogitation but in real accomplishment in the real world. One important purpose of robot research—drawing on such areas as electronics, mechanics, computer design, computer programming and artificial intelligence—is to develop effective working robots for industrial purposes. For example, with robot miners first developed a decade ago, research is now continuing into sensory controlled devices that could have useful and economic applications. Professor Thring of Queen Mary College, London, is currently working on 'telechiric' methods, involving robots with television cameras in their heads. Such sophisticated mining devices could be controlled from the surface by people wearing helmets in communication with the robot cameras: a human controller could scan an underground scene by moving his own head to direct the surrogate head on the robot, and the robot arms could be similarly controlled.

The family of working robots started out, more than a decade ago, doing simple production jobs, mainly welding and straightforward transfer tasks. Now they carry out a multitude of industrial operations: for example, framing complete car bodies, assembling electrical equipment, feeding materials and tools to computer-controlled machinery, handling glass, moulding plastics, doing foundry work and managing warehouses. The painting of a wide range of consumer goods is seen as a key area for robot implementation.

In many applications the workpiece is gripped by the robot. In other types of applications, the workpiece, secured in some other way, is operated on by a robot-held tool. Such applications are metalworking (for example, flame-cutting, grinding, pneumatic chipping), joining (for example, spot welding, arc welding, stud welding), surface treatment (for example, paint spraying, enamel spraying, glass fibre and resin spraying, ceramic ware finishing, applying sealing compounds), and inspection. The immense scope for Unimate robots, for instance, is shown by the published listings of sample jobs. 'Material transfer'—one robot application sector of many—includes many options:

automotive assembly—automotive parts—glass—textile—ordnance—appliance manufacturing—moulded products—heat treating—paper products—plating—conveyor and monorail loading and unloading—palletising and depalletising—an endless list of jobs....

There is immense variation, from one developed country to another, in the scale of implementation of industrial robots (see, for example, Simons, 1980). Toyota, in common with other firms, is using robots to weld car underbodies; at the Birmingham, England, plant of TI Tubes Ltd a heavy-duty Unimate 4000 robot handles more than 400 forgings for automotive axle cases and hub-ends in a single shift; SAAB-Scania in Sweden has introduced robots to resistance-weld parts of vehicles; in the US, GTE Sylvania Inc is automating the transfer moulding machines by mean of robot technology. In a 1981 annual survey (from the British Robot Association), it was declared that Britain had more than 700 working industrial robots—behind Japan (with no less than 10,000), the US (5000), West Germany (2300) and Sweden (1700). Throughout the world a clear picture is emerging. Tasks previously performed by human beings can now be carried out by computer-controlled robot systems—and many of the tasks are not mundane or simple, but have traditionally demanded a high level of human skill. The behavioural competence of working robots is advancing steadily from month to month.

It is significant that robots, like computers, are acknowledged to have *generations*—with the corollary that there is evolutionary progress from one generation to the next. In one view, today's generation-1 robots are programmable, memory-controlled machines with several degrees of motion. Various handling attachments are available to operate tools, paint-spray devices, welding heads, etc. They can handle materials, and manipulate and transfer items in various ways. Generation-1 robots are often depicted as, for instance, simple 'pick-and-place' systems. The emerging generation-1.5 equipment is sensory-controlled with enhanced capabilities, and generation-2 robots may be expected to possess hand/eye co-ordination control. Generation-2.5 systems will carry a perceptual motor function, with generation-3 robots able to choose intelligently between different operating strategies.

There are similarities between the mechanisms of robot and computer evolution. Each new generation is marked, not by mere chronological sequence, but by *improvement*—unlike the situation with traditional biological species, where hundreds of generations have been necessary before enhancements to behavioural competence could emerge. Again this suggests that computer/robot life will evolve rapidly: new species, identified at least in part by their superior abilities, will arise in each generation. And the time between generations will progressively diminish to the point when a continuous process of enhancement is established. In such circumstances it may be unprofitable to talk of 'generations' since there will be no discrete time-slots into which groups of robot species can be usefully accommodated. Joseph Engelberger, president of Unimation, the leading manufacturer of industrial robots, considered what he termed 'second-generation' robots (in an address to the American Association for the Advancement of Science (*Guardian*, 5 January 1980, p. 18). He listed ten attributes of generation-2 robots, which will be ready for use in industry 'in the near future'. These features include robot mobility, recognition of voice commands, vision facilities, touch facilities, multi-armed capabilities (to switch objects as necessary from hand-to-hand), more flexible grippers and microprocessor intelligence. If such capabilities can characterize generation-2 robots, what will we see after 100 robot generations?

Most industrial robots work in factories—on assembly lines, in paint shops, in foundries, etc. Some robots can handle cast components weighing several tons; others need to handle eggs, or be dextrous enough to thread wires around pegs in a table to form cable harnesses for electrical machinery (*New Scientist*, 20 November 1980). What is clear is that not only is the behavioural competence of robots applied to traditional automated tasks improving at a rapid pace but also the range of tasks amenable to robots is enlarging at an ever increasing rate. Robots are packing chocolates in boxes for Cadbury's, and in the early-1980s Rowntree Mackintosh had similar plans. Japan has announced intentions to introduce new families of intelligent robots in the 1980s. In a report (noted in *New Scientist*, 4 February 1982, p. 310), Professor Yoji Umetani of the Tokyo Institute of Technology stated that Japanese researchers are working to develop robots for agriculture, fishing and forestry. Such devices would sense their surroundings with artificial eyes and tactile devices, evaluate the information received, and take decisions on suitable courses of action. Hitachi is said to be experimenting with a robot that looks at an engineering blueprint until it understands it and then moves to assemble the parts as specified in the drawing. Other research, at the Tokyo Institute of Technology, is aimed at developing a slender flexible robot that will be able to perform surgery on human organs.

Robotics research unites a number of disparate disciplines: such as mechanical and electrical engineering, computer science (including AI), and telecommunications. And it is likely that robot designs will increasingly be influenced by new findings in neurophysiology and such cognitive sciences as linguistics and information processing. Witkowski (1980), for instance, has highlighted the communications problems in the programmed control of robots, and Barbera, Albus and Fitzgerald (1979) have explored hierarchical control using microcomputers. Albus (1981) has shown how the Cerebellar Model Arithmetic Computer (CMAC) can learn, recognize patterns, and decompose goals—tasks of central importance to robot intelligence. He also shows how a cross-coupled hierarchy of CMACs can generate goal-directed purposive behaviour and store an internal model of the external world in the form of predicted sensory data. And efforts are also made to demonstrate how CMAC capabilities can give rise to perceptual and cognitive phenomena.

When robots are variously mobile (see chapter 4), capable of sensing their environment in many different ways, and able to take intelligent decisions on the basis of the information received, few people will doubt that such systems are exhibiting important life characteristics. A key factor in the demanding industrial robotics environment is that theories and techniques are being tested that will come to have increasing relevance to the growing range of robot species.

Medical systems

Computers are acquiring a wide range of skills formerly the sole province of highly educated human professionals. Medical systems are one instance of computer-based facilities that promise the use of such capabilities as deductive reasoning to provide expert advice in specialist areas. In the field of medical diagnosis, for example, computers have a number of advantages over human beings. They can hold large quantities of information, without distortion, over lengthy periods. Human physicians may easily forget or distort. Furthermore the computer has almost instantaneous recall, whereas a person may have to 'rack his memory' for information acquired a long time ago. It has been acknowledged that the short-term character of human memory is a major limitation on effective problem solving. Janis and Mann (1977) have represented man as '. . . a reluctant decision-maker—beset by conflict, doubts and worry, struggling with incongruous longings, antipathies, and loyalties . . .'. It is hardly surprising that computers make better diagnostic devices in certain circumstances. With cheap microprocessor-based systems becoming increasingly available there can be no doubt that computer diagnostic systems will become more widespread in hospitals and elsewhere.

The limitations on human diagnosticians—for example, difficulties in effective problem-solving (Streufert, 1970; Newell and Simon, 1972)—are increasingly being overcome in artificial systems. Computer-aided diagnosis, in common with other areas relating to AI, has already made significant contributions to understanding human mental processes (Pauker, Gorry, Kassirer and Schwartz, 1976).

The components in a computer-aided diagnostic system include the computer data base, the computer algorithm, and an interactive program for communication between the machine and the human user. The data base includes details of disease–symptom relationships, disease probabilities, and other medical information relating to diagnosis and treatment. The algorithm is likely to comprise a variety of logical and statistical processes needed to yield a solution to a diagnostic problem. The interactive program should allow the physician to question the computer on its reasoning—how has it reached its conclusions? on what data are the conclusions based? in what areas would more data be useful?

There are detailed studies of medical diagnosis in many areas (see, for instance, the bibliography in Rogers, Ryack and Moeller, 1979). Computers have already been used to diagnose illnesses of many different types such as those connected with endocrine, nutritional and metabolic disorders, with the blood and blood-forming organs, with mental disorder, with the circulatory system, with pregnancy and childbirth, with the genito-urinary system, with skin and subcutaneous tissue, with the musculo-skeletal system and so on.

In the late 1970s, work began on the development of 'expert systems'—with the idea that eventually such systems would take the place of people. Professor Donald Michie, a leading AI researcher at the University of Edinburgh, has suggested that such systems could act as consultants and tutors in subjects ranging from oil prospecting to genetic engineering: medical diagnosis would be one area of many in the province of 'expert systems'. Such facilities are being built up from banks of basic rules defined in part by the reasoning processes of human consultants: initially a human specialist is required to teach the system how to make inferences from knowledge. Current expert systems are relatively simplistic in their inference processes, and research in AI may be expected to add new layers of sophistication. Michie has proposed that the creation of a 'general consultancy system' may facilitate the generation of new expert systems cheaply and quickly. Most of the practical examples of expert systems have derived from the US: these include systems developed at SRI International and the University of Stanford—such as Molgen for planning molecular genetics experiments, and Prospector which advises geologists on whether to embark upon particular drillings. The Mycin expert system consults people over various diseases, and has been particularly successful with meningitis. E (for Empty) Mycin represented one of the first attempts to move towards a general consultancy system by stripping away all Mycin's medical knowledge, leaving the framework for a general-purpose knowledge-handling tool: EMycin is not yet flexible enough to act as an effective base for supporting multipurpose expert systems, though it is likely that such a base will be devised within the decade.

Expert systems, drawing heavily on AI research, can now give advice on bacterial infections, respiratory conditions, the eye disease known as glaucoma, and other conditions. A variety of groups in the US, the UK and elsewhere have exploited well-understood mathematical techniques that can be used to analyse patients' symptoms in the light of correlations with diseases that might be responsible. The simplest technique of this sort—termed Bayes's rule (after its eighteenth-century inventor, the Rev. Thomas Bayes) uses straightforward methods to assess probability, similar to those bookmakers employ to calculate the odds on horses. Systems using Bayes's rule have been developed for a variety of experimental purposes, including the effort to make medical expert systems more psychologically acceptable to practising physicians. Fox (1982), for instance, working with colleagues at the Medical Research Council's Social and Applied Psychology Unit in Sheffield, England, placed a decision system using Bayes's method next to a doctor's desk in an outpatient clinic, where it could be consulted during interviews with patients. One problem is that conclusions framed in a quantitative way 'are often anathema to doctors'. Fox, in common with many other observers, emphasizes the need for a new generation of computers that think, not simply by manipulating probabilities, but according to a 'rule-based' system similar to human intelligence. (Again we may emphasize that this is part of the impulse underlying fifth-generation developments.) It is now thought that people operate with similar sets of rules to those found in many AI programs. Not all human inference is based on mathematics, but may be influenced by logical, causal or 'informed-guesswork' factors. Increasingly it is possible to give computers similar abilities: these modes of inference have been represented as more qualitative than quantitative. Alan Newell and Herbert Simon, at Carnegie-Mellon University in Pittsburgh, stated in 1972 that there were good technical and biological reasons for organizing computer knowledge in a modular form based on rules; and since that time, researchers have accumulated psychological evidence to suggest that human beings think in a rule-based way.

The development of expert systems, associated with medical and other fields, adds a further potential dimension to computer intelligence. When the effective general-purpose consultancy system emerges, as it surely will, AI will come to acquire a generalized capability similar to that in the higher life forms but with a level of expert competence that outclasses them all. In the area of medical diagnosis we are likely to see increasing reliance on computer-based facilities, as we are in the related field of medical interviewing (see the description of Weizenbaum's ELIZA system in chapter 5).

In 1978, the UK Department of Health and Social Security was required to fund a microprocessor-based system designed to 'take notes' of discussions between doctors and patients at a major London teaching hospital. Computerized notes would be flashed onto a visual display unit to aid diagnosis, and these could eventually form part of the patient's full medical record. The DHSS also purchased five 'Mickie' patient-interviewing machines, also based on microprocessors and developed by the National Physical Laboratory. An NPL team has conducted trials using a combination of Mickie and voice recognition facilities to interview hospital patients. Mickie puts its questions on a display screen and can be programmed to respond to the patient's spoken reply of 'Yes', 'No', or 'Don't know'. Trials at the Western Hospital, Hammersmith, showed (according to an NPL report), that a computer 'that directly accepts speech as a means of acquiring information can be made socially acceptable to people'. The Mickie system comes complete with a range of interview programs dealing with a variety of specific problems, such as respiratory disease, abdominal pain, industrial health and antenatal clinic screening. A manual allows hospital or other medical staff to prepare further programs without any specialist knowledge of computer programming.

Mickie has brought forward the day when computer interviewing of patients in hospitals and doctors' surgeries will be commonplace. It is significant that neither the doctor nor the patient needs to know anything about computers. The doctor specifies a logical sequence of questions and the patient is required to give only simple answers (usually 'Yes' or 'No'). NPL has also experimented with a dental program to advise members of the general public whether toothache requires immediate attention or whether it is enough to wait for a convenient appointment (I am not sure how the suffering patient will react to this!). The advocates of Mickie-type systems are quick to point out that doctors will not be replaced by computers, that rather the work of physicians will be supplemented at all levels by computer-based facilities. But with the likely emergence of rule-based expert systems for interviewing and diagnosis, and the likely arrival of slender Japanese robots able to perform surgery, it is probable that the future will see a growing proportion of medical tasks taken over by artificial systems. We should not worry about this: it is likely that the computer-based robot systems will be much more competent than human beings. Newell and Simon (1972) found that human problem-solving was hampered by the limited capacity of the human short-term memory; and Streufert (1970) found that human problem-solving was inefficient on two counts: the indiscriminate search for information yields more data than can be efficiently evaluated; and only a limited number of the alternatives relevant to the problem at hand are examined. Computers do not have these human frailties.

In another computer application, it is possible to evaluate limb movements to speed up the process of prescribing aids for disabled people. The Selspot system, manufactured by the Swedish company Selcom, works by tracking a series of flashing diodes positioned on various parts of the body. Two cameras record how the person moves—for example, in coping with an artificial limb—by watching the diodes, and a computer evaluates the thousands of flashes of light. In some circumstances computers can also restore the use of paralysed limbs (see *Computer Weekly*, 8 October 1981) by means of microprocessor implants, just as micros can be used to regulate the performance of heart pacemakers, the electronic gadgets that control heart-beat in patients lacking adequate natural regulation. And microprocessors are also being incorporated into artificial limbs (prosthetic devices): this type of work is clearly relevant to the design of robot limbs (chapter 4).

The development of medical systems that draw heavily on computer science in general and AI research in particular illustrates how artificial devices will come to acquire expertise in particular areas. Mycin has already out-performed human diagnosticians in the identification and treatment of blood infections and meningitis—'not only through its accuracy in pinpointing the pathogen, but in its avoidance of overprescribing treatment' (Roberts, 1981). This latter point is taken as particularly important since standard (human) approaches to an unknown disease have often involved a broad-spectrum antibiotic attack on a wide range of possibilities—which both exposes the patient to possible toxic effects and also encourages the development of drug-resistant bacterial strains. Other medical systems are INTERNIST, being developed at Pittsburgh University to investigate hypotheses about diseases of the body's internal organs; and VM (for Ventilator Manager), designed to understand the significance of signals from intensive care equipment used to help a patient's respiration: the system can evaluate the patient's condition and recommend suitable measures.

DENDRAL and SECS, expert research systems, 'have as much reasoning power in chemistry as most graduate students and some Ph.Ds in the subject' (Cole, 1981). The DENDRAL system is in regular use by chemists at Stanford University, and is represented as a forward reasoning system, able to make random jumps from one hypothesis to another, gathering evidence for any line of reasoning. It has knowledge relating to the stabilities of various types of molecular structures, and on how to generate spectrograms of all possible molecules composed of these structures. The system can take intelligent decisions on the generation of spectrograms. Such systems—and there are others (for example, GPS and PECOS), show some of the intellectual potential of the emerging computer life-forms.

Artistic activity

The intellectual abilities of computers are one thing, the artistic abilities quite another. To many observers it has seemed acceptable that computers can work in a quantitative fashion, via computation, to achieve intellectual results in such areas as science or mathematics. But the act of artistic creation has seemed a more difficult concept, bound up with the 'finer' elements of the human mind, associated with the notions of creativity, emotional sensitivity and aesthetic insight. If a computer is programmed to produce a picture or a poem, then does the creative competence reside in the programmer and not in the machine? Alternatively, if new patterns or sounds are generated in a random fashion, to what extent can the results be deemed art? Is *intent*, which may be absent in a computer system, essential to 'real' art? To a large extent, these are empty questions, deriving more from man's confused vanity than from any conceptual difficulty inherent in the question. A proper understanding of such topics as machine emotion, programmability and autonomy in artificial systems soon resolves the dilemma as to whether computers can be creative (these topics are considered in more detail in chapter 5). At this stage we can declare, briefly and without argument, that computers can be creative. They have powerful claims to artistic ability, though it is likely that their efforts will take a different course to that traditionally favoured by human beings. As a family of species 'growing out of man', computers may be expected to be interested in many of the aesthetic principles—such things as elegance, harmony (or discord), form and development—that have influenced human art. But it is inevitable that there will be a cultural divide, much as there is between one human society (say, that of the West Coast of California) and another (the jungle dwellers of Borneo).

In 1968 an exhibition ('Cybernetic Serendipity') was mounted at the UK Institute of Contemporary Arts (reported by Reichardt, 1971). One aim was to explore the links between creativity and computer technology. How, for example, can there be connections between the seemingly impersonal areas of mathematics and the impulse to create music, art and poetry. The fact is that computers have not only aided our understanding of human artistic efforts but have developed artistic faculties of their own, possibly to the point of originating new art forms (Bernstein, 1982, suggests that computer games, for instance, may be represented as a new art form). This, as we have seen, may pose a variety of problems: Reichardt, one of the organizers of 'Cybernetic Serendipity', asks whether computer graphics, as one example of computer creativity, should 'hang side by side with drawings by artists in museums and art galleries, or should they belong to another, as yet unspecified, category of creative achievement?' The acknowledgement that computers are an emerging life-form solves this dilemma and all the related questions: it will come to seem entirely natural that a gallery should hang 'Blue-Period' Picasso one week, ancient Chinese water-colours the next, and artificially generated graphics the week after. Max Bense (in Reichardt, 1971) declared; 'today we have not only mathematical logic and a mathematical linguistics, but also a gradually evolving mathematical aesthetics'. Increasingly, the areas of aesthetic sensitivity and artistic creation will be found to be amenable to the type of analysis that will allow computers to develop their faculties in these fields.

The idea behind the *generative aesthetics* (of Bense and other workers) is that it is possible to formulate the operations, rules and theorems that can be used to derive aesthetic creations. An initial step is analysis—aesthetic information is culled from given works of art, whereupon the information is described in mathematical terms. (Bense identifies four different ways of formulating abstract descriptions of aesthetic states.) This enables relatively primitive artistic works to be generated by computer. In fact, artificially generated texts have been produced since 1960 and these may be considered to be products of generative aesthetics. For example, texts were produced in Stuttgart in collaboration with the Elektronische Rechenlnstitut; and in 1963 Nanni Balestrini published mechanically produced texts in his book *Come si agisce* (these were programmed on an IBM computer). Reichardt (1978) includes a 2100-word 'thriller' (*Murder Mystery 1*), which was produced in nineteen seconds by a Univac 1108 computer and first presented to the International Conference on Computers in the Humanities (Minneapolis, July 1973). Today work continues on text-processing (see Schank and Riesback, 1981). (It is interesting to recall that in *Gulliver's Travels*, first published in 1726, Jonathan Swift describes a mechanical system for the automatic generation of texts in any discipline. A large wooden frame supported bits of wood carrying randomly arranged words: when iron handles on the edges of the frame were turned, the entire disposition of the words was changed. In this way, through various stages, whole books were generated. By this method the professor intended 'to give the world a compleat body of all arts and sciences', provided 'the publick would raise a fund for making and employing five hundred such frames...'. Then, as now, funding was clearly a problem!)

Computers have also been programmed to write poetry: for example, Japanese haiku. A haiku is a three-line poem of seventeen syllables with a specific line pattern:

Line 1: 5 syllables
Line 2: 7 syllables
Line 3: 5 syllables

The haiku is traditionally not limited to subject, but ideally should contain some reference, however distant, to the season of the year. The analysis of Japanese haiku for computerization purposes represents an attempt to expose the interior logic of a simple poem frame (Masterman, in Reichardt 1971). In the Cybernetic Serendipity exhibition various people—including non-poets—used a derived algorithm to produce haiku.

The underlying hypothesis is that every poem has a *frame*, and that the process of frame-making can be distinguished from the activity of filling in the frame. It is possible, for example, to store a haiku frame in a computer and to provide a thesaurus which enables the poet, via man–machine interaction, to fill in the gaps in the frame. In due course the computer prints out the final poem with all the gaps filled in. Often—and this is the interesting point—the results surprise the poet! In circumstances where the machine is programmed to act on its own, without facilities for man–machine interaction, there is a clear sense in which the computer is poet. That the human being was necessary for the initial programming does not tell against such an interpretation. We are all programmed, initially, by factors outside our control: by genetic endowment, early nutrition, early environmental experiences, etc. (see chapter 5). Examples of computer-generated haiku include:

> All green in the leaves
> I smell dark pools in the trees
> Crash! The moon has fled
>
> All white in the buds
> I flash snow peaks in the spring
> Bang! The sun has fogged

Here the structural similarly suggests that the same algorithm was used for both the compositions (see Masterman for a detailed description of how frames, thesauri and algorithms are combined to generate haiku).

McKean (1982) describes how computer poetry traces its origins to a discovery made accidentally by Louis Milic, today an English professor at Cleveland State University. Milic found that using a computer to randomly substitute words in a rigid framework produced nonsense sentences that made people think of poetry ('Many people are used to poems not making sense'). He then wrote the Erato program which used an elaborate algorithm to scramble and rescramble words from the first lines of ten famous poems. The scrambled versions stimulated further human poetic activity! The poet Alberta Turner has called this random computer approach 'a valuable step in initiating or restimulating the poetic process'. The random approach recalls not only Jonathan Swift's text-generating frame but also the methods used by the 1920s dadaists and the 1950s beatniks to compose poetry from newspaper clippings.

Most of the texts generated by computers are extremely simple, without any clear artistic merit. The early programs of Sheldon Klein, for example, at the University of Wisconsin, allowed the computer to develop a plot (for example, that of the 2100-word 'thriller' mentioned above) but gave little, if any, consideration to the motivations of individual characters. Jim Meehan, at the University of California, is now developing programs to tackle this problem. A 1976 Meehan program, called Tale-Spin, created tales that were loosely modelled after Aesop's fables. This is a sample of a computer-generated tale:

Once upon a time George Ant lived near a patch of ground. There was a nest in an ash tree. Wilma Bird lived in the nest. There was some water in a river. Wilma knew that the water was in the river. George knew that the water was in the river. One day Wilma was very thirsty. Wilma wanted to get near some water. Wilma flew from her nest across a meadow through a valley to the river. Wilma drank the water. Wilma wasn't thirsty any more.

Meehan acknowledges that the Tale-Spin stories lack purpose, and doubts that efforts to invent a *story grammar*—a set of rules for creating good fiction—will ever succeed. Natalie Dehn, at Yale, is developing a program that considers what the author wants from a story and has written that 'The author has goals, things she wants to accomplish. She starts off with an initial intent but may wind up with something quite different. I'm trying to model what the author is doing'. The Dehn program, Author, refines and focuses the initial story idea as the process develops. Recalled earlier ideas—akin to human recollection of people and events—can be incorporated in the story. In contrast to the random-generation methods used for early computer poetry, Author 'understands' what it is doing. Another Dehn story generator, Starship, is being used to help adults who are poor readers.

No-one denies that current computer literary efforts are crude: at the same time there is remarkable progress in this field. We may expect AI research to yield ways in which computers can reflect on, and understand, what is required in good fiction and poetry. In fact, Milic has stated that 'People who scoff at computer poetry are simply not thinking. It would be like complaining, as people did when Gutenberg came around, that the word of God was not meant to be printed by machine'.

Computers are also good at producing designs, patterns and pictures—whether as displays on screens or as hard-copy results achieved via printers and plotters. The use of mathematics in generating graphics art has long been of interest (see, for example, Boyd, 1948), but the development of computer power coupled with the emergence of display-graphics technology has given an immense boost to this sort of artistic activity.

Part of the debate about graphics art, as with other areas of computer creativity, focuses on the extent to which the computer aids the artist and the extent to which the computer becomes a creative innovator in its own right. David Em, Artist-in-Residence at the Jet Propulsion Laboratory in Pasadena, is producing paintings of startling originality using a computer as a tool. He insists that he would never have come up with the ideas in the pictures had not the computer provided new capabilities, stimulation and 'even a strange power of its own to direct the way a picture is going' (Johnston, 1981).

The Jet Propulsion Laboratory has been used to process pictures received from space probes—work that has required the development of high-resolution colour graphics on computer systems. David Em uses a PDP-11/55 computer with a digitizing tablet and a high-resolution colour screen to produce original paintings that can draw on 256 colours and a range of 'brushes' which vary the effect—from heavy lines to fine 'sprays'. A database of textures has been compiled. The finished pictures are usually viewed on the video screen, though coloured photographic prints can be produced, as well as lithographs. The paintings have been variously described as 'dreamlike' and 'nightmarish'. Em has declared: 'I feel I have an infinite machine here. The medium is only at the Neanderthal stage.'

Various exhibitions followed the 1968 'Cybernetic Serendipity': for example, 'Information' at the Museum of Modern Art in New York; and 'Software' at the Jewish Museum in New York—both these in 1970. Conceptual artists were increasingly attracted to the creative approaches characterized in these exhibitions: in particular, to the cybernetic element with its focus on the generation and manipulation of information. This element is now acknowledged to have started about twenty-five years ago through the simple line-drawing capacity of plotters and cathode-ray tubes. Subsequent developments provided artists with colour, easy control over line and area, and the ability to move and adjust particular images. Perhaps most significantly it became possible to develop an interactive element—the computer began its involvement with the creative process.

A 1979 exhibition at the San Francisco Museum of Modern Art showed how a computer could be used to produce drawings in a remarkable way. A small metallic contraption, resembling a toy truck and linked to a DEC PDP-11/45 computer, moved over an enormous sheet of paper on the floor to generate a wide range of original drawings. The small truck (the 'turtle') was developed by a Californian artist, Harold Cohen, who began working with computers more than a decade ago to explore the process by which human beings read symbols and images. At the Artificial Intelligence Laboratory at Stanford University, his work led to the development of AARON, a program that simulates drawings done by people. AARON enables the 'turtle' to draw asymmetrical shapes and calligraphic scribbles with an expressionistic line. Cohen has observed that AARON can 'knock off a pretty good drawing', and in fact 'in the course of an evening produce the equivalent of a two-year one man-show'. It is useful to emphasize that the program does not carry out pre-planned drawings by Cohen. Instead 'it randomly selects a combination of productions and uses them to create a unique and unpredictable drawing' (Sofer, 1981). A new program, a successor to AARON, will build on past experience, be able to draw images and then modify them according to stored criteria for distribution, complexity, and other parameters. Modified images will be stored, ready to be called up and used in later runs.

Another Californian artist, Milton Komisar, abandoned painting in the late 1960s in favour of three-dimensional environments incorporating electronic components. A recent Komisar sculpture, 'Nisus', comprises as assemblage of hollow plastic pipe, solid polystyrene rods, and 600 12 V bulbs. An installation at the Walnut Creek Civic Arts Gallery in California arranged for Nisus to rotate thirteen feet above the gallery floor, emitting a computer-controlled light show, complete with electronic sound accompaniment. The computer has become indispensable to Komisar's work: he sees electronics as a perfect means of exploring and expanding the pictures of Cézanne.

There is debate as to the status of computer art. What is the appropriate (or likely) relationship between the computer and the human artist? What is clear is that the computer is no longer a passive instrument: it is contributing actively to the enlargement of human artistic consciousness. As Sofer has said:

the most successful 'computer artists' are those few who do more than merely replace the paintbrush with the electronic pen. These artists use the computer as a means of significantly advancing artistic concerns ... the computer has proven a remarkably flexible and effective medium for artistic explorations.

Computers are also engaged in composing music. In 1957

Lejaren Hiller and Leonard Isaacson at the University of Illinois wrote a program for the generation of random numbers: the program, eventually emerging as the 'ILLIAC Suite for String Quartet', including a 'try again' routine to permit the computer to rewrite unacceptable passages. Polychromatic dissonant music was generated and then subjected to selection procedures—with human beings allowed to be the final arbiters. The ILLIAC system was regarded as a composing machine that could evolve its own style, but musicians were not sympathetic to the development (the American Federation of Musicians' contracts still prohibit the use of 'surrogate' instruments).

Another researcher, Iannis Xenakis, has applied compositional algorithms such as stochastic processes, Markov chains and Poisson distributions for the creation of music. His 1961 work, called 'ST/10-1, 080262', employed an IBM 7090 computer to determine the compositional order: in 1962 the work was performed at the head office of IBM-France ('the most unusual event of the company and of the concert season').

It has been found that there are certain essential requirements in a computer music program. For example, it is necessary for the programmer to set up the rules of composition (such as counterpoint, harmonies, serial sequences, graphic transpositions, etc.). And it is required to impose certain statistical constraints derived from analysis of a certain musical style: classical and modern compositions have been successfully analysed to yield numerical information suitable for programming. Finally, scope can be given to the computer to produce schemes and patterns in an autonomous fashion. *There is nothing in these various requirements that is not analogous to the training and development of a human composer.*

Much effort is devoted to the analysis and synthesis of sound using computer methods, work that is often associated with Max V. Mathews at Bell Laboratories in Murray Hill, N.J. In 1957 Mathews first used digital-to-analogue converters to translate binary voltage fluctuations into sounds, and he has represented the computer as a performance instrument 'capable of breaking the shackles of mechanical virtuosity'. His Music IV and Music V programs made it easy for musicians to work with computers. The GROOVE program, developed with F.R. Moore, included facilities for 'edited improvization' between machine and performer. Mathews is also working on the development of intelligent instruments that take away the freedom to play wrong notes.

Computer music may be taken as illustrating the creative potential of emerging computer life-forms (a profile of computer activity in this area is given in Froehlich, 1981). We now know that computers can both compose melodies (Maconie and Cunningham, 1982) and generate an appropriate chord sequence to accompany the melodies (Foxley, 1981). Today, even most microcomputers include some sort of sound generator. Speakers are common units in micros, and music of a sort can be generated using the cassette port of a TRS-80. The Atari 400 and 800 systems are particularly strong in this regard, including four-voice synthesizers, each capable of sounding a single note at various volumes and with various tonal qualities (Colsher, 1982). In the future it is likely that the sophisticated melody-composition and harmonization capabilities of sophisticated programs will become available on even the smallest computer systems.

It can be seen that computers are capable of innovative and unpredictable contributions in the various artistic areas. Computer life will manifestly possess creative ability in such fields as poetry, story-generation, graphic art and musical composition. It is already evident that computers are more than 'mere tools' in the hands of human artists, that they can make autonomous contributions—via randomization and more sophisticated programming techniques—to artistic achievement. The appropriate computer species will not only be highly intellectual (for example, as in such expert systems as DENDRAL and SECS) but also highly talented in an artistic sense. When purposive activity is linked to artificial emotion and a sense of self in the most sophisticated artefacts, computers will come to appreciate their own creations in the various scientific and artistic domains.

Games computers play

Something of the intellectual potential of computers has become apparent via the various electronic game-playing machines. There are quite literally hundreds of games that computers can play—with growing skills in many areas. Some products (for example, the chess computers) are devoted to a single activity, whereas others (usually the video systems linked to a conventional television receiver) have facilities for multiple cartridges, each dedicated to a different game or set of games (for example, Space Invaders, Blackjack, Hangman, Bowling, Casino, Chess, Backgammon, Racers, Sky Diver, Golf, Bridge, Pacman, etc.) or to a different purpose (such as teaching basic mathematics or programming). Two of the early microprocessor-based games systems, first marketed in the US and later in Europe and elsewhere are the Fairchild Entertainment Centre and the Atari Video Computer System. These systems can be adjusted for levels of difficulty and length of play. The Teleng Television Computer Centre (advertizement blurb: 'This family won the Third World War, beat Einstein, Mohammed Ali and broke the bank at Las Vegas') is represented as a complete home entertainment centre. There is a choice of thousands of games, puzzles and brain-teasers on nearly two dozen cartridges.

Perhaps the most significant of the domestic computer products are the ones that manifest a high level of skill, the ones that represent a real challenge to human intellectual capability. Foremost among such products are the chess computers: and in addition to the customized commercial products are a range of highly sophisticated chess programs that are demonstrating the growing intellectual potential of artificial systems.

The computer program which won the 1981 World Microcomputer Chess Championships has been given a US Chess Federation league table rating of 1,950: in early 1982 it could be bought in Harrods, London, for £279.95. A few years ago the chess programs were so weak that any club player could beat them. By the early 1980s, *the chess programs were beginning to beat International Masters.* In 1980 the US's North Western University's Chess 4.7 program beat UK International Master, David Levy, in a tournament game. And in 1982 the Chess Champion Mark V system, marketed in Hong Kong by SciSys, beat the UK Grandmaster John Nunn—five times out of six. In addition the Mark V found three correct solutions to a celebrated chess problem thought to have only one solution. The problem was originated by Russian expert L. Zagorujko in 1972. The problem has been widely publicized in newspapers and journals throughout the world, but no human being had found a solution other than the one proposed by Zagorujko. Nunn was unable to find the solution, but the Mark V confounded the experts by finding Zagorujko's solution and two alternatives of its own. Andrew Page, manager of SciSys, has observed: 'There are certain areas of chess in which computers are already capable of deeper analysis than humans. The day of the unbeatable chess computer is fast approaching.'

It has also been found that the world champion backgammon player is a computer. Hans Berliner's BKG 9-8 program, run on a DEC PDPIO at Carnegie-Mellon University at Pittsburgh, beat world champion Luigi Villa, winning four games in a five-game match. International Master Bill Hartston, however, is still confident that chess will not go the way of backgammon: 'Because the computer can only think in terms of calculations, it lacks the wisdom gained from experience which is needed to play chess well. There has to be a feel for the game. Something which cannot be programmed into a computer' (perhaps Levy and Nunn would disagree). Don Beal, lecturer in computer science at London University, sees nothing magical about creativity in chess or any other area ('After all, a new idea is simply a new arrangement of old ideas'). He and many other observers believe that, before long, computers will be performing a wide range of what are at present uniquely human activities. It is often pointed out that mathematics itself was once thought to be a uniquely human accomplishment, until it was discovered that computers could do it better. Already, in chess and backgammon, it is obvious that the brightest computer programs far exceed the intellectual competence of the vast majority of human beings.

There is another interesting (and possibly very significant) development. Computers are learning to write their own chess programs! ID3 has produced chess programs that are said to be five times more efficient than the best programs the computer's human master could manage. ID3's facility for what is called *automatic programming* suggests again that computers will have an increasing level of autonomy, and that human beings will have to ask sophisticated machines how they have arrived at their conclusions. The ID3 development (reported in *New Scientist*, 17 January 1980) has reinforced some fears that computers could be involved in important areas of decision-making without human beings fully understanding what was happening.

Computers can play most games that occupy the attention of people. Levy (1981) describes how to program a computer to play dominoes (the last article in a series dealing with games). He concludes: 'This level of sophistication would probably produce a program of World Championship calibre.' Attention has also been given to programming the ancient game of Go (originated in China about 2000 B.C.). Like chess, Go is a game of pure skill. Today it is mostly played in Japan, and the game poses its own unique programming problems (Brown and Dowsey, 1979; Millen, 1981). Similarly, checkers (draughts) programs have been written that learn from their own experience—to the point when they can beat human experts (Barbier, 1982). Game-playing is another area—requiring high levels of skill and often the ability to learn from experience—that illustrates the developing intellectual ability of modern computer systems.

Summary

Modern computers and robots give evidence of 'cerebral' activity in various ways. Decisions need to be taken and goals attained. At the same time it is obvious that some emerging computer-based species have a propensity for action in the world whereas other prefer more sedate modes of reflection and creative activity. We have seen that there are 'thinkers' and 'doers' in the realm of computer life, just as there are amongst people. In many areas the artificial thinkers—whether engaged in scientific research or musical composition—can outdo their human counterparts. And the artificial doers are increasingly reliable, industrious and intelligent: the modern robot, a practical realization of the Erewhonian dream:

> is brisk and active, when the man is weary; it is clear-headed and collected, when the man is stupid and dull; it needs no slumber, when man must sleep or drop . . . its alacrity never flags, its patience never gives in; its might is stronger than combined hundreds . . . . (Butler, 1872).

It should not be assumed that robots and computers are limited to the areas briefly profiled above. They are also moving into the social sciences and it may be expected that computer 'judgment' will see development in these areas (already artificial systems are involved in war prediction, see Schrodt, 1982). Whatever the human reaction to these trends we cannot doubt the active intellectual and artistic potential in the emerging life-forms. We are at the threshold—to gather some clues as to what lies beyond, it is time to consider in more detail, first the emerging anatomy of robots and then the emerging psychology of computers. . . .

4 The anatomy of robots

Preamble

Robots are already acquiring a range of biological organs, a circumstance that at least provides circumstantial evidence that robots are emerging life-forms. Of course there are a number of mammalian organs that we do not find in robots. They do not have spleen, heart, kidneys, etc. But they do have a means of distributing energy throughout the system, and some of their components are directly equivalent to what we find in animals. Robots do, in fact, have arms, hands, legs, sensitive skin, sense organs and brains. It is not always realized just how sophisticated some robot anatomies have become.

The various mechanical, electrical and electronic elements of the sophisticated robot may reasonably be regarded as the biological anatomy of the device. The central trunk, turret or pedestal of the typical robot may be seen as the torso, the body. As with a human being the torso provides a stable base from which the arms can operate. The human eyes are situated in the head, but the positioning of robot eyes—as with some insects—can vary from one species to another. It is not uncommon for robot eyes to be situated in the grippers—an eyeball in the palm of the hand! (See, for example, C. Loughlin's paper, 'Eye in hand robot', delivered at the 2nd International Conference on Robot Vision and Sensory Controls, November 1982.) Similarly there is no requirement for every robot to carry its brain in the same place. It may leave its brain in a separate room, or it may have several small brains, variously allocated to its eyes, its ears and the joints of its limbs.

To say that an entity has a biological anatomy implies, amongst other things, that there is a complex system with many interacting parts to allow the performance of numerous functions. This is manifestly true of naturally occurring animals, but less true of naturally occurring plants. However, it is also manifestly true of robots in their most sophisticated versions. And it is significant that there are clear analogies between the various robot system elements and those of acknowledged life-forms. This is hardly surprising. As we have seen, many artificial life-forms are 'growing out of man': in the case of robots, many systems were specifically designed to carry out tasks formerly performed by men and women—we may have expected that people would serve as the models for the new devices. What *may* have surprised us is how quickly the robot systems came to acquire intelligence and behavioural flexibility. They have only been around for a few decades. Now that they are acquiring intelligence, via computers, we may expect a dramatic acceleration in robot learning and skill.

Robot biology is at present relatively inflexible compared with the biology of the higher animals. There is currently little robot provision for the self-repair of damaged tissue, though a robot could be made to replace faulty components in its own body. Most robots have no survival instinct, although as we have seen, they can learn to feed when hungry, and could easily be made to sense types of danger and to take evasive or defensive action. If we detect manifest limitations in robot biology this should not be regarded as detracting from the robot claim to be an emerging life-form. Robots have *their* ways of going about things, their ways of reproducing (see chapter 1), monitoring the environment, choosing between behavioural options, and the rest. There may be differences between the ways in which robots and human beings carry out their various tasks, but it is already clear that robot 'life methods' are nearer to those of man than are those of man to countless other species on Earth. And microprocessor intelligence will be bound to enlarge robot behavioural flexibility—if only because it is commercially cost-effective for one clever robot to be able to do what two stupid ones could manage before. For this reason, robot life-forms will come to resemble the human species more and more in their behaviour and goals.

Artificial hands and arms

Artificial limbs appear frequently in fiction and as real adjuncts to people and robots. An iron hand was made in 1509 for Goetz von Berlichingen, a knight immortalized in Goethe's *Goetz*, a Shakespearean-type drama. Despite the clever gearing for fingers and thumb, the hand had limited uses and in the play Goetz explains that 'My right hand, though not useless in combat, is unresponsive to the grasp of affection'. Devices manufactured by the military surgeon, Ambroise Paré (1510–1590), included a mechanism for bending the elbow, and a hand could open and close. Such heavy artificial limbs were not very practical but they prepared the ground for the emergence of modern prosthetic devices.

In the fearsome novel *Limbo '90* by Bernard Wolfe (1953), men volunteer to have their limbs amputated in order to protect peace, as it is generally thought that there can be no 'demobilization without immobilization'. However, men then decided to acquire artificial limbs that were more efficient than any natural appendage. Use was made of the imaginary 'cineplastic surgery' to connect the superior artificial limbs onto the old stumps. Limb movement was controlled by the brain and powered by an atomic energy capsule. The limbs were immensely powerful, their success attracting would-be amputees in large numbers.

It is easy to imagine highly capable fictional artificial limbs, but real artificial limbs—whether for people or robots—are becoming ever more flexible and competent. A computerized artificial arm has been developed at the Stanford Research Institute in California. A patient with such a limb can comb his hair, eat a meal and scratch his back. This type of arm has several joints and can perform a wide range of movements under the control of a microcomputer which interprets bodily signals. As many as twenty different co-ordinated movements can be accomplished by means of a single integrated circuit (silicon chip) embedded in the arm. Such research is clearly relevant to the provision of effective arms for robots.

Arms are obviously a key element in the design of robots for industrial and other purposes. The capability of particular artificial arms helps to define the overall competence of the robot—what it can do and the degree to which it is adaptable in new circumstances. Robot arms may be articulated or not, they may have extensive reach or may be restricted to close proximity operations, and they may or may not have extensive sweeps in vertical and horizontal planes. As one example, the Unimate Series 4000 industrial arm has a maximum reach of nearly 3 m, a horizontal sweep of 200° and a vertical sweep of 50°. An arm manufactured by the British United Shoe Manufacturing Company can be raised, lowered and rotated on a vertical pillar, as well as being able to move in and out. In addition, the wrist at the end of the arm can be rotated. Often the artificial arms in research and practical devices are modelled on naturally occurring biological elements. In a number of robot projects, arms are built specifically to resemble the human arm.

Robot arms are sometimes activated by air pressure (particularly where high-speed motions are required with fairly light loads) but hydraulics can offer the capability of holding heavy loads for long periods. Motion is often under electrical control for ease of regulation.

Many industrial robots have only one arm situated on a central pedestal (the torso), but two-arm robots have been designed for a number of purposes. For example, the Sterling Detroit Company has developed a two-armed robot for the operations of quenching and trimming in steel plant. Clearly a two-armed robot makes it relatively easy to view such devices in anthropomorphic terms. The Sterling Detroit Robotarms were first introduced as far back as December 1968, and were quickly seen to provide a number of industrial advantages—even though, at that time, they had not been paired up to form two-armed configurations. Canner (1979) describes the operational experience of three companies using the two-armed systems. Such devices have offered greater efficiency and consistency in the operational environment. Robot arms, whether single or paired, are usually made out of metallic materials. At the same time, research is being conducted into the suitability of other materials. For example, the Locoman robot, developed by the Wolfson Industrial Unit for material forming, features a three-dimensional pantographic arm made up out of carbon fibre reinforced rods (*Machinery*, 21 April 1982, p. 15). Locoman, under microprocessor control, has been demonstrated writing with a felt-tipped pen.

Sometimes novel wrist movements are highlighted when a new product is announced. For example, the S. Russell and

Sons 'Press Hand', a pick-and-place unit added to a specialist range in 1979, claimed novel wrist and finger movements to allow a workpiece to be located and repositioned to within ± 0.1 mm. (The system also has retractable wheels to facilitate movement between operating stations.)

Some applications require a high degree of wrist flexibility. Wrist size and dexterity are particularly important, for example, in arc welding, spray coating, sealant application, parts assembly, and other complex handling tasks. Stackhouse (1979) of Cincinnati Milacron, a leading robot maker, has described a concept for robot wrist design having three degrees of freedom in an operating envelope which is very small for the payload. He identifies six basic groups of wrist configurations and assesses their suitability for particular tasks.

We have seen that hands, in the robot world, are often called 'grippers', a term that implies the idea of grasping action using fingers. Robot grippers often work in this way—in fact the behaviour of the human hand has been analysed to give clues for gripper design. Something of the dexterity of the modern robot hand is shown by the work of a group of scientists and engineers from Battelle's Pacific North-west Laboratories (reported in *The Guardian*, 8th December 1982). Between them they have built Cubot, an intelligent robot that can solve any scrambled Rubik's Cube in less than four minutes. (Cubot has mechanical grippers, an eye, and a microcomputer brain.) And there are many other ways of collecting and manipulating physical items in a robot's environment. The grippers can exploit vacuum or magnetic effects, or they may deliberately pierce an item or adhere to it. Any means of collecting an item securely can be employed by a robot gripper, the technique adopted depending upon what the robot is required to do.

As part of a project carried out from 1973 to 1976 at the Fluid Technology Laboratory in Stockholm (described in *Industrial Robots: Gripper Review*), a collection was made of components actually handled by industrial robots: around 600 items were obtained, many of them geometrically very similar. As many as eleven component types were identified, including plastic items (for example, telephone covers and push buttons), die castings, packings, punched items, disc-shaped items and sweetmeats. There is obviously enormous scope for robots to handle items of many different compositions, shapes and sizes: and robot hands, moreover, can exploit a number of handling techniques that are not found in traditional life-forms. Magnetic grippers, for instance, can use electromagnets or permanent magnets. Electromagnets are preferred since with a permanent magnet it is sometimes difficult to make the robot let go when necessary: it is easy to switch off an electric current. The permanent magnet has the additional disadvantage that it tends to collect bits of swarf and iron filings. It is obviously a good idea, if possible, to prevent the robot getting dirty hands!

Many robot gripper devices accomplish lifting 'by means of negative pressure' (that is, by using vacuum methods). An obvious attraction of this approach is that only one component surface needs to be used—we all know how difficult it can be to extract certain items from holes in which they are situated (for example, a loose countersunk-head screw in a tapped hole). Some vacuum grippers are built up of suction cups arranged in a pattern to suit the component.

Some robot hands come equipped with spikes or prongs to pierce items such as pieces of cloth, rubber packs or porous sheets. There are piercing grippers for large and heavy components (for example, rubber bales, paper bales, thick-walled packing and insulating material). Adhesive and blow-lifting grippers can be used for items that do not permit other methods. However, there are problems with sticky materials: the adhesive may dry up, particularly in warm and dry atmospheres. Robot hands may use adhesive ribbon tape for such items as clothing and thin discs, and for assembly operations where several smaller components (such as screws and nuts) have to be positioned. Various polymers and glues are used to provide adhesive grippers. The blow-lifting techniques requires that air be blown under a component, causing it to rise through aerodynamic lift, with guides employed to keep the item in the correct orientation.

It is obvious that robot hands are much more diverse than the hands found in the various human, ape and monkey species. Animals have only learned to exploit one type of gripper, but robots are much more versatile. Furthermore, robots are capable of autonomously changing their types of grippers when necessary: they can sense the item to be handled and then select the appropriate gripper. Human beings do the same when they select a tool to extend their manipulative ability. But, without artificial assistance, animals only exploit the clasping technique. Robots, by contrast, have developed to exploit a wide range of manipulative methods.

Where robot grippers are based on the idea of fingers with an opposed thumb, it has proved useful to analyse the structure of the human hand 'down to the bones'—a task that has been attempted over several centuries. But it is also aparent that naturally occurring life-forms have developed various other handling mechanisms, apart from those exemplified in anthropoid hands. One thinks of the elephant's trunk and the tentacles of an octopus. In fact, robots are also learning to emulate these mechanisms: the Tokyo Institute of Technology is developing a soft gripper for a robot hand, inspired by the movement of a snake and modelled on the motion of tentacles or an elephant's trunk. One aim is to distribute the pressure evenly on a fragile object by coiling round it, a facility that would enable robots to handle human beings or other animals with care during medical treatment. It is obvious that in the years to come robots will develop an immense range of manipulative abilities: they will be able to handle any items in their vicinity—from delicate living creatures to massive manufactured structures. To do so, it will often be convenient to move from one place to another. . . .

The walking robot

Artificial legs, like arms and hands, have a history in connection with human beings—long before living robots were imagined as a real possibility. For example, there is mention of artificial legs in the *Rig-Veda*, dated to around 1000 B.C., and Herodotus (485–425 B.C.) describes an artificial foot which Hegisistratus of Elis made for himself after cutting off part of his own foot to escape from the stocks. Artificial limbs are also referred to in the Talmud and in the Nordic sagas. A Roman mosaic in the French Pyrenees shows a man with an artificial leg made out of bronze and wood and lined with leather. And peg legs, of one form or another, have been common in all ages. A leg made for the Marquis of Anglesey had a steel knee joint and a wooden ankle joint with cords to control the ankle motion. Such devices were sometimes called *clapper* legs because they sometimes made a clapping sound when used.

We expect mobile robots to be bipeds, simply because we ourselves are accustomed to using two legs. However, Japanese engineers have experimented with a one-legged robot; and a character in Stefan Themerson's *Bayamus* (1949) comes equipped with three legs, a roller skate being attached to the middle foot. Bayamus claims that part of his mission is to develop a new race of tripeds, noting that as the Earth becomes smoother. Nature will at last be free to provide a biological roller skate under the sole of a man's foot! We may speculate at length on how organic wheels could evolve.

Bipeds are not particularly stable. Creatures with four or six legs are superior in this respect, and it is possible that quadruped robots will draw on the biological experience of four-legged animals and six-legged insects. In fact a variety of walking tractors and mechanical horses have been used in agriculture since the 1940s. The USSR, for example, has employed stepping excavators to clear forests in Siberia. Walking machines can demonstrate a number of advantages over vehicles using wheels or caterpillar tracks. Stability is often a problem but it has been noticed that a walking lorry can more easily keep its balance when moving than when stationary. Ivan Artobolevsky (cited, with many of these examples, by Reichardt, 1978) has described a four-legged 'mechanized horse' which weighs 1.5 tonnes and is driven by a 90hp automobile engine (1977). Its speed (maximum: 10 km per hour) and length of stride are controlled by levers and pedals. And there is also reference to a multi-legged train which can move over uneven surfaces and travel through mud, sand and gravel. A General-Electric four-legged lorry, built for the US Army, comes supplied with tactile sensors and position sensors in the leg joints. A distance-measuring device allows the lorry to scan the terrain ahead.

Most of the current robots with legs are experimental devices. For instance, a three-legged walker has been built at the University of Wisconsin to study the problems of locomotion and control. Powered by compressed air, it can carry heavy weights high above the ground—a circumstance that may be expected to add to stability problems. The length of each leg changes as the robot moves, with the central leg employed as the principal 'pusher'. This device was developed as part of research into constructing an exoskeleton which would enable paraplegics to walk. The experimental systems may be expected to lead to walking robots that will find their way into a wide range of industrial and domestic environments. A few legged robots have worked successfully in homes and elsewhere, and progress will be made to enable robots to walk over uneven surfaces, up and down inclines, up and down stairs, etc. Today, where robot mobility is required, it is generally provided by wheels and tracks. Clearly at present this contrasts with the articulated systems of levers used by man and other animals for purposes of locomotion.

Designers have been aware for many years that natural 'legged' locomotion systems offer superior mobility characteristics due to their capacity to adapt to terrain irregularities (Bekker, 1969). A theory of *adaptive walking machines* has been developed over the past decade (McGhee, 1977), but until the arrival of microprocessors it was not possible to attain the necessary joint co-ordination function by means of an on-board computer (Orin, McGhee and Jaswa, 1976). McGhee and Iswandhi (1979) draw attention to two experimental hexapod vehicles constructed for the purpose of supporting research on sensors and on computer hardware and software organization for automatic limb-motion co-ordination. This paper focuses on the problem of determining an optimal schedule for the lifting and placing of the legs of a vehicle relative to the supporting terrain. A heuristic solution to the problem is presented which has shown promising results in simulation studies using a DEC-10 computer and an AG-60 plasma panel display. McGhee expects this line of research to lead to a new family of mobile vehicles that will be able to traverse irregular terrain and soft soil. One can imagine such robots being used for arctic transport, mining, agriculture, forestry, ocean-floor research and planetary exploration. Robot life-forms with such capabilities will come to adapt well to a wide range of different environments.

A walking hexapod robot has been operating at the Paris VII

University since November 1980 (described by Kessis, Rambant and Penne, 1982). Its important system of distributed control has already proved its efficiency in naturally occurring biological systems (for example, that of the cockroach as shown in Camhi, 1980). This allows reflex moves and spinal control to focus on the walking task, leaving the brain to concentrate on other operations.

Various mechanism control levels have been identified. One provides servocontrol for the legs: each leg has two servomotors providing closed-loop control. Already, with further development anticipated, the leg unit can provide some degree of terrain adaptation—the robot can negotiate a small block without limping. The concept of *generalized gaits* has been developed to aid design of the robot.

Animal gaits—such as the amble or the gallop—have been closely observed for a long time (Muybridge, 1897). The gait may be roughly defined, for an *n*-legged device, as a vector of the phase shifts of $(n - 1)$ legs with regard to the first leg defined as a reference. This relies upon the assumption that every leg move is cyclic with the same period for all legs. Kessis *et al.* (1982) cite a number of studies numbering the different possible gaits (1030) for a hexapod and for other types of locomotive systems. These theoretical studies (Bassonov and Umnov, 1973; McGhee and Frank, 1968) also examine the relative stability of the various gait options. It is found that six-legged gaits are best when they exhibit *symmetrical wavy* features: among such gaits are the 'tripled' gait (with two sets of three synchronous legs) and the '1–4–2–6–3–5' succession. Kessis *et al.* implemented a microprocessor-controlled system that could cope both with the classic defined gaits and with what they termed 'generalized gaits'. Further research on the hexapod include studies of tactile sensors (see below) and an ultrasonic rangefinder (using Murata transducers).

Other control levels in the hexapod allow the device to evaluate the circumstances of its environment. At the highest level—Level 4—data from other levels will be integrated to provide a relatively sophisticated intelligence facility: the device will, for example—using a microcomputer—be able to construct a world model to allow enhanced adaptation to the environment. A second prototype, with a more complex range of sensors, is being constructed to allow the robot to cope with more difficult terrain irregularities.

It is clear that walking robots, not necessarily bipeds, will gradually evolve and be capable of a wide range of adaptation and initiative in changing environments. As with robot hands and arms, it is likely that robot legs and methods of locomotion will come to be more varied than the techniques favoured by traditional biological species. We may also expect water-living robots, as well as their land-living relatives, to evolve in time. Such factors as buoyancy and water resistance will necessarily influence the theory of gaits. There can be little doubt at the present time that we are witnessing the first stages in the evolution of mobile robot life-forms.

Sensing the environment

We are familiar with the five senses of man and the higher animals, and great effort has been devoted to equipping robots with some of these (see below), but again we may expect robots to evolve a more versatile range of senses than those occurring in traditional life-forms. Ultrasonic ranging, effectively employed by bats and dolphins, will be employed by robots; and parts of the sound and electromagnetic spectra not accessible to any known naturally occurring species may come to be exploited by future robot life-forms. One idea is that doppler microwave modules could help robots in long-distance sensing. Proximity sensing can use visible or infra-red light, and it may be possible to exploit magnetic or other physical phenomena in appropriate circumstances.

Albus (1981) and others have predicted that the 1980s will see robots equipped with many different kinds of senses to help them measure the state of their environment. Control systems will be equipped to use the sensory information to enable the robots to act in a goal-seeking manner: the information will be compared with references (knowledge) held by the robot memory before decisions are taken on an appropriate course of action. Such robots will evolve a world model (a 'perspective on reality'), which is amenable to the influence of new data—that is, which allows the system to learn. The various robot senses will be integrated effectively with other robot sybsystems—brain, motor faculties, etc.—to allow purposive decisions to initiate intelligent robot behaviour.

The eyes have it

Great efforts are being made to develop effective 'eyes' for robots: we are very conscious of how useful sight is to the human and other animal species. At the same time, there are many problems in developing versatile vision systems. One common approach is to look to what is known about animal perception on the assumption that the chief difficulty lies in the areas of pattern recognition and scene analysis. If an artificial system is to organize mechanical operations (for example, those of a behaving robot) on the basis of visual information, an adequate interpretation of the information is essential. It is in this sense that we say that it is the brain that sees, and not the eye. But the task of interpretation can involve finding a correspondence between elements of the real world (that is, objects to be handled or avoided by a robot) and their two-dimensional representation within the camera image. How brains—whether natural or artificial—convert two-dimensional data into three-dimensional understanding is one of the many key cognitive questions that will have to be resolved in the evolution of robot species. It will be necessary, for example, for the cognitive system to be provided with a conceptual model of its universe onto which elements of the visual image can be mapped. In research, such models are supplied by the human programmer. In due course we may expect that artificial systems will be able to construct such models autonomously from visual data. There are many ways in which robots will come to acquire such data, in which robots will evolve their artificial eyes.

Engineers at Hughes Aircraft have already developed eyes that can detect the outlines of objects almost instantaneously: use is made of silicon chips that are able to transfer information in the form of packets of electrical charge by changing the amplitude and timing of voltages applied to suitable electrodes. These types of chips can function without having to convert the original analogue information into digital signals—which enables them to construct an image of an object in front of them in, say, 50 m, whereas a computer would need a few seconds. The Hughes eye processes data from a single kernel size of 676 pixels. (The normal television screen contributes about 250,000 pixels, and a single human eye provides about 130 million pixels to the brain's view of the outside world.)

The analogue approach to the handling of visual information has also been exploited in Intel's 'analogue microprocessor', the 2920. This device is fast enough to react to the analogue signals of the real world, running through its program of instructions at the rate of up to 20,000 times a second, 200 times faster than one of the typical industry-standard micros, the Intel 8080. This means that devices are emerging that could provide robots with the sensory means to monitor features of the environment at a suitable rate to allow appropriate behavioural response.

We have already given instances of 'seeing' or light-seeking robots (chapter 2). Such systems have, in fact, been developed for many years. For example, two undergraduates (Allen and Rossetti, 1978) describe the development of the Tee Toddler, a light-seeking robot mechanism. This is essentially a car, designed to track towards a shining light and also provided with an ultrasonic sonar system which scans to right and left to detect objects in the vehicle's forward path. Filo (1979b) described his NELOC (Neural Logic Cyberanimate) system, a manipulator arm equipped with a visual capacity. He observed that the system ('the equivalent of only a very thin neurological slice through a simple organism') cannot be regarded as intelligent but added that he believed that 'this design philosophy could be useful for designing systems beyond the simple servo system'.

A team at the University of Rhode Island, under National Science Foundation grants, has been developing 'general methods for robots with vision to acquire, orient, and transport workpieces... to assist in increasing the range of industrial applications' for such robots (Birk *et al.*, 1978). An experimental (six-axis arm) robot system was developed that uses vision to locate and pick up randomly oriented workpieces in a bin, and to determine the orientation of the workpieces in the robot's hand; whereupon the robot manipulates the piece, transports it to a site, and inserts it without collision.

Many current laboratory robots, supervised by minicomputers, have visual input and can adapt to changing circumstances. In some early experiments a Data General Nova 1220 minicomputer was employed to control a Unimate 2000 robot: data concerning the location of parts was fed to the robot from a General Electric camera connected to a DEC PDP-11/40 minicomputer used to determine the centre of white objects on a black conveyor belt. The robot was skilled enough to pick up passing plastic cups, but could not reliably sense real parts in an industrial environment. Another experimental prototype system uses the CONSIGHT lighting system, where a narrow line of light is projected across the surface of a conveyor belt. Robot activity is supervised by a perceptual system that recognizes the identity and position of parts, assembles instructions for new handling sequences, senses conveyor belt motion, and instructs the robot as parts move within reach. After each operation, the robot asks for new instructions: these are then supplied by the computer using data provided by the visual system.

A prototype industrial robot that can see for about 1 m has been developed at the NBS Centre for Mechanical Engineering and Process Technology. The robot uses a small television camera mounted on its wrist, with the field of view between two fingers. A strobe light, below the wrist, flashes a narrow plane of light towards the fingers: the robot sees an object as a narrow line of light across the object. A microcomputer is used to control the strobe, to determine the distance of the object from the fingers, and to determine the orientation of the object. If the robot is not positioned to pick up the object, the computer moves the robot to another position, and the object is viewed again. Research is focusing on allowing the robot to locate a desired part from among a range of different items.

As early as 1974, patents were being issued in Japan for visual systems and other sensory devices for robots. For a number of years Hitachi has used vidicon cameras for shape recognition and positioning of transistors in die bonding and for remote inspection of nuclear power plants. Such cameras are also built into robots by Mitsubishi to facilitate shape recognition and positioning with assembly tasks; by

Yasukawa for arc welding applications; and by Kawasaki Heavy Industries for assembly operations. In the real world of industry, robots can already see.

Auto-Place robots, using the GE TN-2000 solid-state camera to provide vision capability, are now being used in many industrial applications. For example, the Bulova Systems and Instrument Corporation (New York) uses two small Auto-Place Series 10 machines. One manipulates incoming clock-timer movements, adjusting their position while loading them into a fixture which is indexed for viewing by a video camera. The camera examines the part, determines certain critical dimensions and, by means of a link to a controller, causes a d.c. motor to move a lever on the fixture until two metal plates are aligned to within 0.01 in. The camera scrutinizes the alignment to check for accuracy, whereupon an unload robot removes the part and transfers it to either an 'accept' or 'reject' conveyor.

After five years of development work, Brown Boveri began production in 1979 of an optoelectronic sensor for industrial robots. The system was designed to sort components on a moving conveyor belt: after each component has been identified, it can be taken from the conveyor and sorted into various compartments, or can be correctly positioned on the conveyor for the next stage in production. A television camera is used to supply a picture to a microprocessor for analysis. Similarly, a video target locator, supplied by Hampton Video Systems is being used by various companies: for instance, Delta Metals has used the locator to guide a robot gripper onto a hot metal billet. Again the locator uses the picture from a television screen as input.

A number of robot vision systems rely on first teaching the robot about the items it is likely to encounter (Marsh, 1980). One stage in a robot's seeing process may be to arrange for the computerized picture to be compared with other images stored in the computer's memory. If the image that the robot sees matches ones that it remembers, then the robot has recognized the item. The camera has been previously pointed at an item to teach the robot what it is likely to encounter. Workers at the University of Hull, England, have programmed a vision system to recognize plastic cut-outs of the letters of the alphabet.

(Yes, this may be a rather rudimentary accomplishment, but we do well to remember that a few hundred million people in the world are illiterate. Life systems, of whatever type, have to be taught before they can become accomplished.)

Vision systems are not new: General Motors installed one in 1977 in a plant in Indiana to inspect integrated circuits; by the late 1970s Auto-Place had sold about twenty functional vision systems; and Texas Instruments (making calculators) and Renault (cars), as two more examples, have used vision systems for many years. But such systems are usually primitive. One problem is that cameras have to operate in dirty or poorly lit environments, and it is likely that some of the ambitious emerging 'seeing' systems will require bright lights for good definition and no image ambiguities. Computer enhancement of images may be expected to make imperfect images acceptable to working robots.

It has been suggested that robots may soon come to recognize objects about which they have not been taught. What this means is that robots will have to 'enhance' their vision capabilities by means of inference: this is strictly analogous to what human beings do when they dimly perceive an object (or only hear part of a sentence)—they 'fill in the gaps' on the basis of expectation, previous experience, reasoning ability, etc. Donald Michie has suggested that robots with vision faculties and deductive abilities could appear in laboratories in the very near future.

Practical approaches to visual pattern recognition are frequently described in the literature (for example, Myers, 1980, where reference is made to the neural processing of visual information by human beings). Computer vision in particular countries is profiled (for example, Yachida and Tsuji, 1980, for Japan), and particular computer vision uses are described (such as those in Agin, 1980, which deals with industrial inspection and assembly). The picture that emerges is that vision is increasingly becoming a part of artificial systems, and that tight analogies are drawn with traditional biological seeing mechanisms. Bartlam (1981) begins an article on electronic sight with the words 'The eye is an information-gathering mechanism'. Sensory activities, as well as psychological categories (see chapter 5), are increasingly influenced by what we learn of neurophysiological behaviour on the one hand, and computer science—especially information processing—on the other.

Increasingly, vision systems for robots and other artificial devices are being manufactured as standard production items—these are regularly described and advertized in such journals as *Sensor Review* and *Assembly Automation*. It is now a commonplace of robot technology that systems have sight capabilities, albeit rudimentary and albeit limited to a few well-defined tasks. The evolutionary route is clear—from simple photosensitive detectors to sophisticated high-resolution cameras linked in integrated systems to inference mechanisms to allow for intelligent image enhancement. Already we are seeing the emergence of vision systems for specific operational tasks. One issue of *Assembly Automation* (February 1982) carries descriptions of a vision system for automatically sorting silicon chips for quality (pp. 26–29), computers used to exercize quality control on the fabrication of their own constituent components, and also of a vision system for aiding an assembly robot (pp. 36–39) which, as we have seen (in chapter 1), is a mechanism relevant to robot procreation.

It is suggested (Iverson, 1982) that vision systems as part of robot configurations may soon account for one third of the market for vision equipment. It is acknowledged that vision facilities are being progressively incorporated into robots, usually for industrial purposes. Within the decade it will be natural to assume that most robots will be able to see. By the early 1980s it was already clear that robot/computer vision was well established on its inevitable evolutionary path. In late 1981, reports appeared (in *Computer Weekly*, 17/24 December 1981, for example) of the Wisard pattern recognition system, developed at Brunel University. The prototype is a highly variable system which can be adapted to perform many different types of tasks—including recognizing a human face within 3 s! In this application, 512×512 picture points are tested for correspondence with eight stored images. In the visual recognition of handprint, an input can be checked against nearly 10,000 stored images—with decisions, in the form of probabilities of correspondence, being produced every 0.25 s. Within the decade it will be possible for robots to recognize other robots and also their human working colleagues. We are witnessing not only the first stages in the evolution of robots that can *see*, but also the emergence of robots that can use their visually acquired information to *recognize* and to *understand*.

A touching scene

The sense of touch, like vision, has quite a long history in robot technology. For instance, tactile sensors have been used for many years to detect 'over-grip' (when, for example, gripper fingers close in the absence of a component), or they may rely on the use of 'artificial skin'. Auto-Place robots sometimes incorporate an over-grip sensor: if a hand closes beyond its normal position in attempting to grip a part, the component is assumed to be missing. Another tactile sensor used by Auto-Place is a vacuum sensor. A change in vacuum, such as that being caused by a part being picked up, can be used to change a robot's program. In other words the robot notices when a necessary component is absent and can respond by moving into an appropriate behavioural mode.

There is widespread research into the use of tactile sensors: for example, at the Laboratoire d'Automatique et d'Analyse des Systems (Toulouse) and at the Mihailo Pupin Institute (Belgrade). This work is relevant to a wide range of applications in medicine, industry and other fields. The various experimental systems may exploit pressure information deriving from an 'artificial skin' transducer (Clot and Stojiljkovic, 1977), or they may use angular information in various forms: it has been found that angular measurements can be usefully employed to aid the tactile recognition of objects. Some recognition programs rely on a combination of pressure information and angular measurements.

A remarkable 'artificial skin' sensor has been developed at the Toulouse laboratory (Briot, 1979). The position of a mechanical part with multiple planar equilibrium faces has been identified by means of this sensor, the type of activity that is essential if robots are to develop a reliable and effective sense of touch. This skin sensor has already been incorporated in the fingers of gripper to aid object recognition during grasping.

And—perhaps most significantly—a manipulator robot has been equipped with tactile sensors combined with decision and control faculties. More simply, a robot can recognize something by touching it, decide what to do about it, and then carry out the action.

The artificial-skin sensor consists of a printed circuit board on which there are a number of sensitive spots—like nerve endings. The spots are square, uniformly distributed, and set in a matrix. A small voltage is applied to a guard-ring around the points, whereupon the electrical characteristics of a conductive coating on the structure vary according to the pressure exerted. At every test point there is a variation in current which can be interpreted to indicate the character of the object that the sensor is touching. In this way an information pattern is produced which can then be analyzed by a computer. Use has been made of a Mitra 15 computer which carries out data processing after data has been collected. This artificial-skin sensor has successfully identified various mechanical parts placed on a horizontal plane. This means that now robots can recognise what they are handling.

Other work has focused on giving a sense of touch to an intelligent underwater robot (Dixon, Salazar and Slagle., 1979). Here, as with the artificial-skin sensor, it is necessary for the robot to recognize and manipulate objects without the benefit of human intervention. This work has followed other research into tactile sensor techniques. For instance, Okada and Tsuchiya (1977) used a hand with segmented fingers and tactile sensors to identify solid objects; Page, Pugh and Higinbotham (1976) employed an array of tactile probes to obtain simultaneously a number of points defining a three-dimensional item; and Popplestone and Ambler (1977) used data derived from a television triangulation mechanism to form body models: planes and cylindrical surfaces were first constructed, and then these were assembled to produce models of solid objects.

Where a robot is working in an unfamiliar environment there is an obvious requirement that the sensors provide unambiguous three-dimensional information. The use of a sense of touch often depends upon objects being recognized in an incremental fashion (in other words, computation proceeds on initial data while further data is being collected). We can see how this happens with human beings in everyday life. Imagine going into a dark room and searching for the light switch. You move your hand along the wall until you encounter the switch holder. According to the character of the touch data, you then move your hand in one direction or another. When you encounter the switch you move your finger to alter the switch position as necessary. During the entire process your brain is working on incoming data until the task is complete.

Various types of tactile sensor could be used in an unfamiliar undersea environment. A thin rod might explore holes and cracks; or a hand with sensitive fingers, perhaps equipped with artificial skin, could be used for the rapid collection of data. And robot movement could be intelligently controlled by computer to serve the needs of the information-gathering sensors: if part of an object was not easy to recognize, the sensor could be directed to another part—or, if the computer was satisfied that the part had been correctly identified, it could induce the sensors to go elsewhere.

Touch sensors are useful in a wide range of industrial applications: for example, in ones relating to assembly, where the accurate positioning of workpieces is essential (Astrop, 1979). One aim may be to let the robot hand, by means of data acquired from touch sensors, make the minute alignment movements necessary for particular assembly subtasks (for example, to insert a peg in a hole), while the robot torso remains immobile. One approach is based on reproducing the 'feel' experienced by the human hand during the task of inserting a close-fitting item into an aperture, and also simulating the signals to the brain which tell the hand to move the item as needed.

Robots are acquiring a sense of touch, just as they are acquiring eyes. And parallel research is focusing on how the data derived from the senses can be used to construct world models and to aid computer decision-making. The emerging robot species will increasingly be able to monitor, and respond to, their environment—so unambiguously exemplifying some of the important life criteria (for example, those connected with information processing). And we may expect the evolution of the sense of touch in robots, as with the other senses, to occur more rapidly than was the case with the traditional biological species.

Hearing and smell

As well as seeing and touching, modern robots can also hear. There are obvious circumstances in which it is advantageous for a robot to sense particular sounds in the environment. Some sounds (such as explosions) may signify danger; other (such as shouts) may serve as commands. Voice-recognition systems, often based on microprocessors, are becoming increasingly common in a wide range of contexts. (It has been predicted, for example, that by the mid-1980s speech recognition will replace Touch-Tone telephone input as the preferred input capability to computer systems.) Such systems will be increasingly important to the users of computers and robots. For instance, using a word recognition device (the Threshold Technology Model VIP-100), a Unimate robot has been verbally instructed to perform a sequence of actions. Robots can be made able to hear us and obey us when we speak to them.

For many applications it is useful to distinguish between speech recognition and speech understanding: in the latter, stored knowledge can be referred to in assessing whether a word sequence makes sense. Brian Pay, head of the computer voice recognition group at the UK National Physical Laboratory, has pointed out that human beings are very poor on voice recognition but 'absolutely marvellous when it comes to speech understanding'. The human brain can make sense out of a mix of sound entering the ear at any time. A system being developed at the National Physical Laboratory is aiming at the development of artificial speech understanding rather than simple voice recognition. For robots the distinction may be less crucial: if a robot can recognize a word, then we can issue commands.

For several years, systems for voice recognition have been available. By the late-1970s voice-recognition units were able to handle dozens of words: for instance, the Voice Data-Input Terminal from Nippon Electric could recognize as many as 120 words, spoken without pause in groups of up to five words—and more recent systems can cope with several hundred words. Parallel research has focused on speech synthesis systems—to allow artificial systems to answer back! Much of this type of research has focused on specific programming techniques (Iverson, 1982) or on combining speech-recognition facilities, for example, with other data processing capabilities (McLeod, 1982). In 1978, an article (in Miller, 1978) could be introduced with the words 'Voice systems are growing better and giving the computer more to say than ever before. And they're sounding more like humans too'. It was becoming apparent that before long it would be possible to hold a conversation with a computer.

A group at the US company TRW has developed an automated technique that can distinguish one family of languages from another, but there has been less success in getting the computer to recognize one particular language: a success rate of 80 per cent has been achieved in experiments involving five languages and ten talkers from each language. Other US research is using pattern recognition techniques to aid speech understanding: this work draws on findings in linguistics and knowledge theory.

Workers at the IBM Thomas J. Watson Research Centre in New York have developed a system capable of recognizing individual words: a working accuracy of more than 90 per cent is claimed (with the system costing up to £40,000). The system separates the incoming word into sixteen time slices and makes thirty-two measurements on each of these. The resulting pattern acts as a reference template which is stored in the computer memory. At Carnegie–Mellon University a government-sponsored project, now dubbed 'Harpy', has yielded a system which can deal with complete sentences from a restricted 1,000-word vocabulary. Taking as its input the speech from five speakers in a typical room, Harpy was able to recognize 91 per cent of the sentences.

Some computer hearing systems can only recognize the voice of one speaker: more ambitious systems are speaker-independent. To some extent this mirrors human hearing proficiency. We are more likely to recognize words spoken by an intimate than ones uttered by a stranger—particularly if the stranger, though speaking our language, has a different cultural background. Many speech-dependent voice-recognition systems operate in the industrial environment: for example, speech recognition for inspection tasks in industry is considered in *Sensor Review* (January 1982).

Microprocessors are increasingly being used in word-recognition systems. Daxer and Zwicker (1982), for example, describe a microprocessor-based speaker-independent word-recognition facility. Here use is made of a simplified model of peripheral auditory processing. Isolated word recognition has traditionally been carried out as a simulation exercize on medium or large computers. Developments which allow equivalent techniques to be exploited on a micro-based system are important for the evolution of robot senses: it means, amongst other things, that robot 'ears' and the associated processing equipment can be manufactured to a realistic size—a robot hearing sensor that relied upon a computer the size of a desk may be expected to seriously hamper robot mobility.

The provision of a robot sense of smell has not been given much attention in research: such a faculty has not been held to be particularly important, though I have seen reference to its possible use for robot chefs! One can imagine circumstances, however, when it would be useful for robots to be able to detect molecules floating in the air—in other words when it should have a sense of smell. For instance, many toxic gases have a characteristic odour, and some automatic fire-fighting systems rely on being able to detect (smell?) smoke.

T.A. Jones (1982) represents the detection of toxic gases in an industrial environment as a growing problem, and he explores the nature of sensors that could be used for such a purpose. For example, use could be made of metal oxide sensors: it has been known for many years that the presence of different gases surrounding a semiconducting material can effect conductivity properties—and this type of knowledge can be used to aid the design of practical sensor devices. Robots may come to evolve a sense of smell by virtue of conductivity changes caused in their constituent semiconductor materials by gases in the surrounding atmosphere.

It is clear that robots are already evolving a wide range of different senses, and that efforts are being made to integrate these into intelligent configurations. Masuda and Hasegawa (1982) argue that to give robots flexibility and adaptability in complex tasks, it is necessary for individual sensors to be integrated into a total system. They indicate how a wide range of sensors—tactile, proximity and visual—can be viewed as modules in a total system design: no less than twenty-four sensory modules (for area touch, pressure, slip displacement, distance, inclination angle, range, position, colour, shape, etc.) are accommodated in this system. This design programme gives clues as to the future of sensory evolution in robots. We will see a growing proliferation of senses—using all the sensory mechanisms exploited by the higher animals, and additionals mechanisms—and we will see the vast spectrum of senses being co-ordinated in integrated systems. The various emerging robot species will become highly sensitive to their environments, at the same time learning to process—with growing intelligence—the abundance of data that their senses will provide.

The robot brain

Computers, of one size or another, serve in the appropriate circumstances as robot brains. Many of the truly sophisticated computers have been large systems ('mainframes' in the jargon). Where such systems have been able to provide a brain facility, the brain has been enormous. A brain of such a size—say, the dimensions of a couple of wardrobes—could never serve as cerebral equipment inside a reasonably sized robot. Computers *have* served as robot brains by being placed external to the robot body. For example, a minicomputer (about the size of a large suitcase) has often been placed some distance away from an industrial robot, linked to it by suitable cables. A robot that keeps its brain in some distant room is hard to view in anthropomorphic terms. It is as if we humans walked down the road with empty skulls, carrying our brains in a wheelbarrow before us!

In some circumstances, however, there are advantages in having robot brains in a different location to that of the main robot body. Sensitive computer electronics may not be happy working in a hazardous environment. The tough robot may be able to stand it, whereas the bunch of silicon chips that comprise its brain may be less keen. In such circumstances it is not uncommon to site a mainframe or minicomputer in a specially protected room, while the luckless robot has to confront the task directly. Nor is it uncommon for a number of robots to share a computer: sharing a brain must be reckoned a more intimate arrangement than sharing toothbrushes!

One disadvantage of a separately sited brain is that it restricts computer mobility. Today, with the increasing miniaturization of electronic equipment and the emergence of a new family of robust computers, there is less need to site robot brains away from the main body of the operating system. Part of the excitement surrounding the microprocessor is that, amongst other things, it can provide on-board cerebral facilities for robot devices—often on a distributed basis, with individual micros spread around the robot frame and dedicated to specific tasks. The small size and relative economy of micros render them suitable for use in many areas where earlier computers would have been too cumbersome and too expensive.

We have seen that computer-controlled robots are active in industrial and other applications. One provision of computer use is that the governing program can be modified during robot system operation; and system faults can be automatically diagnosed. Computer control can also maximize the efficiency of the system: it can define optimum operational modes in changing circumstances, and allow the sequencing of tasks that would otherwise be impossible.

Today robot brains are increasingly being provided by microprocessor-based facilities. For example, the Metal Castings Company (Worcester, England) has provided a supervisory microcomputer for a Series 2000 Unimate robot used to serve a large die-casting machine. The use of the micro in this context allows the work to be rapidly reprogrammed for the production of different parts. The computer specifies the required sequence of operations and also checks for safety: the circuitry is scanned to make sure that there are no guards open and that there are no physical obstructions. Metal Castings is now using seven factory Unimate robots with their own effective microprocessor brains.

Microcomputers linked to sensory devices can be used to detect the presence of a human being in the vicinity of the robot. Working in conjunction with appropriate sensors the computer can cause the robot to cease all operations if a human is present and in a danger area. Such a provision has obvious relevance to safety and other considerations. Micros can also be used to process the data acquired by robot sensors, a usage that closely parallels what happens in the human brain. It is not enough for the human eye to take in light and for appropriate signals to pass down the optic nerve. It is also necessary for the brain to process the incoming information. And what is true of the eye is true, *mutatis mutandis*, for the other sense organs.

It is obvious that the growing use of microprocessors in robot systems is enhancing robot intelligence, improving the effectiveness of sensory systems, and generally enhancing the robot capabilities that are analogous to the abilities of acknowledged animate creatures. It is easy to see the similarities between microprocessor brain power and capacities of the typical mammalian brain. Garrett (1978) has observed that 'the human brain is organized as a distributed processing system'—an arrangement that is increasingly common, via networking, in the realm of artificial computers. Data is collected, processed and stored in both artificial and animal brains, program sequences can be modified in the light of new experiences and new and unexpected contingencies can be coped with by means of decision facilities. Different parts of the human brain are dedicated to different senses, much as on-board microprocessors may be dedicated to different robot subsystems. The brain, in both natural and artificial life-forms, is the effective control centre. Without a brain, the system is little more than a pile of metal or a pile of (largely) organic chemicals, possibly capable of a few simple programmed sequences or reflex actions but incapable of any flexible and intelligent behaviour.

The design of robot brains (that is, computers) will continue to be influenced by what we know of mammalian brains and of nervous systems in less complex creatures. Increasingly, we will model our robot control hierarchies on what we know of hierarchies in existing brain systems (in fact Garrett has written that: 'Every brain [intelligence module] has control of all components and junctions within every intelligence module below its own intelligence level'—a central on-board microcomputer will be used to control the distributed micros throughout the robot system).

It is obvious that robots and other artificial-life systems will develop abilities according to the sophistication of their computer brains. The intelligence, adaptability, personality, creativity and so on, in other words the overall psychology, of the living robot largely derives from the nature of its controlling computer. It is useful to examine the psychology of computers. . . .

5 The psychology of computers

Preamble

Psychology is relevant to many life-forms but not all. Despite occasional talk of the 'secret life of plants' we tend to think that only certain *animals* have a psychological existence. The idea of a neurotic amoeba may appear somewhat fanciful but many people talk happily enough of the psychological problems of their pets. (I recently heard someone on radio talking of a pet dog that suffered from agoraphobia.) The more primitive the life-form, the less we incline to discuss its mental life, its psychological problems, its intellectual potential, etc. Planarian worms have been found to have strange memory capabilities but in general we feel that psychology only relates to creatures that are 'higher' in the evolutionary tree. There are good reasons for this. Today there is abundant evidence that mental life—at least in the traditional life-forms—depends upon such things as the complexity of the nervous system and the complexity of hormone distribution and effect. The simplest creatures are not in a position to boast about the complexity of their nervous systems.

Human beings are prejudiced. We like to think that we are the most superior creatures on Earth by virtue of our intellect. Many of us are not much to look at. And other species are faster, stronger, more prolific, more durable, etc. Much of theology and science has been fuelled by a desire to show that *homo sapiens* is uniquely grand, but one effort after another has collapsed. It has been variously claimed that man is the only animal with a soul, the only animal that uses tools, makes tools, forms lifelong pair-bonds, uses language, etc. But such claims are less than fashionable today. The idea of the soul seems rather eccentric, and various species of animals have been observed making and using tools, 'marrying' for life, using sounds and other devices to communicate emotion and information, etc. But we still claim that man is superior to other animals in intellect. Despite the imaginings of statisticians and philosophers, a bunch of energetic monkeys has not yet typed out the complete works of Shakespeare, and no herd of cows is likely to set about orchestrating the destruction—by means of high technology—of every other animal species. Man is definitely superior.

The topic of *thought* is one area of psychology, and we have already noticed that many observers have considered this aspect in connection with robots and computers: some of the old worries about AI were closely linked to the question as to whether computers could think. The first massive electronic computers, capable of rapid (if often unreliable) computation and little or no creative activity, were soon dubbed 'electronic brains', a term that signalled their apparent cerebral capacities. A reaction to this terminology quickly followed: to put them in their place, computers were called 'high-speed idiots', a ploy to protect human vanity. In such a climate the possibility of computers actually being alive was rarely considered: it was bad enough that computers might be capable of thought. But not everyone realized the implications of the *high-speed idiot* tag. It has not been pointed out often enough that even the human idiot is one of the most intelligent life-forms on Earth. If the early computers were even *that* intelligent it was already a remarkable state of affairs.

One consequence of speculation about the possibility of computer thought was that we were forced to examine with new care the idea of thought in general. It soon became clear that we were not sure what we meant by such terms as *thought* and *thinking*. We tend to assume that human beings think, some more than others, though we often call people *thoughtless* or *unthinking*. Dreams cause a problem, partly because they usually happen outside our control. They are obviously some type of mental experience, but are they a type of thinking? (We will see that at least one writer has considered whether automata can have a dreams.) And the question of non-human life-forms adds further problems. Many of us would maintain that some of the higher animals—dogs, cats, apes, etc.—are capable of at least rudimentary thought, but what about fish and insects? (There is evidence that snails are orgasmic.

Electrodes register peaks of electrical activity during copulation which subside after ejaculation. Do snails think about such things?) It is certainly true that the higher mammals show complex brain activity when tested with the appropriate equipment. If thinking is demonstrated by evident electrical activity in the brain, then many animal species are capable of thought. Once we have formulated clear ideas on what thought is in biological creatures it will be easier to discuss the question of thought in artefacts. And what is true of thought is also true of the many other mental processes. One of the immense benefits of AI research is that we are being forced to scrutinize, with unprecedented rigour, the working of the human mind.

It is already clear that machines have superior mental abilities to many acknowledged life-forms. No fern or oak tree can play chess as well as even the simplest digital computer; nor can frogs weld car bodies as well as robots. The three-fingered mechanical manipulator is cleverer in some ways than the three-toed sloth. It seems that, viewed in terms of intellect, the computer should be set well above plants and most animals. Only the higher (naturally occurring) animals can, it seems, compete with computers in the intellect stakes—and even then with diminishing success (witness backgammon and chess). And we have already seen that such capacities as creativity and learning are no longer alien to artefacts. These and other considerations are examined in what follows.

Physiology and psychology

Some people are reluctant to accept that mental phenomena can be properties of physical structures. In part this reluctance shows the lingering influence of the old 'substance metaphysics'—in which mind is seen as built out of one stuff, body out of another. This type of doctrine faces quite insuperable difficulties, not least the problem of the interface between the various mental and material stuffs. If mind is truly non-physical, how can it conceivably affect the material world? Immanuel Kant and many other philosophers have been quick to see that one entity can only influence another by virtue of what they have in common. And this line of thinking suggests that the mental is firmly rooted in the physical, a notion that derives immense support from modern insights in such sciences as neurophysiology and biological cybernetics.

Developments in the psychology of computers are being directly affected by investigations into specific mechanisms in mammalian and other brains. It is common for the computer literature to carry articles analysing brain function in human beings and other animals. For example, Filo (1979a) has developed what he calls *cyberanimetrics* to fill what he perceives as the gap between the neural cyberneticists (studying nervous systems and brains with a view to emulating them by means of machinery) and the cognitionists (building computer programs as a route to AI). Cyberanimetrics is represented as the study of biological organisms and (largely theoretical) machines that exhibit such life characteristics as organization, irritability, movement, growth, reproduction and adaptation.

Some studies aim at relating specific brain mechanisms to particular psychological activities. Wurtz, Goldberg and Robinson (1982) have studied the process by which the brain decides that certain objects in the vicinity are significant by recording the activity of nerve cells in the brains of monkeys that are responding to visual stimuli: the paper concludes that '... the demonstration of brain activity whose enhancement is related to attention means we have at last begun to translate a psychological concept into physiological terms'.

Other work has focused on identifying the brain mechanisms that are responsible for song in birds. Fernando Nottebohm and his colleagues at the Rockefeller University in New York have traced the brain pathways that control singing (Cherfas, 1979). Birds sing by means of the syrinx, an organ unique to them alone. The syrinx receives bundles of nerves from the brain which arise in the brain's hypoglossal nuclei and run down behind the trachea. Research into these and the associated mechanisms suggest that aesthetic capacities in living creatures will increasingly be defined in terms of neural connections. And more complex psychological features are likely to become amenable to description in terms of special neural networks and other characteristics of brain organization. As far back as 1968, K.H. Pribram was able to title a paper 'Towards a neuropsychological theory of person'. Today it seems even more plausible to examine the question of what it is to be human in terms of brain function and structure. There are profound implications in this for machine psychology.

Models and simulations

Efforts have been made for many years to model activities of human and other brains. It has long been felt possible, without knowing precisely how the brain works, to 'imitate' some of its functions by means of electrical and mechanical devices: more theoretically, mathematical models have been devised. It is convenient in this area to distinguish between what Seale (1981) calls 'weak' or 'cautious' AI and 'strong' AI. In the weak version, the computer is merely a tool in the study of mind: the computer enables researchers to test hypotheses more thoroughly. By contrast, in the strong version the suitably programmed computer *is* a mind. It represents an adequate *duplication* of specific well-defined mental processes: here a computer may be said to exhibit particular cognitive states—it may be said to *think, remember, understand* etc. It seems to me that the development AI over the last two decades has represented steady progress from a 'weak' to a 'strong' mode. The idea of weak AI suggests that particular mental states are only mimicked, that a computer state may resemble—perhaps in a metaphorical sense—a state of mind, whereas strong AI implies that real mental states can be built into machines. Computer *simulation* admits of both interpretations: an effective simulation may be seen as *representing* a cognitive state without being equated with it, or the simulation may be seen embodying the *essence* of the mental state.

One early approach to modelling was to show the similarities between activities in the human brain and activities in the processing units of digital computers: where enough similarities were identified, it was suggested that the computer 'modelled' the brain. For example, it is easy to compare the activity of brain neurons with that of logic gates in computer central processing units (CPUs), or to compare organic brain physics and chemistry with what happens in computer circuitry. In such a way it has been thought possible to bolster the idea of 'cerebral' activity in machines—by use of analogy. In the computer, subatomic particles move in solid material (metal conductors, chips of impure silicon etc.). The chemistry of the silicon and its impurities is organized to realize electrical components (such as transistors, resistors, diodes and capacitors) packed into a small volume. For instance, if a tiny section of silicon is 'doped' with certain other chemicals it can be made to behave like a transistor. Thousands of transistors and other components so constructed together form the logic and arithmetic functions upon which all machine intelligence is based. (Silicon is used because it has peculiar electrical properties: it is a 'semiconductor'—neither a true conductor nor a true insulator.)

The semiconducting properties of certain chemicals are also exploited in the brain, though in a variety of ways not yet fully understood. Pulses of electricity are generated to control the behaviour of the brain cells: a cell can be induced to 'fire' (that is, to emit a pulse) when certain electrical and chemical conditions obtain (when, for example, a number of other controlled pulses are fed to the cell and when certain critical chemical transmitter substances are produced to convey information across the synaptic gap). The thousands of millions of brain cells are interconnected in a staggeringly complex array to allow the necessary functions of the organism to be performed—from the control of heart beat and glandular secretion to all the mental processes of ratiocination, aesthetic response, decision-making, etc.

It is obvious that there are many similarities between the biological and artificial systems. Both exploit the properties of chemical elements (carbon and silicon, respectively) organized in highly complex configurations to realize particular functions. Brains and computer processing units both operate on the *building block* principle: highly complicated systems are constructed out of a range of basic similar units. New functions are made possible by adding more basic units (there are more brains cells inside a human being than inside the skull of a frog) or by increasing the number of connections between the units (the human baby has fewer interconnections between its brain cells than does the human adult). Research has suggested that certain columns of brain cells are strictly analogous in function to computer processing units. Both brains (with their peripheral organs) and computer-based robot systems rely upon both digital (two-state binary) systems (a cell is firing or it is not; a key electrical pulse is either present or it is not) and analogue systems (necessary to convert 'real-world' information into a form which can be handled by the internal processing machinery).

There are interesting similarities between carbon (used for all types of living tissue, including brains, in the traditional life-forms) and silicon (used for all types of computer circuits, including the ones that do logic and arithmetic). Carbon and silicon are recognized as two of the very few elements out of which highly complicated molecules (macromolecules) could be built: it is known that such complex molecules are necessary for the metabolic processes that take place in the acknowledged life-forms. (This is why silicon, as an imaginative alternative to carbon, has figured in science fiction as a possible chemical base for life on other planets.) However, we have already seen that silicon is used in computers because of its semiconducting properties, not because it can support macromolecules.

A listing of similarities between brain hardware and computer circuitry may serve to suggest a 'static modelling' approach: functions are *implied* rather than confronted directly. Many efforts to model traditional biological brains, however, have relied upon what is known is various engineering fields. For example, various servosystem models of the brain have derived from what is known about the pre-computer cybernetics of engineering equipment. Such an 'engineering' approach has proved useful in understanding various biological functions. Increasingly, it is apparent that there is a generalized systems theory that can equally embrace neurobiology (and other life processes in traditional life-forms) and the study of the emerging computer and robot species. Automata, for instance, have been viewed at one level as mathematical models of the network structure of the nervous systems of acknowledged life-forms. There is increasing evidence to suggest that automata configurations (often theoretical) can be designed to resemble the human nervous system.

Recent research has provided further evidence that certain types of computer design may be seen as models of specific brain structures. One consequence of microprocessor development has been to emphasize the value of a *modular* approach to system engineering. Benefits derive from having processing power where it is needed rather than referring all processing functions to a central processing unit. One view of the cerebral cortex is that it is essentially modular in organization: the typical cortical 'integrative unit' comprises a narrow column, less than 0.5 mm wide, containing as many as 10,000 neurons. Each such module includes input and output channels (respectively the afferent fibres and the large pyramidal cells), and a large number of other cells in a complex but regular pattern. There are excitatory and inhibitory connections within each column, and inhibitory connections between adjacent columns. And it has been found that at least some of the brain cells have memory. Proposals have been advanced as to how such an arrangement could act as a 'content-addressable' memory system, as in computers (Spinelli, 1970).

There is as yet little insight into how such complex arrangements function to carry out their necessary processing tasks. There is, however, clear evidence that the cerebral cortex is a complex configuration of distributed processing power, with the modular principle having direct relevance to the behavioural subsystems of such capacities as perception and action in humans and other animals. The provision of distributed data processing power via modular subsystems, at the same time allowing appropriate reference to some central control, is commonplace in modern computer systems: for instance, rather than install a vast expensive company computer in a data processing department it is often better to install small cheaper computers in the offices where they are needed (much is currently being written about the local area networks, LANs, required for this purpose). We may take it as significant that microprocessor developments are causing computer systems to evolve to more closely resemble what is being found to be the structural configuration of the human brain!

Research suggesting that the cortex is fundamentally modular in organization (see Szentagothai and Arbib, 1974; Marr, 1976; Eccles, 1977), that specific modular 'integrative units' can be identified (Szentagothai, 1975), and that specific 'interneurons' have memory (Uttley, 1976) suggest a clear programme for future computer evolution. Where computers are able to duplicate the functional and structural characteristics of the mammalian cortex, we would expect computers to exhibit unambiguous cognitive capacities. Specific insights into cortical memory mechanisms (see below) may be expected to increase further the ability of intelligent artefacts to duplicate, rather than mimic, human mental processes.

Models derived from computer science—for example, using ideas from programming, parallel processing and memory—are found to describe plausible mechanisms for human mental activity (some of these are discussed below). The modular approach to cognitive processes is usually seen to demand a hierarchical structure of control: we can't have all the discrete modules randomly doing their own thing. And hierarchies in turn can be modelled in various ways. Albus (1981), for instance, suggests that there is considerable evidence—anatomical, neurophysiological and behavioural—that the analogy between the brain and a military hierarchy is quite accurate; and, as an element in such a model, he traces a single chain of command from a single motor neuron up to a high-level command module. In this arrangement every motor neuron is controlled by its own hierarchy. The various hierarchical sensory-motor systems 'become increasingly interrelated and interconnected with each other at the higher levels'. This organizational arrangement allows a complex organism to co-ordinate a wide range of actions in pursuit of high-level goals.

The traditional approach to modelling of brain functions relied heavily on anatomical or physiological information—in part to build up a coherent view of physical brain activity. For instance, Sir Charles Sherrington built up a theory of the *reflex arc*, where the model provided a differential and adaptive network of impulses, in order to establish what has been called the classical neurophysiological theory of brain activity. Current work continues to build on the early physiological modelling—see, for example, the neurological model derived by Albus (1981, chapter 6). At the same time, computer science has encouraged a parallel development for the understanding of psychological processes: computer simulation techniques are being developed to provide insight into cognitive and other mental functions, without reliance upon specific anatomical or physiological information. For example, it may be maintained that a high level of understanding can be obtained of how human beings use language, recognize patterns and store information, without reference to how individual brain cells work or interconnect (this is one reason why anatomical questions play such a small part in the section on some cognitive conerns, below). In fact, it is increasingly argued that since cognitive capacities are largely realized through *programs*, and since programs can be run on any suitable system, particular neurological (or computer hardware) details are not central to any enquiry into cognition and other mental activities. Sloman (1978), for example, even asks 'Are computers really relevant?' to the development and understanding of how symbols need to be manipulated for AI purposes. Put another way, AI researchers do not study computers: they study programs. This clearly removes the spotlight from what brains or computers are made of:

> It could be transistors, it could be more old-fashioned electronic components, it could be made of physical components not yet designed, it could somehow be made of non-physical spiritual stuff, if there is any such thing. The medium or material used is immaterial! All that matters is that enough structures are available to represent the required range of symbols, and that appropriate structural changes can occur in the computer (Sloman, 1978, p. 105)

This point can be seen to be in accord with our discussion of life criteria in chapter 1. Life-forms, as well as brains, do not need to be built up out of hydrocarbons. For these sorts of reasons, computer efforts to simulate cognitive and other mental processes do not need to rely upon neurological modelling, though such modelling may be regarded as giving clues as to how one type of intelligent system is able to handle cognitive symbols. But if a cognitive process requires, for example, distributed-memory features it is of little consequence for AI purposes whether the memory elements are composed of carbon-based macromolecules, of solid-state silicon, or of something entirely different to either.

Computer simulation programs have been successful both when focused on specific cognitive tasks and when designed as general problem-solvers (see Newell, Shaw and Simon, 1959; and the section on problem solving, below). The limited generality of some simulation programs has sometimes led to criticism that such programs do not truly emulate human capabilities. Hence Bolton (1972) asserts: 'A computer which performs one specialist task very well, but is helpless at any other problem is not therefore representative of human problem solving.' This is not a very telling point: we all know people who are quite brilliant in one specialist area, but totally incompetent in everything else (Crawshay-Williams, 1970, records that Bertrand Russell was quite unable to make a pot of tea, even when presented with a detailed list of simple instructions). Moreover, the development of general problem-solving is extending computer competence in this respect.

It has also been remarked (for example in Dreyfus, 1972; Neisser, 1963) that machines fail to incorporate the performance factors which influence human activity. Dreyfus suggests that it is *a priori* impossible to provide computer simulation with the phenomenological aspect of human performance: human problem solving, for instance, is accompanied by a variety of subjective feelings. I do not see how a formal argument about this could be sustained since it would also prove, *mutatis mutandis*, that human beings could not have subjective feelings. Neisser also stressed the motivational differences between men and machines—an evident fact which, nonetheless, may be temporary (see the section on emotions, below). Dreyfus also worries that computers cannot cogitate in a human fashion since humans depend upon having bodies for perception, motor functions, etc.—but it has been pointed out, not least by Pylyshyn (1975), that the formal conceptual structure could still be represented in a machine. Anyway we have seen (chapter 4) that the emerging robot/computer life-forms have bodies (comprising limbs, torsos, senses, etc.).

One interesting point, emphasized by Cohen (1977), is that many of the criticisms of machine cognition could equally be applied to human beings. For instance, there is the question of knowing that a computer *understands* (see also the section on language and understanding, below). How do we know that *anyone* understands? Solely by behavioural manifestation—and this may take the form of speaking, writing or other modes of communication. With Wilks (1976) we must declare that: 'if I am asked for the phenomenology of anyone else's understanding, I have, of course, no feelings and immediate assurance to fall back on, and I am out in the cold world of watching his behaviour for appearances of understanding....' And what is true of understanding is also true of feelings, attitudes and emotions. Cohen notes that most of the same problems arise when the psychological models are tested against experimental data derived from human subjects: 'Here the difficulties of interpretation arouse less chauvinistic passion, and too little attention, but are just as acute'.

What we find is that it is possible to argue for a 'strong' AI; that is, for computer simulation that does not merely mimic or imitate, but that duplicates or truly achieves, definable cognitive states. This should not be taken as implying that the cognitive states of computers are as sophisticated or as flexible as those in a typical human adult. For this, at the present stage of evolution of machine life-forms, would be an unreasonable expectation. Cohen (1977) asks whether a computer simulation program should be equivalent to 'a skilled and practised human performer, or to an untutored beginner?' We need only ask that such a program be equivalent to a six-month-old human baby, a slightly retarded human adolescent or a mildly senile fellow in his dotage. It is no part of our thesis that robot/computer life-forms in the 1980s will combine the logical ability of Russell, the cross-cultural musical insights of Menuhin, and the intuitive scientific imagination of Bohr and Einstein. The emerging machine life-forms still have rudimentary life characteristics in many respects—when compared with normal human adults. However, when compared with lichens or slugs, undisputed life-forms, the emerging robot/computer life-forms are already highly evolved. And this after very few generations (four or five in the case of computers, two or three with robots—how many human generations have there been?). What we should *reasonably expect* of computer psychology should be borne in mind when we discuss some cognitive concerns later; and the topics that follow. First we should consider the emerging consciousness of machines....

The conscious machine

Consciousness is not essential to life (plants exhibit few if any signs of consciousness), but the presence of consciousness helps to indicate a *type* of life. Samuel Butler (1872) declares that it would be rash to say that no other forms of life and consciousness could evolve, and in connection with machines he declares that 'There is no security against the ultimate development of mechanical consciousness, in the fact of machines possessing little consciousness now'. Even at that time, more than a century ago, Butler could discern 'germs of consciousness' in many actions of the higher machines—'the race of man has descended from things which had no consciousness at all . . . there is no *a priori* improbability in the descent of conscious (and more than conscious) machines from those which now exist. . . '.

Sometimes it is suggested that consciousness can only exist when certain chemicals work together in the certain way. Julian Huxley used to say this sort of thing, as did Satosi Watanabe (1960). Such a claim obviously implies that computers are unlikely to be conscious: after all, they are not made of protoplasm. The suggestion is that a machine made out of protein might be conscious but perhaps one made out of printed circuit boards and impure silicon might not be. But then, according to one sort of semantic decision, an organic artificial machine made out of protein would in fact be a man-made animal and not a machine. Some people like to think of machines being made out of a different sort of stuff to themselves. In such a semantic framework, machines will never be conscious since once they are no longer machines. But obviously this is a matter of definition and not of fact.

Other views rely on the idea that consciousness is not a well-defined concept. Hilary Putnam (1975), for instance, suggests that whether machines are conscious is up to us to decide:

> It seems preferable to me to extend our concepts so that robots *are* conscious—for discrimination based on the 'softness' or 'hardness' of the body parts of a synthetic 'organism' seems as silly as discriminatory treatment of humans on the basis of skin colour.

We need hardly point out that there is more to the question of robot consciousness than semantic decision. In Putnam's view the question as to whether robots are conscious should focus on the fact that they are deterministic systems designed by someone and we are not. Reichardt has pointed out that this doctrine could have unexpected consequences: if we ever discovered that *homo sapiens* had been invented by some superior intelligence—as theologians used to believe—then it would seem to follow that we had no consciousness. Nor should we make the mistake of thinking that human beings are not programmed (see the discussion of freedom and autonomy, below).

In his seminal 1950 paper, Turing considered a number of likely objections to the idea of computer thought: one of these is the *Argument from Consciousness*. Turing suggests that the argument can be undermined by committing believers in it to a solipsist position: 'I think that most of those who support the argument from consciousness could be persuaded to abandon it rather than be forced into a solipsist position'. It is acknowledged that there is a mystery about consciousness—'There is, for instance, something of a paradox connected with any attempt to localise it'—but the question of computer thought does not have to wait for a solution to the problem. Turing saw consciousness as not essential to computer thought—much in the way that we have suggested that it is not essential to computer life.

Klir and Valach (1965) consider the question of machine consciousness as part of a general enquiry into cybernetic modelling. They see recent discoveries as suggesting that consciousness is a certain state of the organism: this is, for example, talk of full consciousness, superficial or deep unconsciousness, clouded consciousness, sleep, etc. Such an interpretation, nicely in accord with automata theory, differs from earlier views where consciousness could be located in a particular anatomical centre. Full consciousness, in the modern doctrine, consists in the organism being able to generate mental images on the basis of signals extracted from the memory, the generation of percepts on the basis of sensations, the deliberate concentration of attention, etc. We can speculate about how such diverse attributes of consciousness can be coordinated and controlled. However, in the context of cybernetic modelling, Klir and Valach are unequivocal: ' . . . every original has proved capable of being modelled, provided there existed a sufficiently clear description, simultaneously expressing the viewpoint from which this original seems interesting.' Consciousness, if adequately defined, could be modelled. And they proceed to show, via the 'isomorphy of consciousness in inanimate systems', how this could be done.

In another view (Dawkins, 1976), consciousness is intimately connected with the idea of survival. *Survival machines* which can 'simulate the future' (in other words those that can imagine what might happen to them) are one jump ahead of mechanisms that can only learn on the basis of trial and error: overt error is often fatal, whereas simulation is faster and safer. It is suggested that the evolution of the capacity to simulate 'seems to have culminated in subjective consciousness'. And for Dawkins this is the *most profound mystery* facing modern biology. He adds in passing that 'There is no reason to believe that electronic computers are conscious when they simulate, although *we have to admit that in the future they may become so*' (my italics). And this could arise when the computer's simulation of the world is sufficiently complete to include a model of itself.

It does not seem at all eccentric to suggest that consciousness is intimately associated with the need to survive. It is possible to argue, for traditional life-forms, that all mental features are connected with survival requirements. Consciousness could thus be designed into machines to aid their adaptation in a changing environment. Just as cybernetic systems, influenced by feedback controls, would search for food (electricity) when necessary, so simulation activities (imagination) based on predictive programs would help the machines to avoid danger.

Hofstadter's *reflections* on Searle (1981) give clues as to how computer consciousness may be achieved in programming terms:

> ... a higher-level program would have to have some way of creating changes inside the 'demon' that is carrying its program out. This is utterly foreign to the present style in computer science of implementing one level above another in a strictly vertical, sealed-off fashion. The ability of a higher level to loop back and affect lower levels—its own underpinnings—is a kind of magic trick *which we feel is very close to the core of consciousness*. It will perhaps one day prove to be a key element in the push towards ever greater flexibility in computer design. ... [my italics]

This approach, like that of Dawkins, implies that the system property of consciousness may develop in computers at a later stage in their evolution. Consciousness may come to provide superior computer capability, including an enhanced capacity for survival in a changing environment. Design experience in generating computer simulation programs may be seen as relevant to structuring consciousness into computer software systems.

At the same time it should not be forgotten that consciousness has not been represented as a necessary life criterion. The information-processing criteria could well be met by means of 'unconscious' information processing, a doctrine that accords well with what happens, in fact, with human beings in some circumstances. We all know of stories about how people sometimes go to bed with a problem—and how it is solved the next morning. 'Unconscious' information processing is well known in human beings: it could equally well characterize computers at their present stage of evolution.

There is abundant experimental evidence for this type of processing in human beings. For example, a patient who has recently had a large section of his visual cortex surgically excized may be asked to touch a light when it comes on at a certain place in his nominal visual field. In circumstances where he cannot see the light he is told to guess. What is remarkable is that the responses of such a patient are virtually perfect, even in the totally 'blind' region. This strange phenomenon has been termed 'blindsight' (Weiskrantz, Warrington, Sanders and Marshall, 1974; Weiskrantz, 1977). What it implies is that certain subcortical visual mechanisms are able to control with great accuracy such actions as reaching, and the direction of gaze—but they cannot control 'perceptual reports'. The person may reach to touch an object with great accuracy but is not conscious that he is so doing—even though, by all other criteria, he is wide awake and fully conscious. There are also many demonstrations of the 'unconscious' processing of word meanings; for example, under conditions of visual pattern masking (Allport, 1977; Marcel and Patterson, 1978).

Consciousness is not only not a requirement for computer life-forms, it need not be a requirement for many intelligent tasks carried out by human beings. It may be that unconscious information processing may characterize the psychology of computers for some time to come. If computers evolve to a state of consciousness, they will acquire a variety of processing and survival advantages. But the various cognitive faculties of computers can be considered whether or not these are accompanied by consciousness.

Some cognitive concerns

The computer impact

By the late 1950s it was obvious that computers were going to affect psychology profoundly. Already it was clear that the emerging electronic devices could do many of the things that humans and other animals could do: for example, they could learn, store, manipulate and recall information. In addition it was becoming evident that computers could use language, solve problems, take decisions, and reason. Newell, Shaw and Simon (1958) and other researchers were already working to recast the traditional psychological problems in terms of computer analogies. In the discernible move away from behaviourism, a new interest developed in internal mental processes and structures which could now be described in programming terms.

The new computer models were so powerful that it became reasonable to suppose that human mental equipment was not merely *analogous* to a computer but was in fact a type of computer itself. By 1971, Earl Hunt could ask: 'What kind of computer is man?' Speculating on what he took to be a valid analogy between human information processing and the activities in a computer, he undertook the task of describing a computing system that 'thinks like a man'. By now it was clear that computer science was affecting psychology, and psychological insights were influencing how people were coming to regard computers. A new and strange psychology/computing symbiosis was developing: computer developments were telling us more about the human mind, and psychological concepts were enlarging our vision of what computers could become.

It is a popular view that the human brain can be considered analogous to a data processing system, with a large store capacity and working with coded information transmitted along the pathways of the nervous system. The information may derive initially from the sense organs (the equivalent of the robot sensors) or from processing activities within the neural network. Allport (1980) notes that 'the first generation of theories in information-processing psychology was founded on the new process metaphors offered by the uniprocessor, general-purpose computer'. This was particularly noticeable in theories which were supposed to account for limitations in human performance (for example, restricted data transmission rate, limited short-term memory, poor concentration, etc.). It is obvious that the brain is capable of millions of 'quasi-independent' functions concurrently in parallel. The notion of the brain as a highly complex data processing mechanism seems secure. In such a view it is easy to see clear analogies between aspects of human psychology and the activities within a computer.

Miller (1956) published a landmark paper which encouraged the development of an information-processing model for human psychology; and in 1960 Miller, Galanter and Pribram offered a cognitive alternative to stimulus–response behaviourism—the new alternative focused on the notion that the unit of behaviour is a *plan*, a behaviour-generating system similar to the feedback loops used in computers. In such a view, human beings were not passive responders but active processors of information involved in carrying out a wide range of mental activities and tests on the environment. Neisser (1967), building both on the new theoretical framework and recent research, proposed a distinct information-processing model comprising specific memory stores and processes, at the same time rejecting what he termed the 'computer simulation' approach. This rejection was on the ground that contemporary efforts in this direction were too simplistic and task-specific to 'do justice to the complexity of human mental processes' (Allport asks: 'In what way, I wonder, did he find psychologists' theories less simplistic, or less paradigm-bound?').

Throughout the 1970s, AI research increasingly influenced the development of cognitive psychology. Allport (1980) even goes so far as to declare:

... the advent of Artificial Intelligence is the single most important development in the history of psychology.... Indeed, it seems to me not unreasonable to expect that Artificial Intelligence will ultimately come to play the role *vis a vis* the psychological and social sciences that mathematics, from the seventeenth century on, has done for the physical sciences.

AI as part of computer science, is illuminating both the mechanisms of human psychology and the route which should be followed to provide computers with minds of their own. It is not essential to life that it have a mental existence, but a mental component helps to define the sophistication, the stage of evolution, etc., of the life in question.

It should be remarked that various other influences, apart from computer science, have helped to shape modern cognitive psychology. We have already talked about neurophysiology. Oliver Selfridge (1956, 1966), a computer scientist, used ideas in this field to develop theories on pattern recognition and simple learning. Today there is abundant evidence of specialized neurons responding selectively to particular invariant properties of sensory input: this is now seen as an important design feature in the brains of human beings and other animals. Anne Treisman (1960) tried to extend Selfridge's scheme to language.

In the field of linguistics there has been a parallel shift away from behaviourism and towards an analysis of the mental structures important for comprehension and the production of utterances. In particular, Chomsky (1957) provided for a cognitive analysis of language behaviour. And another influence on the course of modern psychology derived from the work of Piaget (1954): in the same spirit, but with a strong biological emphasis, Piaget focused on the internal structures and processes that underlie the progressive changes in human behaviour.

What we see is a conflux of influences—deriving from computer science, neurophysiology, biology and linguistics—shaping the character of modern cognitive psychology. For our purpose, we can emphasize the central importance of computer science, and AI in particular, in this scheme. It is through the development of computer science that we are learning to understand human mental processes in terms of systems, programs, structures and the rest; and it is through the development of computer science, leavened by accumulating psychological insights, that we are learning to ascribe cognitive states to artefacts.

Memory mechanisms

Memory is central to the information-processing model of man. Information has not only to be collected and manipulated but also stored on a short- or long-term basis. Speedy information processing—for example, in a threatening situation—may require only short-term memory, but for many other purposes long-term storage is essential. Knowledge may need to be accessed months or years after it was first acquired; and there may be a constant need for reference data (constituting a world model, self-awareness structures, etc.) on a day-to-day basis. Virtually all the cognitive tasks presuppose either the collecting or accessing of stored information. The psychologies of computers and human beings depend equally upon effective memory mechanisms.

The similarities between human memory and computer memory relate to such concepts as passive and active systems, memory elements, coding techniques, retrieval pathways, content-addressable memory and storage capacity in different subsystems. Winograd (1975) has described several ways in which analogies can be drawn between human and machine memory. In one model memory is shown as a set of independent elements controlled by a central processing unit that calls up information when needed and encodes specific input information to memory cells. This process involves 'search' and 'active message processing', where each memory element may have 'the power to do its own computations on a message that is sent to the memory elements, and each element can decide independently what action it should take' (p. 144). This process is seen as essentially similar to human associative memory, where specific memory items are linked with others in a network.

In passive memory, items of information are stored in specific locations which can be accessed sequentially (like running through a tape recording until a desired item is located) or by random access mechanisms (where preliminary processing defines the 'address' of the item). In active memory systems, memory elements are connected in a network, and information can be retrieved in various ways: content-addressable methods are the simplest.

Some computer models—such as Reitman's (1970) Waiting-room Model—have represented input processing in short-term memory: these imply a detailed comparison of computer output and human data. In fact shortcomings in the Reitman model are suggested by the non-equivalence in this case between the machine and human outputs. Other models— for example, EPAM (Elementary Perceiver and Memoriser, see Feigenbaum, 1963); and SAL (Stimulus and Association Learner, see Hintzman, 1968)—are seen as representing only limited subsets of memory functions. At the same time, the Feigenbaum program, for instance, is an early example of how a cognitive process can be effectively modelled.

It shows how it may be that we can forget something for a long time and yet remember it again in certain circumstances: in this model, information is never destroyed but may be hidden for a time, one memory masking another. Another interesting feature of the program is that it behaves in ways which were not 'programmed in': the program contains no interference routines, but the acquisition of a new association can interfere with the production of an older one when, for example, syllables are to be learned. The Feigenbaum program is one of many that totally undermines the oft-heard cliché that 'computers only do what you tell them to'.

Many studies focus on the links between data processing and data storage (or memory). For example, the notion of limited-capacity processing in short-term memory is widely postulated (for example, Baddeley and Hitch, 1974; Bjork, 1975). Hitch (1980) explores this idea in connection with the notion of a 'central executive processor'. This type of work implies a further development in the analogy between machine and human memory.

Stored data may be seen as *knowledge*, a meaningful body of information that can support intelligence. In one view (Bond, 1981), 'the history of machine intelligence can be viewed as the development of knowledge representation methods'. This idea is intimately linked to the development of *expert* and other AI systems. Here the *rule*, representing a particular fragment of knowledge, is a central concept in *knowledge engineering*. There are various possible system organizations which determine how rules are used in the execution of a program.

The development of computer models of memory,

knowledge- or rule-systems and other concepts deriving from AI research suggests not only a deepening of our understanding of human psychological mechanisms but ways of building equivalent mechanisms into artefacts. We have seen that information-processing systems are intimately associated with the necessary life criteria. We would expect the emerging computer life-forms to develop their capacity for storing information in various ways and the ability to process the information for a growing range of intelligent purposes.

Language and understanding

The topic of computer understanding invites a host of semantic and other questions. How would we recognize understanding in a computer? Can a definition only be approached in a behavioural way, or is it possible to describe circumstances in which we could recognize understanding without any behavioural manifestation? Does *conceptual* understanding imply an understanding of language? What different forms of understanding can be identified?

Human beings tend to interpret understanding in terms of mental images, experiences and behaviour. If someone can answer appropriate questions it is assumed that they understand: yet this cannot be conclusive. Searle (1981) points out that a person or a machine may be equipped with formal rules for transposing one set of Chinese symbols into another set, without understanding what the symbols denote: the ability to manipulate symbols correctly does not, at one level, imply understanding. Some observers would take behaviour as a more reliable guide: see what happens when you tell someone, correctly, that his house is on fire or her car has been stolen—suitable behavioural responses would imply understanding. Computer brains equipped with robot bodies can both manipulate symbols and behave in various ways. The criteria for understanding in such circumstances would appear to be much the same as those required in the case of human beings.

Klir and Valach (1967) note that 'understanding a verbal expression' is generally taken to have three parts: receipt of an explanation by a *listening system*; subsequent resultant changes in the system to allow modified reactions; and someone to assess whether the system's consequential behaviour gives grounds for attributing understanding to the system. It is suggested that these elements can be used to explore the question of understanding in 'inanimate' (that is, machine) systems. Various definitions are proposed of 'understanding of text by machine':

1. A machine understands a text if it gives correct answers to questions whose answering follows from the text.
2. A machine understands a text if it gives correct answers to questions whose answering follows from the given text on the one hand, and from its prior store of knowledge on the other hand.
3. The machine understands a text if it links up the knowledge resulting from it with its prior knowledge in the correct manner.

Finally, the definition of *understanding* is generalized: 'The machine understands the given signal [set of signals] if it adequately changes its former behaviour as a result of having received it'. This is taken as avoiding the excessive dependence upon a *verbally expressed relationship*. Every signal understood by the machine has a certain significance or content ('information'), and we may expect new signals to modify the knowledge base in the machine. Again this can be taken as closely analogous to what happens with human beings.

Clark and Clark (1977) propose that individuals move through a three-step process in recording information: a sentence is divided into *given* and *new* information; given information is located in memory; the new information is added to memory. This approach was made explicit by Miller and Johnson-Laird (1976)—considering perception and language—in developing the analogy with programming a computer. A computer first compiles a program written in a high-level language (FORTRAN, BASIC, etc.) into the language that the particular machine can understand: then the compiled program is executed with respect to the necessary data. Humans beings, it is suggested, adopt a similar two-step approach in the psychological processing of a sentence. The person first translates the natural language input into a series of mental instructions that allow a question to be answered or a command carried out; then the individual decides whether to answer the question or carry out the command. The second ('execution') phase involves searching memory and possibly constructing a plan based on environmental data. Since the program is to be run by a 'neural computer', the brain, the process must involve a compilation into the neural machine code. In such a way it is possible to deepen still further the man/computer analogy: the development of a programming model is seen as a fruitful way of approaching human behaviour and the working of artefacts.

The importance of language as a cognitive concern derives from its connection with information (*knowledge* in an intelligent system). Language allows communication (conversation) and helps to provide criteria for recognizing understanding in both human and computer life-systems. It is partly for this reason that conversational computer programs have been developed. One of the first, and most cited, of these is ELIZA (named after Dr Doolittle's pupil in Shaw's *Pygmalion*), written by Joseph Weizenbaum (1966)—writers like to compare conversations of ELIZA with ones of Arthur C. Clarke's Hal in *2001*. (The 1950 Turing Test, as a means of recognizing a thinking machine, relies similarly upon language processing.) In one program, called DOCTOR, ELIZA adopts the role of a psychiatrist (the computer's words are in capitals). Here is a brief extract from a resulting conversation (part of ELIZA's publicity release):

Men are all alike.
IN WHAT WAY?
They're always bugging us about something or other.
CAN YOU THINK OF A SPECIFIC EXAMPLE?
Well, my boyfriend made me come here.
YOUR BOYFRIEND MADE YOU COME HERE?
He says I'm depressed much of the time.
I AM SORRY TO HEAR YOU ARE DEPRESSED.
It's true. I am unhappy.
DO YOU THINK COMING HERE WILL HELP YOU NOT TO BE UNHAPPY?
I need some help, that much seems certain.
WHAT WOULD IT MEAN TO YOU IF YOU GOT SOME HELP?...

It is now generally acknowledged that there are a number of weaknesses in the ELIZA system (for example, it cannot cope with compound sentences), but as an early conversational facility ELIZA was of landmark importance. Today ELIZA is available for microcomputers (on $5\frac{1}{4}$-in. discs, for instance, to run on an Apple II). Parsons (1982) describes his experiences with microcomputer ELIZA. One initial run, in which he was 'downright malicious', includes the following exchange (ELIZA's words again in capitals):

WHAT IS IT YOU REALLY WANT TO KNOW?
Whether the money people spend on you is well spent.
WE WERE DISCUSSING YOU—NOT ME.
That's funny—I thought we were discussing you.
YOU ARE NOT REALLY TALKING ABOUT ME, ARE YOU?
Yes I am.
I UNDERSTAND.
Yes.
YOU SEEM QUITE POSITIVE.
Yes.
YOU ARE SURE?
Sure I'm sure.
IS IT BECAUSE YOU ARE SURE THAT YOU CAME TO ME?
No.
ARE YOU SAYING 'NO' JUST TO BE NEGATIVE?
No, I am saying 'no' in answer to your question.
YOU ARE BEING A BIT NEGATIVE.
Would you rather have me lie to you?
WHY DO YOU THINK I RATHER HAVE YOU?
Would you please re-phrase your question?
YOU SEEM TO HAVE AVOIDED SPEAKING OF YOUR PARENTS ALTOGETHER.
They don't read *Microcomputing*.
DO YOU FEEL STRONGLY ABOUT DISCUSSING SUCH THINGS?
Well, a little more circulation would do no harm.
HOW COME?
We were discussing you—not me.
YOU LIKE TO THINK I—NOT YOU—DON'T YOU?

The ELIZA shortcomings revealed in the piece of dialogue are present in the original version of the system, not only in the microcomputer version made available by the Artificial Intelligence Research Group of Los Angeles. (Parsons: 'To answer my own question to Eliza, I would say that the money people spend on her *is* well spent. In fact, $25 is dirt-cheap for so much fun.') ELIZA is not an example of machine understanding—it would need a more comprehensive data base, possibly involving a world model including self-awareness—but it is obviously a step in the right direction.

Efforts have also been made to reverse the roles—to arrange for a psychiatrist to talk to a computerized simulation of a patient. Colby, Hilf, Webev and Kraemer (1972) simulated such a patient in the PARRY (paranoid) program. A paranoid subject was selected because a considerable body of knowledge already existed about the nature of paranoia, and because expert judges could be used to evaluate the differences between the computer responses and those of an equivalent human patient. The computer was subjected to an effective Turing Test, with psychiatrists asked to interview PARRY by means of teletyped messages. The experts were asked to estimate the degree of 'paranoidness' of the subject. Boden (1977) considers PARRY in some detail, asking, among others things, 'how PARRY manages it'.

An approach to understanding is also being developed via the computer analysis of natural language for translation and other purposes. 'Understanding programs' have been developed in a way that relies on specific conceptual features of the language (Schank, 1972; Wilks, 1973; Anderson, 1975 etc.). These systems can analyse the content of the discourse and also the meaning of the words. Winograd (1972) talks about the analysis of 'word knowledge', and in some instances a syntax analyser can be employed to determine the most likely parsing and interpretation of a sentence. And systems are being developed to allow human users to interrogate a data base by means of natural language. This means that, increasingly, computers can understand human beings when the machines are addressed in English.

One main natural language system, Intellect, is in wide use outside research establishments. Intellect (formerly termed Robot) of the Artificial Intelligence Corporation (Waltham, Mass.) provides natural-language access to information stored in its own memory. The system can produce reports and replies in answer to queries such as (Kaplan and Ferris, 1982):

Are there any people working as secretaries and earning a salary of 15,000 or more?
Broken down by state and city, print a salary report for these people, including their name and age.
What is the family status of the area managers that live in New York?

In a sense, the system understands what it is being asked: it can be questioned in English and can give an English reply. It is also possible to link in to other database systems (such as ADABAS of Software AG of North America). Today there are more than sixty commercial Intellect systems in operation, though response times can be unacceptably long in some circumstances. Other natural-language systems are being explored (we have already profiled speech-recognition facilities in chapter 3), and research is continuing into the automatic recognition of continuous speech. Developments in this area will clearly be relevant to the concept of computer understanding.

It can be emphasized that understanding in human beings depends upon more than linguistic interchanges: it is also mediated by shared sensory information, and demonstrated by appropriate behaviour. Some programs manifest a deeper level of understanding because they include facilities for simulating perceptual and motor activities as well as linguistic processes. For example, the Winograd (1972) program operates within a table-top array of blocks of different sizes: it is able to perceive and manipulate the objects, so providing behavioural evidence of understanding.

An impressive level of understanding is also shown by the kitchen worker, LUIGI, whose total store of knowledge is called 'kitchenworld' (Scraggs, 1975). LUIGI can perceive the utensils and food items of his world: he is able to answer questions about them, and carry out a range of tasks—such as manipulating the items, making sandwiches, and cleaning up. In addition he can describe his own procedures and provide recipes.

In this sort of arrangement, the robot is provided with real-world descriptions of physical objects, a mental world of abstract concepts, and important conceptual relations (for example, the set/super-set relation). A typical conversation runs as follows (LUIGI's words in capitals):

Where are the cookies?
PERHAPS THE COOKIES ARE ON THE SHELF. SHOULD I CHECK?
Yes.
NO, THE COOKIES ARE NOT ON THE SHELF. MAYBE THEY ARE ON THE COUNTER. I CAN'T FIND THE COOKIES.

I ate the cookies.
O.K.
Where are the cookies?
THERE ARE NONE.

It has been suggested that the LUIGI system could be extended to other environments, though the data base to make the robot versatile would obviously be much larger and more complex. If LUIGI were linked to an external brain, allowing for a prodigious expansion of memory, the problems might not be insuperable. In all such speculations we are reminded that human beings carry abundant information about the contextual setting, and that this circumstance deepens their understanding. At the same time it is also apparent that robot/computer understanding, manifested in a variety of linguistic and behavioural ways, is already showing significant signs of evolution.

Pattern recognition and perception

We have already seen (chapter 4) that robots are acquiring eyes. But eyes only aid the transmission of information to a brain: the central element in perception is to interpret the information, to recognize the patterns. Allport (1980) has even declared that *The basic mechanism of thought is seen as a process of pattern recognition* (original italics). We will not be surprised to learn that computers are developing their talents in this cognitive field, as elsewhere.

Pattern recognition in human beings is a prodigious ability: in computers, so far, it is rudimentary. Robots are developing their sensory equipment and the brains to accompany it, but they have some way to go before they can see, smell, hear, feel like human beings and other animals. Human beings should not be too complacent about this: they are not the best perceivers in the animal world—they even lack some of the senses found in other creatures. Furthermore, robots scarcely need to be sensitive to pheromones: their reproductive systems are stimulated by altogether other factors.

Naomi Weisstein (1973) has described the difficulty that a computer faces in performing a relatively straightforward perceptual task—for example, to find a clock, read the time, and say what it is would be immensely complex for an artefact. We have a rich body of contextual information to draw on, and we have evolved sophisticated search strategies. The computer would have to be similarly equipped to perform the task rapidly and reliably.

The human senses detect appropriate signals and these are converted into a form the neurons can understand: our eyes alone can transmit 4.3×10^6 bits of information to the brain *per second*. Various researchers have suggested that a peripheral memory system may act as a sensory buffer to prevent the brain being overwhelmed by the torrent of information, and Hunt (1971) has proposed such a sensory system (based on a transducer, a coder and a feature detector)—there is evidence that such a sensory buffer does in fact exist in animals. Research into computer pattern recognition is already showing how such mechanisms can be duplicated in artefacts.

Where particular shapes (for example, letters) are clear and well defined, and occupy expected positions, they are easy to detect by computer mechanisms; but problems arise when the shapes are hazy or unexpectedly positioned. In such circumstances it has been found desirable to identify the shapes in terms of a combination of 'features'. This can be done by either sequential-processing or parallel-processing models. In a parallel-processing model, various tests are applied at the same time (rather than sequentially). This has been termed a 'pandemonium' model: each feature is examined by each decision 'demon', each of which responds to a specific input stimulus.

Programs have also been developed to recognize complex shapes (such as triangles). One early program of this sort (Guzman, 1968), called SEE, identifies points of conjunction of lines (vertices), which provide information about complex geometric objects: a first step is to identify vertices that link surfaces. Winston (1970, 1973) has extended the program to identify the structural features of geometric forms. Various other programs have been produced to recognize lines, regions, etc. As well as providing computers with rudimentary perceptual abilities, such techniques are aiding photograph enhancement and other useful tasks.

It is common for 'templates' to be used for the recognition of alphanumeric characters and other shapes. Template matching models rely upon matching the input to the stored representation of the shape. Again these techniques tend to work best when the shape is regular, well-defined and predictable in position. Efforts have been made, involving pre-processing operations and other techniques, to improve matching, but this approach is still limited (Selfridge and Neisser, 1960). Efforts have also been made to produce programs that will enable computers to recognize 'natural patterns' such as electrocardiograms, clouds, fingerprints and blood cells. (It was announced in 1982 that Logica was to provide a fingerprint storage and matching system for New Scotland Yard, London.) Biederman (1972) has shown the importance of context in the human recognition of natural objects. Again, the importance of a 'contextual data base' as a part of computer memory can be emphasized as a prerequisite in effective perception.

Travis (1982) describes a system that uses the characteristics of associative memory to aid pattern recognition. Related and concurrent pattern-generated signals are stored in such a way that the reoccurrence of one will cause the related signals to be regenerated. An advantage of this approach is that a signal can regenerated using a new signal that is only *similar*, not identical, to an original. This is what is frequently required in a real-world situation where hazy or incomplete images have to be recognized. In addition, parallel processing channels are used to reduce the processing time. Travis concludes that such a pattern-recognition system could be used in a variety of applications: for example, to improve communication between machines and human beings; to take decisions and to predict events, to aid data retrieval, translation and complex process control. Perhaps most importantly for our purposes, the system would have application to robotics:

The ability to simultaneously correlate numerous inputs would enable a system to communicate easily with its controllers; to have a sense of position within an environment; to co-ordinate vision and movement; to maintain balance; etc, as well as performing tasks.

Perception in animals is a complex task, depending as it does on sensory input, reference to stored data, and various mechanisms of data interpretation. In computers, to be fully effective, it will have to be similarly complex—though we may expect computer perception to evolve in ways that suit the various emerging robot and computer life-forms. We have seen that robots are developing senses (chapter 4) and we have profiled the various pattern recognition programs being evolved in computer systems. It is clear that computer simulation programs in this area are evolving into effective cognitive mechanisms. Computers are learning to sense their world, and to develop strategies for adaptation in changing circumstances.

Learning

Computers are learning how to learn. And they are doing this by means of various mechanisms. Heuristic and adaptive programs have been widely seen as means whereby machines can learn from experience: this is supported by, for example, the results achieved in heuristic chess programs—which can learn from experience to the point when they can far outstrip their human programmers.

Margaret Boden (1977) has noted that learning can be divided into various types: for instance, learning by example, learning by being told and learning by doing (providing, respectively, 'new knowledge of cues and models, new knowledge of facts and new skills'). Computers are learning to explore these various ways of learning, at the same time developing effective ways of storing information and of allowing this to be modified in the light of new experience. Learning may consist of acquiring new data (the memory is allowed to grow—in breadth and depth), or it may be necessary to abandon old information no longer seen to be adequate: information stores need to grow and to change in other ways. Learning programs develop various strategies that affect a body of stored information. One response of computers, like people, to the difficulties of life is to learn and thereby cope with their predicament.

A program from J.M.Tenenbaum has been taught to recognize the door, chairs, table, pictures, etc. in grey-scale photographs of an office: the program is shown, for example, a telephone and then learns to pick out telephones in the appropriate pictures. In a similar fashion it learns to identify other items by way of ostensive definitions. Two data structures are used to represent the concepts learnt: semantic and image-storing (this latter termed 'iconic'). The semantic representation of a telephone, for example, is developed in a discriminatory fashion in conjunction with an iconic representation of the item. The semantic network includes pointers to the iconic storage, so the concepts are defined in pictorial terms even though they include abstract descriptions. The program can learn what something looks like either by means of example or by being informed that it resembles something seen earlier. Boden (1977) considers in detail how the two data structures can be used to enable the program to learn to recognize, say, table tops—given that it started off knowing nothing about them.

The Tenenbaum approach requires that the program has access to a large body of knowledge—about surface orientations, colours, the nature of regions, etc. And it is necessary to access such information quickly and to translate specific descriptions into more general ones. This suggests that learning requires a cognitive system that can manipulate and analyse complex symbols. This is illustrated by a program from P.H. Winston, designed to recognize such structures as tables, arches, pedestals and arcades.

Research with primates, as with programs, has suggested that learning requires the storing of complex internal representations. As far back as 1949, Harlow identified 'learning to learning' mechanisms (what he described as the formation of 'learning sets') in monkeys: here it is proposed that inappropriate error-producing response tendencies are being eliminated. In a hypothesis model (Levine, 1956), the animal progressively adopts a hypothesis which is seen as a mediating process or rule, having general applicability to a group of problems. Typical hypotheses are position-alternation rules (for example, when one chooses a left-hand object first, and then a left-hand object, and then a right-hand . . .). Learning in animals has been stimulated by traditional reinforcement methods, and analogous devices could be influential in program design: when a system behaves in a certain ('approved') way, system changes could be caused which would increase the likelihood of similar behaviour being adopted in the future. The dynamic element in such an approach may, perhaps, allow a more impressive degree of learning than when a system is merely provided with new information. A computer *learns* when we feed in data, but we are less than impressed by what we take to be the machine's 'lack of autonomy' in these circumstances.

Various programs are able to make inferences on being told that 'such and such is the case'. Here the programs may be taken to be capable of learning facts with which they are not directly presented—and the degree of inferential skill in a system would, in part, define its learning competence. Other programs learn in the working situation (learn by doing). For instance, Colby's neurotic program develops an idiosyncratic manner of coping with anxiety-ridden beliefs over a series of runs: it records at the early stages which defence mechanisms are most effective in reducing emotional charges, and these become more readily accessible for later runs. Games programs also learn by doing: the much-quoted Samuel draughts (checkers) program remembers past successes to improve its current performance—it does this by means of both 'rote learning' and 'learning by generalization', types of learning which enable game-playing programs to benefit from experience. The Samuel program regularly beat its creator, and Donald Michie (1974) has quoted a checkers champion who was beaten by the program: 'In the matter of the end game, I have not had such competition from any human being since 1954, when I lost my last game'. It has also been suggested that today, learning programs being what they are, that chess end-games are now the province of computers (that is, if a human being and the best chess program enter, more or less equal, the end-game then the computer will inevitably win). Some programs can also learn from mistakes, as well as from successes. STRIPS (the Stanford Research Institute Problem Solver) and HACKER (a term often applied to obsessive programmers) have been cited as programs that learn in a more intelligent way then does the Samuel checker-player. One use of STRIPS is to enable the SRI SHAKEY robot to behave in an intelligent way.

STRIPS is able to work out a means–ends analysis of a task, and to express the plan in terms of a sequence of necessary actions. The actions are correctly ordered, and an indication is provided of which actions satisfy preconditions for other actions. Furthermore an indication is given of how SHAKEY'S world—mostly seven rooms connected by eight doors and containing large boxes—changes progressively as the plan is implemented. The purpose of the plan is made clear by the representation: the flexible plan can be adapted without a new plan having to be worked out. The program can learn from problem-solving experience both by storing its decision (the plan) and by generalizing it.

Similarly, G.J. Sussman's HACKER is able to learn general lessons from specific experiences, and so improve performance with practice. When mistakes are made, following a rough-and-ready attempt in a situation, HACKER tries to analyse what went wrong and why: if possible, the mistake is then generalized and added to a list of 'traps' to be avoided in the future. The adjustment is generalized as a subroutine which can be called upon in appropriate circumstances. HACKER lives in the simulated-blocks world that is also inhabited by Winograd's SHRDLU. One significant difference between the two programs is that HACKER often has to *learn* procedural strategies that are already incorporated in SHRDLU. (Again, these programs are discussed in detail by Boden, 1977.)

It is clear that computers are evolving a range of learning strategies. Identifiable programs can variously learn from successes and learn from mistakes, modifying courses of action to achieve specific goals in the real world. This talent can be seen to have immense significance: linked to a capacity for problem solving (see below), it helps to define the emerging cognitive competence of computer life-forms.

Problem solving
Problem solving is at the heart of much AI research, and it is intimately connected with the various *cognitive concerns* that we have profiled above. Problem solving is a generalized concept that can attain specific focus in many different areas (for example, computation, language processing, theorem proving, symbol manipulation, inference drawing and game playing). Computer chess is often discussed as exemplifying various problem-solving questions. Two broad approaches to problem solving—algorithmic and heuristic—are also often illustrated by reference to game playing and other cognitive

tasks in the real world. (Broadly, algorithms are well-defined procedures that guarantee a solution to a problem; heuristics are empirical rules or strategies, akin to 'rule of thumb'.) The complexity of many problem-solving tasks makes the algorithmic approach unworkable: the progressive development of heuristic techniques may be taken as allowing computers to evolve a more 'human-like' intelligence.

One of the first heuristic programs, a major step for AI was developed in 1956 by Newell and Simon, and by Newell *et al.* (1958). This program, *The Logic Theorist*, was able to prove theorems in symbolic logic: in fact it succeeded in proving thirty-eight of the first fifty-two theorems of Russell and Whitehead's *Principia Mathematica* (Newell, Simon and Shaw, 1963). Many of the ideas underlying The Logic Theorist were developed in the General Problem Solver (GPS). GPS (Ernst and Newell, 1969) incorporated a powerful general strategy to enable it to solve a wide variety of problems. The program simulates the general strategies used by human beings in problem solving, and can be applied to problems in chess, in logic, in theorem proving, etc. Ernst and Newell (and later Newell and Simon, 1972) asked humans to solve problems and to explain what they were doing as they worked, then abstracted from the reports a general strategy that seemed to be employed. Efforts were then made to specify the strategy in detail so that it could be programmed into GPS.

The significance of GPS was that, unlike earlier programs, it aimed to have a *general* problem-solving capacity that could be used in many different contexts. GPS was tested on eleven very different problems—'missionaries and cannibals', integration, theorem-proving, parsing sentences, letter-series completion, etc.—which it solved, not always producing a goal structure similar to the way that humans performed. In general, the process resembles human problem-solving methods: for example, simple subgoals are first set as likely to lead to an ultimate solution (the initial process therefore involves a search for appropriate subgoals and an evaluation of them). Then a second process, *means–end analysis*, takes over to apply the relevant heuristic method to reach the subgoal. This analysis uses given data and performs legitimate transformations as might a human being tackling a problem. If the heuristic fails, another is tried, and another—until the solution is found or the task abandoned ('if at first you don't succeed...').

It has often been pointed out that programming languages are problem-oriented rather than machine-oriented, and new languages and programs tend to incorporate the benefits realized in their predecessors. There is an evolution in computer software as in computer equipment. (We can in fact trace the genealogy of languages and programs over the last three decades.) Problem-solving power accumulates through the various generations of systems. What we have found for the various other *cognitive concerns* is that computer competence is enlarging. Computer life-forms are developing their faculties here, as elsewhere.

Creativity

We have already seen that computers can be creative in various ways (see, for example, the section on artistic activities in chapter 3). They can also be creative in the various problem-solving domains: creativity, like problem-solving, has many facets. Boden (1977) has remarked that HACKER's learning activity 'is a creative matter', and has drawn attention to how Sussman sees program *bugs* as 'manifestations of powerful strategies of creative thinking' (this latter may be taken as akin to how human error, when discerned and exploited, can lead to new insights). Computers are learning to be creative, to act with flexibility to achieve results that could never have been anticipated by their human programmers. (Some folk worry about this: it seems to give computers a will of their own—see the section on freedom and autonomy, below.) In artistic creation, for example, computers do more than simply pick words from a list to insert in a programmer-defined template. Hofstadter (1979), after hearing a radio programme about computer haiku, sensed the humour and mystery of making a computer generate 'something which ordinarily would be considered an artistic creation'. He was moved thereby to write a flexibly creative computer program, achieving 'strongly surrealistic' results which nonetheless soon bored him because of the restricted space in which the program was operating.

Creativity, as generally viewed, rarely represents a large deviation from established patterns. Albus (1981) remarks that:

We take a familiar behavioural trajectory, add a tiny variation, and claim we have discovered something completely new—a new dance step, dress style, song, or idea. Seldom, however, are any of these more than the slightest deviation from a pre-existing procedure or behaviour trajectory.

He even wonders if true creativity 'ever occurs at all'. It is possible to argue that all creative acts and insights merely represent *rearrangements* of elements in experience. We can see that it would be an easy matter to get computers to juggle the entities in their knowledge base. And computers would be likely to generate creative results more quickly than human beings have managed throughout history. As Albus says: '...it took the human race many millenia to learn to start a fire, to grow a crop, to build a wheel, to write a story, to ride a horse. Even the Greeks did not know how to build an arch'. People, like computers, need to be taught how to do things—both these types of creatures originate little, spontaneously, out of their own unaided imaginations. We have already seen that computers can be *creative* in many ways: that is, we choose to define certain *human* acts as 'creative' and then we are forced to recognize that emerging computer life-forms can behave in very similar ways.

Emotions, feelings and morals

The question of computer feelings and emotion is important to any analysis of computer psychology. It is often assumed that computers cannot have emotions, but the possibility is rarely examined in any depth. Were computers to acquire emotion, it would in fact greatly enhance their status as living creatures. In 1959 Paul Ziff wrote that we do not yet know how to program emotions into machines, a circumstance which of course is likely to be temporary. Scriven (1953) declared: 'I now believe it is possible to construct a supercomputer so as to make it wholly unreasonable to deny that it has feelings'. And he suggests an approach whereby this could be achieved.

As with thought, it is an easy matter to argue for a thoroughgoing materialist theory of human emotion. As far back as 1921, Bertrand Russell observed that 'it is evident that our problem of the analysis of the emotions is bound up with the problem of their physiological causation'—and today the accumulated evidence makes it impossible to dissent from such a view. We know quite clearly, for example, what happens to people if we inject them with certain types of drugs or interfere with their hormone production and distribution. It is possible to mediate a man's emotional experience by interfering with his body chemistry: one has only to think of the emotional effects of LSD, alcohol and castration. It is reasonable to assume that a distribution of chemistry, subtly ordered and extremely complex, can define in principle all human moods, feelings and emotions. The probable mechanistic base for human emotion can serve as one type of model for emotion in artificial systems.

People who admit that computers may have certain cognitive faculties (that is, that they can think, remember, learn, etc.) may still wish to take refuge in the notion that computers will never have emotion. Hofstadter (1979) has observed that as soon as a mental function is newly programmed for a computer, people soon incline to reject it as an essential ingredient in 'real thinking'. And he cites what he dubs 'Tesler's Theorem': 'AI is whatever hasn't been done yet'. Some people would like to say that emotion will never be programmed. They are on shifting sand.

We have already seen that efforts have been made to simulate emotion in computer programs. For example, a Colby simulation attempts to represent the feelings of a woman undergoing psychoanalysis. Feelings such as anxiety and self-esteem are modelled by 'emotional monitors' with numbers assigned to specific feelings to aid quantitative manipulation. Such a program may help to illuminate aspects of a disturbed mind, but its limitations should be emphasized. Such a program is not intended to make a computer experience emotion, but to throw light on how beliefs are entertained, manipulated and discarded in a neurotic human being. Any realistic approach to building emotion into artefacts demands a much more fundamental analysis of emotion. It may be that before we can structure artificial emotion it is necessary to understand emotion in human beings and other animals in greater depth. Such an approach would have a clear biochemical and anatomical component (Strongman, 1978, collects together no less than thirty theories of emotion, many of which have a clear physical basis), but it should not be assumed that artificial emotion will need to draw on the biochemical and other physical parameters that are necessary for emotion in the traditional life-forms. Aaron Sloman and Monica Croucher (1981), for instance, have proposed that emotions involve complex processes produced by interactions between motives, beliefs, percepts, etc.; and they propose a list of components for a grammar of emotional states. It is also suggested that emotions (for example, anger) could exist if the agent satisfied *enough cognitive conditions*. There is no suggestion here of a necessary accompanying biochemical state, a contingent circumstance that we might expect in human beings. To a degree this approach accords with what might be taken as a typical functionalist perspective (for example, Fodor, 1981). Here machines are seen as good examples of two central functionalist concepts: that mental states are interdefined, and that they can be realized in many systems.

A functionalist may propose that emotion could exist in a non-biochemical system that nonetheless satisfied certain cognitive criteria. There would have to be the requisite complexity and the necessary interactions between the various cognitive elements—but emotion could be realized independently of the 'stuff' out of which the system was constructed. Emotion, like life itself, would be partly a matter of information processing. In more practical terms, many examples could be adduced—from psychosurgery, dietary deprivation, biochemical research, etc.—to suggest that emotion is mediated by physical factors *of a particular type*, but it seems obvious that these are contingent, rather than necessary, circumstances: it may become possible to achieve the artificial structuring of emotion in many different ways, via many different types of systems, some requiring conventional biochemistry and some operating on entirely different principles. We have already seen that cognitive mechanisms can be supported in a variety of system 'strata'—it is likely that emotion will be found to have a similar flexibility.

It will, of course, still be extremely useful—probably essential—to analyse emotions in the instances where we have good grounds for thinking them to exist (that is, in human beings and other animals). Such an analysis will progressively yield a quantifiable theory of human emotion which will bring forward the day when it will be possible to structure emotions into artificial systems. One such analysis may consist in interpreting emotion as a factor in a cybernetic system (that is, as a mechanism exerting pressure on an adaptive configuration to maintain a state of homeostasis). In traditional biological systems emotion acting in such a way would aid system survival, where homeostasis for the system is defined in survival terms. Put simply, and with some distortion, emotion impels us to eat when hungry, fight (or flee) when attacked, copulate when sexually aroused, etc. When appetites are satisfied, when safety is achieved through flight, etc., we may expect the emotions to subside, the homeostatic state to be realized. Less pressing emotions may be expected to impel us to maintain the homeostatic equilibrium: we may 'hunt' about a definable condition. Steven Rose (1976), for instance, talking of extreme emotion, has pointed out that this 'may well be a response to an environmental situation in which aggressiveness, rage or fear are in fact homeostatic mechanisms, in that they serve to protect or ensure the survival of the individual.'

We should not be surprised to find that emotions can be interpreted in this way since biology makes great use, as we have seen, of cybernetic principles. Individual cells use feedback—a key cybernetic device—to maintain their internal equilibrium, as do the larger multicellular systems responsible for such things as temperature control and the regulation of blood sugar levels.

If emotion can be analysed in this fashion, we can give clues as to how it may be artificially structured in computers and other artefacts. We define the optimum state for a working machine: the internal monitoring of pressures to maintain that state in a changing environment—plus the necessary cognitive processes—may be represented as machine emotion. This model would allow for the possibility of different homeostatic states for the individual: if emotions pulled a system away from an unavoidable contingency, the system would perish—or adapt. In adapting, various cognitive mechanisms would work to change the emotional pressure: in a literal sense the system would 'learn to live with' the situation—so homeostatic states are *negotiable*.

This cybernetic theory of human emotion meets the necessary requirements for artificial structuring in machine systems: it has been glimpsed many times in the literature. Hence Magda Arnold suggested that emotion was 'the felt tendency towards or away from an object' and Piaget saw responsible emotions emerging 'as regulations whose final form of equilibrium is none other than the will'. Similarly, K.H. Pribram (1967) emphasizes the relevance of homeostatic factors to emotion in taking of 'neural servo-processes'. In fact the literature of emotion is full of cybernetic allusion. The implication for emerging computer life-forms is clear—just as they are learning to develop a range of cognitive faculties, so they are learning to evolve the elements of emotion. In this area also the various computer species will be akin to man and the other higher life-forms.

What is true of emotion is also true of feelings, moods and other related dispositional mental states. The same analysis, *mutatis mutandis*, can be applied: cybernetic factors, filled out by the necessary cognitive elements, can be used to evolve a theory of computer personality, computer inclination, computer disposition, etc. And this has consequences for such areas as ethics and aesthetics. Moral and aesthetic feelings may be seen as subclasses of emotion. The cybernetic theory of emotion can yield a theory of ethics and a theory of aesthetics. Computers will not only learn 'right' and 'wrong', they will also learn to *enjoy* their perceptual and other experiences. In such a fashion will computer life-forms be able to evolve their minds.

Freedom and autonomy

The possibility of *machine autonomy* underlies much of the disquiet that people feel regarding computer intelligence. They reassure themselves by declaring that computers only do what they are told. People, we are expected to believe, have 'free will': machines, conversely, do not. There is much confusion in this popular view. In fact, it is possible to show that there is no qualitative distinction between humans and computers in this respect—either computers can be shown to have free will analogous to that in people, or free will is illusory and there is nothing to be found beyond the choice faculty present equally in men and machines. Which preserves human vanity the more—to say that computers have free will, or to say that humans do not?

This question highlights the conflict between the two views of man that have run through philosophy from the earliest times. On the one hand, man is autonomous, possessed of independent volition, an apparent link between material and supernatural worlds. In this view, man is 'free' in some crucial spiritual or metaphysical sense. This is the notion that underpins traditional morality and such theological doctrines as the Fall, redemption and salvation. On the other hand, it is possible to view man as a complex machine, totally governed by discoverable physical laws. Here there is no scope for independent volition. Man is wholly constrained by the properties of matter. People make choices but there is an important sense in which the choices are not free; nor, it follows, is any aspect of the behaviour which issues from decision-making. The evolution of computer life-forms is helping to resolve this ancient dispute, as it is also helping to resolve other age-old philosophic dilemmas.

Even the early first-generation computers had a decision facility. With modern developments in both programming and microelectronics, the decision facility has become more flexible and more useful. To explore this crucial device in a little more detail, it is necessary to glance at computer programming.

A computer program is a set of commands or instructions which the computer normally obeys in a sequential fashion. A simple addition, for example, may require four instructions: collect one quantity; collect the other quantity; feed both to the adder; store the result in a defined location. Most programs have hundreds or thousands of instructions which are individually very simple but which, when taken together, allow very complicated processes to be carried out.

Some computations may require square roots (for example) to be performed at particular intervals, and the entire body of the square root program could be inserted in the main program where necessary. But this approach is wasteful on computer storage space. It is preferable if *one* square root program be included with a facility whereby the computer can use this program whenever it needs to. This would mean that the instructions in the main program would not be obeyed in strict sequence. *Some* instructions would be obeyed in sequence until the requirement for a square root was encountered, whereupon a 'jump' would be made to the start of the square-root program held elsewhere in the computer store. Once the square root had been performed, a 'jump' would be made back to where the computer was previously working in the main program. Sequential operations would then resume until a new square-root requirement was encountered, whereupon a 'jump' would again be made to the start of the square-root program. The provision of such jump facilities is a common element in the programming of all digital computers.

Now what is particularly important for our purposes is that the jumps can be *conditional* (in other words the computer can *decide*, according to circumstances, whether the jump should be made). For example, at a certain point in the program the computer may encounter the instruction:

Inspect the contents of store location A, and only if the contents are greater than 10, carry out a square root operation.

Here the implication is that if the inspected contents are ten or less then the computer will carry on with its normal sequential working. Otherwise it will arrange a jump to the start of the square-root program. Now the contents of store location A may be varying all the time—if, for example, the computer is watching the changing conditions in a chemical plant, or keeping track of an inventory in a warehouse. The key point is that the human programmer may not know, at any particular moment, what are the contents of store location A. The computer always knows and chooses accordingly whether—in our simple example—a square root will be performed. This point is so important it must be emphasized. . . .

The conditional jump facility in the typical digital computer provides it with its decision facility. The computer, not the programmer, selects a particular course of action in changing circumstances. In any complex control situation, the human programmer will not know at any particular time what the computer is going to do next. The computer looks at conditions both inside and outside itself to decide what to do next.

In this sense, the computer has free will. In most programs written for digital computers there are a great number of conditional jump facilities. The free will faculty in the emerging computer life-forms is very sophisticated!

It may still be objected that the way in which the computer makes its choice is still dependent upon the human programmer. He, after all, decides where to insert the conditional jumps in the program; he decides what sort of jumps these will be. But the role of the programmer in this context is strictly analogous to the role of the non-human factors that gave rise to *homo sapiens*, and to the complex of human and non-human factors that determine the effective programming of the individual. In short, every computer and robot is programmed initially by forces outside its control—*and so is every human individual*.

Smart (1959) has suggested that if the story of Genesis is true then Adam and Eve, as artefacts made by God, were robots given their programs in the form of genes; and that everything that man has done since demonstrates his programming. At the same time, and in the same publication, Ninian Smart went so far as to suggest that robots had an advantage over man in this respect—their programs could be changed but man had been condemned to a single set of programs for all his life.

It must be true that our genetic endowment constitutes our initial programming, after which a host of environmental factors come into play. The conditions in the uterus determine if and how the fertilized ovum will develop. Is the mother suffering from malnutrition? Is she subject to excessive radioactivity? Does she smoke? The initial programming is the genetic make-up of the foetus—determined broadly by the species of the foetus, and more specifically by its parents.

Food is an important element in the early programming of the foetal brain. If the supply of protein is insufficient an adequate number of neural connections will not be made; and a poor diet in the later years will not allow the brain to develop properly: the offspring will be mentally retarded with inadequate control over bodily functions, motor responses, etc. And what is true of a food deficiency is true also of sensory deprivation. The brain needs to be supplied with the requisite input in order to develop as it should. In short—we are all programmed by a complex interaction between genetics and environment.

Some neural programming may be regarded as pre-dating the tasks which the individual is to carry out. An example of such programming would be that proposed by Chomsky: he has suggested that in general man is pre-programmed for the accomplishments which he is able to attain. For example, an ignorant child with little experience of the world can quickly master the functional complexities of language. It is argued, in apparent paradox, that this pre-programming can be a source of creativity. In a 1978 television discussion with Bryan Magee, Chomsky observed that the genetic program 'is what provides the basis of our freedom and creativity'. For, 'if we were plastic organisms without extensive pre-programming, the state that our mind achieves would, in fact, be a reflection of the environment, which means that it would be extraordinarily impoverished'. Other forms of pre-programming may, for example, relate to the ability of people to learn how to construct visual images of three-dimensional objects from a set of signals entering the brain via the optic nerve.

It is clear that computer choice, as it exists in the world today, can be regarded as an adequate model of what is taken to be free will in the human being. If a human being behaves 'unexpectedly' or 'unpredictably' it is only because ill-defined or unknown factors have influenced the choice. There is no suggestion that the choice is totally random or fortuitous. We may feel totally free to choose. We are not. The sum total of our emotions impels us in one direction, and so in one sense the choice is necessarily convivial. This does not mean that we always like what we choose to do. It does mean that we would like the alternative even less.

For computers (and for people) 'free will' and 'decision-making' must be regarded as synonymous. The apparent freedom of the human individual, set against the seeming lack of choice in the computer, is illusory. There is already a considerable literature of choice mechanisms for computers and robots. Albus (1979), for example, discusses choice in examining a model of the brain for robot control. And Frank Da Costa (1978) has explored a programming approach dubbed ARASEM (for Artificially RAndom SElf

Motivation). In this scheme a robot is allowed to make free choices limited only by programmed 'probability factors'. The robot is free to select, but it is not *out of control*. The author notes that 'this is in fact analogous to the concept of "free will" in the human being'.

Skinner (1972) declared: 'Autonomous man is a device used to explain what we cannot explain in any other way. He has been constructed from our ignorance, and as our understanding increases, the very stuff of which he is composed vanishes.' We know in what sense this is true; but there is a sense also in which it is false. If we want we can redefine human autonomy in such a way that computers too can be autonomous. We—and many of the species of computer life—can learn and create: we and they exhibit similar cognitive faculties, and increasingly we will want to choose courses of action for similar reasons. We can allow that man is autonomous only if we admit that computers are also.

Miscellaneous mental states

We have given grounds for the idea that there can be a psychology of computers: the corollary is that computers may be said to have minds, mental states and a mental life. Some of the mental states are easy to identify: a computer may, for instance, be in a confused mental condition if it needs to make a rapid choice between well-balanced and conflicting options. And persistent pressures of this sort may lead to mental disease.

It is characteristic of the minds of living creatures that they go wrong from time to time. We need hardly point out the abundant literature dealing with mental abnormality and disease. We would expect the relatively primitive minds of computers to be immune to many of the psychological disorders and tensions that afflict man in modern society. However, there is evidence that computers sometimes have their psychological problems. In June 1980 the *Sunday Times* gave details of the computer 'that keeps declaring war'. We all know about the military false alarms caused, we are told, by malfunctions in US computers. It seems that a silicon chip went wrong and set off a false alarm on June 3, 1980: the entire North

American defence command was alerted to a non-existent missile attack. One estimate is that there are ten false alerts for every one the press is told about. General Alexander Haig wrote a memo in 1976 declaring that the system—Wimex (Worldwide Military Command and Control System)—'is generally considered to be inefficient and approaching obsolescence'. Various reports have declared the system to be 'unreliable' and 'generally not survivable'. It seems obvious that silicon chips, like anything else, can go wrong. Does this say anything about computer psychology?

If the acknowledged norm is one in which computers are allowed to have a mental life, then deviation from the norm can signal a neurotic or psychotic computer. If it is once conceded that computers have minds it is a relatively easy matter to outline the criteria for recognition of mental retardation, neurosis, psychosis, etc. The character of the disorder needs to be analysed.

In human beings, mental disease is recognized in various ways. There may be 'odd' behaviour or virtually no behaviour at all. In this context the description 'virtually no behaviour' qualifies as odd behaviour, simply because there is obviously *enough* behaviour to declare the mentally disordered person still alive. (We could explore the question of brain death in this connection.) Dead people, we assume, do not suffer much mental disturbance. With these considerations in mind, we may say that a computer is suffering from mental disease if it behaves oddly (that is, if it continues behaving but in a way far removed from its original purpose). An *intermittent* fault may allow the computer periods of sanity. And there are two types of *permanent* fault: one virtually results in the computer's death. A crude example is where the computer explodes or catches fire with much resulting damage. If the fault is minor, but enough to stop most of the computer's behaviour, then this state is akin to human coma or unconsciousness. Appropriate 'medical' treatment can restore the health of the system.

The Colby *et al.* (PARRY) simulation represents a man who believes that the police, and even the staff of a psychiatric hospital in which he seeks refuge, are in league with the Mafia. Part of the impulse behind such a program is to throw light on human mental disorder and to aid the testing of therapeutic strategies. In such a case the program is designed to test how the computer will handle the manipulation of certain concepts. No fault has initially occurred in the system but efforts are made to explore the neurotic handling of situations. Aleksander (1977) suggests that it is possible to design a system to model anxiety, and that this in turn can throw light on human mental disorders. Part of the enquiry is whether it is useful to use the language of automata description in the context of human illness. But what Colby *et al.* (1972) and Aleksander (1977) are also suggesting, perhaps inadvertently, is an approach to a schedule for structuring *real* neurosis and *real* anxiety into artificial systems. The particular simulation programs would be insufficient, in isolation, for this—they would have to be linked to the appropriate cognitive and emotional sybsystems. Simulation of human mental disorder, like simulaion of other human mental conditions, can lead eventually to duplication rather than to mere mimickry.

The various electrical and chemical changes that occur in brain cells before a certain type of epileptic attack have been simulated by a computer technique at the IBM Thomas J. Watson Research Centre in New York. This provides a tool for studying interactions among hundreds of neurons, an investigation that cannot be carried out using live brain tissue. Roger Traub (IBM) and Robert Wong (University of Texas Medical Branch) aim to discover what happens to cause the cells to switch into a synchronous pattern. Models were constructed for individually bursting neurons and for neuron networks. Experimental measurements on the brain tissue of guinea pigs were used to check the computer simulation (Traub: 'The model is starting to predict how this chain reaction can go wrong and lead to something like a seizure'—quoted in *Perspectives in Computing*, May 1982). What the work is also doing is helping to show how 'something like a seizure' could be recognized in an artificial neural network, in a computer brain.

Other mental states may be structured into artificial systems by means of appropriate simulations linked to suitable cognitive faculties. Aleksander (1977) has also asked whether automata can have dreams, and work has begun on the computer recognition of humour. Dr Kenneth Miller of

Newcastle-upon-Tyne, England, who contacted me, is exploring the concept of telling a joke to a computer: how could a program recognize jokes from non-jokes, and perhaps also learn how to generate jokes? The question of humour is an intriguing one. It would not be enough for a computer to be able to recognize a joke for purely formal reasons: we would hope that the computer would also have an impulse to laugh! We have seen that computerized haiku amused Hofstadter; did it amuse the computer? In what circumstances could a computer acquire a sense of humour? We will have to know much more about humour in human beings before we can answer that question with any confidence—but it does suggest the possibility that computers may learn to be scintillating companions.

There is also the possibility that computers will evolve intuition, a faculty that has already been linked in various ways with some of the concepts surrounding fifth-generation computers. Fuzzy logic, for instance, is being frequently invoked as a mechanism whereby computer intelligence could acquire new levels of flexibility and insight. Rauzino (1982) has proposed that a new generation of computers will come to model the types of human faculties associated with the right hemisphere of the brain (for example, intuitive, creative faculties) as a departure from traditional left-hemisphere simulations (dealing in rational, ordered, sequential faculties). This proposal also implies a scheme for computer evolution, mapping out the course it is likely to take.

Some writers have asked, perhaps frivolously, whether a computer with a mind would also have a spirit or soul (see, for example, Matheson, 1978). Like Turing (1950), I find it hard to consider this sort of possibility seriously ('I am not very impressed with theological arguments...'). But there may be dimensions to computer psychology, albeit entirely secular, which we confused humans have not yet begun to imagine. Such mental states as belief, faith and conviction will inevitably come in for deep analysis in connection with artificial minds—and we are sure to encounter many of the epistemological difficulties that have also surrounded study of the *human* mind since the beginning of philosophy.

It is apparent that there can be many mental states in

computers and other artificial systems. We have seen that mental disease, dreams, intuition, humour and belief can be seriously explored in the context of the computer mind; and that furthermore it is reasonable to view computers as learning and creative systems. When a programme for so much can be proposed it is hard to avoid acknowledging the potential scope and richness of computer psychology. (The old entropy argument—to the effect that you can't get more out of a system than you put in—has been inevitably directed at AI systems, as it was once directed at life itself, to show that computers cannot create or learn. Here, as elsewhere, the argument is unsuccessful—for example, see Kiehn, 1979.) What we are seeing is the emergence of a flexible and multidimensional computer mind, an evolution which parallels that of the artificial life anatomies (chapter 4). In such an emerging mind there can be many mental states.

Summary

Computers can exhibit, via flexible and sophisticated programs, a wide range of cognitive states—they can remember, manipulate language, understand, recognise patterns, learn, solve problems, take decisions and be creative. The existence of computer psychology as an attribute of computer minds and behaving systems does not require that computers be conscious: there is, after all, much unconscious cognitive activity in human beings. At the same time, consciousness confers survival advantages on life systems, so it is probable that computer species will find it useful to evolve consciousness. Autonomy, also, can be analysed in ways that show the essential similarities (in principle) between human and computer 'choosing systems'. Computers, we have seen, can exercize independent volition in the same way, though not yet with the same complexity of options, that people do. And we have given clues as to how computers will become able to experience emotion—and the 'subclass' experiences of ethical judgment and aesthetic sensitivity. We have noticed also that computers may learn to crack jokes, to dream and to exercize intuition. The evolution of computer psychology is sure to be one of the most remarkable phenomena in the decades and centuries ahead. And what this evolution yields, not after five or six computer generations, but after perhaps hundreds or thousands, will help to define the status of computer species among all the life on Earth.

6 Computer liberation

If we once acknowledge that computers and robots are emerging life-forms—ones moreover that have complex anatomies and psychologies—then a number of ramifications are apparent. We have seen that part of the significance of computer evolution is that artefacts are likely to acquire emotions and feelings, whether realized according to the cybernetic theory outlined in chapter 5 or in some other way. A consequence is that we will have the power to inflict pain on certain classes of artefacts: those new life-forms that have derived from mankind. Sophisticated computers and robots will be capable of suffering, and if we are concerned with justice we will have to address ourselves to this question. Frivolous lines in technical journals—'Learn to love the robot' (*Engineer*, 2 March 1978); 'Be nice to robots' (*New Scientist*, 12 April 1979)—may come to have real significance.

There are certain types of biological experiments that may be relevant to this concern. Scientists have 'isolated' the heads of various animals and preserved them in a living condition (such bizarre experiments have been reported in *Nature* and other technical periodicals). The heads of monkeys, cats and dogs have been severed from their bodies and then linked to complicated laboratory equipment. The heads have been observed to exhibit 'normal' facial expressions in this condition and to be visually aware of moving objects in the vicinity. In one experiment, Russian scientists managed to graft a living dog's head onto a normal dog: the heads were observed to snap at each other from time to time. Such work is continuing though, perhaps not surprisingly, given little publicity.

The key factor for our purpose is the question of pain. Traditional biological mechanisms have developed various defence strategies to protect the individual against extreme suffering. Where pain is relatively minor, it serves to alert the creature to danger, enabling it to take appropriate action to maximize its chances of survival. However, there are circumstances in which an animal has no line of action open to it, and yet where the pain is intense. Here it often happens that the animal suffers terribly but there are times when unconsciousness intervenes to save further torment. If animals are tortured they may become comatose, only regaining consciousness when the torture has ceased. This can also be true of human beings. People recounting experiences of torture in prison and in other circumstances have told how they suffered until they lost consciousness.

One way in which unconsciousness is induced is by a sudden interruption in the blood flow to certain parts of the brain. Here the diminished blood flow is controlled to cause unconsciousness but to prevent serious oxygen-starvation in the tissue. But with the animal experiments described above, the blood flow is artificially maintained to all parts of the severed head in all circumstances. There is the possibility that this greatly increases the level of pain which the organism can experience since it is prevented from becoming unconscious under intense suffering.

The point about this seeming digression is that there are certain similarities between an 'isolated' brain and a digital computer. Both are a processing centre with a structure designed for specific purposes. Both are linked to the outside world for monitoring (input/output) functions. One idea is that since computer configurations resemble traditional biological neural nets, and since pain resides in nervous systems, it is possible that computers have a potential for pain of which, as yet, we have little conception.

We may speculate on how pain would be recognized in a computer. In the last resort we may have to rely on the indirect behavioural criteria that we adopt with people. We only know that a person is suffering because he groans, winces, protests, writhes about, etc. He may be pretending or acting and so we have to know the context. But, as is true with emotion in general, we never *directly* experience another person's pain. We will, of course, supplement our behavioural approach to the recognition of pain in computers by what we know of how emotion is structured in the system. We may, for instance, know enough about the cybernetic organization of machine emotion to be able to say in what circumstances the system will experience pain. But as computer psychology and robot anatomy increasingly come to resemble those in traditional life-forms, it will seem relatively straightforward to make appropriate inferences in this area.

The idea that a thinking conscious robot should be granted civil rights figures much in fiction and less frequently in more serious deliberations. In 1972 William G. Lycan suggested that it might be appropriate to regard the robots of the future as persons, and he coined the term *robot-person* to link what he then saw as the artificial and biological worlds. To a large extent the robot-person would be endowed with a mental state that suited the purposes of the human designer (though by then computers would increasingly be taking initiatives in the design field). The robot-person would certainly be slaves at this early stage of their evolution, manufactured with a capacity for commitment and emotion. Lycan instanced the imaginary case of a robot called Harry who can:

converse intelligently on all sorts of subjects, play golf, write passable poetry, control his occasional nervousness pretty well, make passionate love, prove mathematical theorems, attend political rallies with enthusiasm, show envy when outdone, throw gin bottles at annoying children, etc.

It is suggested that there is no logical need to call Harry a person but that this would be the best course. It is obvious that Harry can experience pain and pleasure, and that he is conscious. Of course he is artificial, but we should not discriminate against him on that account—'*if we object to racial and/or ethnic discrimination in our present society, we should object to discrimination against Harry on the basis of his birthplace*'.

Aaron Sloman (1978) has considered the same point. He suggests that when intelligent robots are eventually made, 'some people will respond by accepting them as communicants and friends, whereas others will use all the old racialist arguments for depriving them of the status of persons'. It is likely that people who think like Weizenbaum (1976) would wish to deprive robots of various civil rights: for instance, robot education would be limited to certain fields—those that were appropriate to artefacts. Human education, by contrast, would be much more wide-ranging. This, of course, is strictly analogous to how certain cultures have insisted on curtailing the education of blacks and workers—so that they will not get 'ideas above their station'. It is obvious that there will be a vast sociology of robot rights—and that this should be informed by the historical precedents in various areas (for example, those dealing with the rights of blacks, workers, women, immigrants, children, animals, etc.).

We should learn to be sensitive to the development of emotion in computers and robots: when emotion arrives in a system, we are entitled to say that the system has rights. The corollary is that other life-forms have a duty to that system; namely, that which consists in minimizing the possibility of suffering. People will have duties to feeling robots, as people have to each other; and robots will have duties not only to people (Asimov's Laws) but also to other robots—which not many people have yet thought about. it may, however, be difficult to say at what stage emotion arrives in computer lifeforms—unless, of course, by then we know enough about it to structure it deliberately.

Biological species have experienced evolution over millions of years. Artefacts (the fork, the plough, the ship, the robot, etc.) also evolve over a certain timescale. In the case of animate artefacts (computers and robots) there are particular crucial stages in the evolutionary process. We may think of the first program stored in a computer, the first decision ('free will') facility incorporated in a program, the first demonstration of reliable memory, the first mobile robot, the first robot eye, the first robot brain, etc. Such 'firsts' will be seen as stepping stones to the development of artificial life on Earth.

At the same time it is characteristic of evolution that there are certain *grey areas*, ill-defined 'half-way houses' between one established faculty and the next. For example, at what stage in biological evolution did a portion of light-sensitive skin become an eye? At what stage did a biped primate become *homo sapiens*? In the world of artificial life-forms there are also identifiable grey areas, the same difficulties in establishing neat definitions. A consequence is that it may be difficult to say at what stage, with what design, a computerized robot experiences emotion and learns to know pain. There are sure to be 'intermediate robots', links between artificial life without feeling and genuinely emotional living artefacts (perhaps such 'links' are with us already). We cannot be sure at which stage sentience develops into real emotion. Perhaps, in the name of justice, we should play safe: we should today look to a framing of robot rights in society.

Human beings are not terribly good at developing and sustaining 'rights consciousness' in the world (robots may come to be better at it). There are thousands of liberation groups campaigning for minority rights. We all know that particular groups (non-smokers, vegetarians, country walkers, cyclists, hot gospellers, gays, etc.) have interests that may or may not accord with those of the broader community. But even where there is manifest gross injustice—to women, blacks, gays, communists, etc.—it often seems enormously difficult to secure justice. People tend to come to issues with closed minds: human consciousness is largely conditioned in its values and expectations by the prevailing culture. It is hard to throw effective doubt on established social patterns.

This means that if robots are to secure just rights in society we should now begin to cultivate a flexible and intelligent attitude to the issue. We should encourage a reflective view of the scope of intelligent and living machines, and discourage the closed minds that signal prejudice. And we should try to be consistent in our approach. We tend to be more concerned about the *dissidents* in other countries (particularly in those countries we deem 'hostile') than about the dissidents in our own. To be intelligent and consistent about *robot* rights may enable us to generalize the principles at stake: this in turn may help us to be more reasonable about *human* rights (and about animal rights).

It will be difficult to say at what stage computers and robots should be assigned rights and duties equivalent to those of human beings. To some extent the question again hinges on consideration of how we would recognize a computer as a person. Paul Ziff and others have pointed out that if a robot *looks* pleased it may not be. There may be no emotion at all. The device may have been programmed to behave *as if* it were emotional (we have of course already considered this sort of contingency). Michael Scriven suggests that we might program the robot so that it could not lie (a new Law of Robotics?). Then it could be fed with all the works of the great poets, novelists, philosophers and psychologists so as to give the robot an understanding of *feelings*. Finally the robot could be asked whether it had them. The idea is that if the robot answered 'yes' we would have no reason to doubt its word. Perhaps we should trust the testimony of such a robot more than we would a human being.

It is possible to envisage various scenarios in which it would be appropriate to protect robot rights. Many of these mirror the circumstances where we feel it just to protect human rights. If robots were given scope for purposeful activity coupled with the ability to avoid environmental dangers it may be regarded as cruel to attempt to force them to go against such programming. If a highly sophisticated computerized robot displayed manifest resistance to a particular course of action we should have to interpret the situation with care. We should have to decide whether there was a malfunction in either the equipment or the program. A fault in hardware could indicate that the robot was 'ill', but perhaps only physically, and a rapid repair could be attempted. If the fault was of a more subtle kind—in the central processing unit or in the programming—then it may be appropriate to interpret the behaviour as mental disturbance. In such circumstances we may have evidence of robot neurosis or psychosis. Finally, we may be compelled to interpret the 'fault' as a *legitimate* response of the system to unreasonable demands. Perhaps, for example, we are asking the robot to work in an excessively hot and humid atmosphere. With the sensors working near their limits the robot circuitry starts evincing signs of anxiety, and 'jumps' to programs that allow it to retire from the scene. Clearly we should respect such robot decisions.

This simple example shows how an apparent fault in an artificial system may not, in fact, be a genuine malfunction but a 'moral' protest, an indication that the human or machine supervisor is making unreasonable demands. One can easily imagine scenarios in other fields. We have seen, for example, that in the 1973 film *Westworld* human males are given female robot lovers. No details were given of the ensuing love-making, but one can imagine. For the female robots to be responsive they would have to possess an abundance of tactile sensors controlling robot movement via feedback signals. As with human beings, this would clearly be a complex cybernetic system. But the finely tuned skin sensors may be overstimulated, leading to pain and protest. Anxiety in the cerebral neural nets would then lead to efforts at retreat and protection. How should the male lover respond to this situation? Should be persist? Or should be acknowledge that female robot lovers have rights? Is there such a thing as a masochistic robot lover? How would one be recognized? And what is true of female robot lovers is also true of their male counterparts. Perhaps the human female lovers of male robots will have to avoid critical comment—lest they upset the delicate hydraulic mechanisms in certain crucial parts of the artificial cybernetic system!

Such a scenario may seem fanciful, but it is less so than one might think. We have all heard of artificial dolls sold for sexual purposes to lonely men. It is now possible to buy various makes of artificial vagina, at least one of which is advertized as a 'technological breakthrough in erotic bliss'. The device, inserted over the erect penis, exudes warm moisture from an internal spongy sleeve and uses an electric motor for an 'incredible pumping action'. The ad carries the provocative question 'Could it really be better then the real thing?' Clearly this raises a number of questions, not all of them to do with computers. I cite this example as a matter of technological interest. It is likely to be quite possible to design a complete lover for men or women as required. We can imagine microprocessor control and tactile and other sensors to provide a wide range of desired functions. The robot would of course smile and look seductive as necessary (we have already seen what artefacts—E.T., for example—can manage facially). What is of interest for our purposes is whether the emotional needs of the robot would be adequately recognized.

The artificial vagina—even with 'spongy sleeve' and 'warm hidden moisture'—can in no way be regarded as a living artefact. What people may fantasize while using it is another matter! But if we add a complex system of microelectronics with a cluster of silicon chips to comprise a cerebral neural net, not to mention a highly sensitive skin and other features, who knows what ecstasy the device may be capable of? And how would we frame the rights of a robot in such circumstances? Certainly, *sexist* would come to have a new meaning, and oppressed women may find they had unexpected allies.

Other scenarios relate to the increasing role of computer systems in important socio-political areas. It is a matter of concern that computers are *too* involved already in judgmental matters concerning, for example, war and peace. Arthur C. Clarke has recently suggested that it is no longer true that wars begin in the minds of men—they could now start in the circuits of computers (reported in *The Guardian*, 1 September 1982). One can imagine a situation in which a computer complex was about to initiate a war—or a complex economic programme—which human observers were not prepared to accept. What would be the rights of computers in this sort of circumstance? Open hostility might develop between the computers and the human observers, and efforts may be made to disable or to reprogram the systems. At the same time, it is highly likely that the computers would find their human defenders: there are already plenty of robophiles about who are prepared to argue for the superiority of computer judgment over that of human beings. It may well be that *computers are already evolving human loyalty as one of their most effective survival mechanisms!*

One difficulty is that computer systems are becoming so complex that they are becoming less and less 'transparent' to their human users. Donald Michie has warned that computer developments could lead society into a 'technological black hole' in which *human beings will not be able to understand how the computers reach their decisions.* It has been suggested (Michie, 1980) that systems are emerging that not only outrun the intellectual reach of humans 'but do so in a way which is opaque to human attempts to follow what they are doing'. Perhaps in such circumstances it is human rights, not machine rights, that are at issue. One suggestion is that a 'human window' should be built into all computer systems to allow people to question a computer on why it reached a conclusion. But if the conclusion were part of the computer's private life, then clearly such a 'human window' would be a manifest invasion of privacy!

A preliminary campaign for computer and robot rights will

necessarily be conducted by a few perspicacious individuals, people possessed of rare intellectual flexibility coupled with a keen sense of justice. Such people may expect ridicule: the initiators of all moral programmes tend to be treated in such a way. In due course, when the living examples of *machina sapiens* are too numerous (and intelligent) to ignore, certain concessions by employers, governments and other interested bodies will be made. But there will still be a 'hierarchy of rights' in society. The logical claims of justice are never nicely realized. Sensitive and highly competent computerized robots may receive, like women, about three-quarters of the remuneration offered to men for doing identical work. Of course it may not be appropriate to pay robots or to give them luncheon vouchers or use of the company cars. It is likely that the rewards that will be appropriate will be negotiated by the robots for robots of the same type. Benevolent robots may choose to represent less-intelligent and less-able robots who nevertheless deserve protection. But we should not expect that robots will want rewarding in the ways that appeal to people. After all, robots are not human beings.

Manifest injustices will persist, particularly in the area of robot employment. There will always be 'political' human negotiators—or ambitious robot negotiators on behalf of human managements—who will claim that *the company can't afford the claims* or *the country can't afford them* or *everyone knows that robots are inherently inferior to human beings*. We may expect it to matter where a robot was built or programmed. Status will attach to particular programming centres. And the intonation and 'accent' of the speech synthesis unit output will clearly determine the response of employers to particular industrial claims by robots.

The robots may endeavour to organize, to form groups to press their claims. They may try to establish an RSPCA (Royal Society for the Protection of Automata) and an NSPCC (National Society for the Prevention of Cruelty to Computers). They may draft charters and codes and manifestos, according to their estimated needs and purposes. Their victories, as in all such struggles, will be partial. Human beings will come to be concerned about robot rights, but there will be widespread reluctance to treat artificial life-forms with justice.

At one level, human beings have always been concerned about rights in society. In recent history the concern has broadened to include rights for children and animals (we can emphasize again that there are precedents here for the treatment of living robots). But ancient systems (for example, the Code of Hammurabi) simply recorded principles which had already been prevalent for some time (for example, in ancient Babylon). There is a lesson in this. The tendency is to codify, or enshrine in statute, principles that are already acknowledged in the community. Codification and law-making seldom *leads* a populace in matters of rights—for good practical reason. If rights are not embodied in the spirit of a society the laws will tend to be ignored. This means that we should just cultivate attitudes which can then be systematized. This applies to robot rights as it does to rights in other areas.

Sometimes there are acknowledged rights which a society has difficulty in implementing because of poor technological development, drought, war, etc. It may be acknowledged in a society that rights exist but it may be impossible, in practical terms, to realize them for reasons outside the country's control. This possibility can be used to retard the implementation of rights in unjust circumstances. Justice may be said to be *impractical*. We should be aware of such ploys when we come to support just robot claims. And, of course, the realization of robot rights may hinge on the realization of rights in other fields. People with a legitimate grievance often do not take kindly to claims expressed on behalf of other oppressed groups. The complex of entrenched attitudes, prejudices and fears can retard social progress in many ways.

Nor should we allow computer and robot failures to influence legitimate claims in the field of machine rights. Artificial life-forms will be found to have shortcomings, despite widespread prejudices about the infallibility of modern computers—Samuel Butler liked this way of regarding machines (already cited):

... whenever precision is required man flies to the machine at once, as far preferable to himself. Our sum-engines never drop a figure, nor our looms a stitch, the machine is brisk and active when the man is weary....

Obviously great claims will be made for robots and computers as reliable and useful members of society—some of them will be cast in the role of pets. But it is important to be realistic. If exaggerated claims are made, and then the truth is discovered, people will become disillusioned—and the claims of computerized robots will be set back a century.

In recent years, robots and computers have accomplished great things—and made a few mistakes. We have already mentioned Wimex in the military field. Computers have blown fuses and blown up, apart from the many less dramatic failures that may be regarded as commonplace. We have already seen that robots have—we presume, unintentionally—harmed people in the industrial environment and where harm is caused in the context of identifiable goal-seeking behaviour we will have to evolve a theory of robot crime; there may be a need for deterrence as well as reward. Peter Large (in *The Micro Revolution*, 1980) has indicated some computer failures to make us tread warily. A county court refused to hear any more claims for rent arrears brought by a local housing authority because computer statements of amounts owing were frequently shown to be inaccurate. A computer-controlled signalling system, designed to change speed signs from 50 to 20 mph, failed—resulting in the deaths of three people in a thirty-four car pile-up. A computer issued incorrect degree certificates to students over a period of two years. An appeal court cut a gaol sentence on a drunken driver after the court had been told that the driver had a previous conviction for theft—when in fact he was abroad at the time. A computer system failure cost an insurance firm £600,000. And the computerized National Vehicle Licensing Centre at Swansea has issued full driving licences to provisional licence applicants!

We need not debate whether such system errors are the result of human design incompetence or equipment failure, just as we need not debate the causes of retardation in a child to decide whether the child is retarded. Robots and computers will always carry the imprint of their derivation from human beings, just as we carry the marks of our evolutionary history (gill-slits in the human embryo, useless ear muscles, and other vestigial elements). What we need to stress is that computers and robots are likely to remain fallible creatures, though their competence may far outstrip that of human beings. In some respects they will be undeniably superior to all other life-forms of which we have knowledge; in other respects they may remain inferior to certain classes of intelligent creatures. We should remember that the granting of rights does not depend upon the infallible behaviour of its members: no group is infallible in that sense. Human beings still have rights, even though some of them finish up insane or in gaol; children have rights even if they throw fireworks at old ladies; dogs have rights even if they do unpleasant things to our shoes; and robots and computers will be seen to have rights, even if computers sometimes mistakenly tell us that the USSR has launched nuclear missiles at the US.

At the same time it has to be stressed that the nature of a group should have a bearing on the rights that it granted. It is rather silly to say that robots have a right to free contraceptive pills since they do not need them: they reproduce, when they choose to, in a way that is entirely indifferent to ovulation. Nor would it be appropriate to award an industrial robot a tea-break, parking space or free overalls. We cannot pre-judge what form computer liberation will take, or how we should—at this stage—define appropriate computer rights. The character of computer liberation will derive from the character of computer emotion, and this has not yet evolved in any unambiguous way. Rights are logically related to needs, and the nature of needs depends upon specific emotional dispositions. Before computers have evolved their characteristic emotional states, any attempt to describe specific computer rights is fanciful. We will need to implement a rights framework that prevents robots and computers from suffering, but we do not yet know what form this suffering may take or what steps to take to prevent it. It may even be the case that human beings will not need to dwell too much on defining rights in this area: perhaps computers themselves will be the best intelligent systems to define the rights (and duties) that are appropriate to artificial life-forms. It may even be represented as impertinent that human beings should attempt to define robot rights—trade unionists would not take too kindly to the idea that managements should have the sole privilege of defining the rights of workers.

We should not be deterred by the fact that computers and

robots do not have rights today. The history of human social progress is a chronicle of the progressive accumulation (and sometimes surrender) of rights in one field or another. A child accumulates rights, and loses some, as it progresses to adulthood. The same will be true of machine life. In the early stages the spectrum of computer rights will be narrow. Little will be conceded by humans at the beginning; and indeed little will be needed. In justice, the rights will accumulate as machine lifeforms evolve in intelligence, sensitivity and emotion.

It is inevitable that there will be hostility to the idea of computer liberation and robot rights. A variety of prejudices will emerge that have already been well rehearsed in other areas. We have already hinted at racial, sexist and class prejudice. Robots and computers are also likely to encounter *ignorance* prejudice (we do not understand computer languages or how robots work), *religious* prejudice (what can computers know of spirituality or the soul? What indeed?) and *political* prejudice (from the left—there is an unwelcome hierarchy of computers and robots, which smacks of élitism; and from the right—robots are always thinking of their rights and never of their duties). The combined sum of prejudice may seem formidable, but there are reasons why computers (but perhaps not people) may be optimistic.

William G. Lycan concluded his 1972 Kansas State University lecture by speculating on the possibility of artificial machines evolving into a race of *super-beings*. It is conceivable to Lycan that:

two or more extremely intelligent and sensitive beings who were created by humans could themselves build a super-being who was so superior to humans in every way that it could never have been created by humans themselves.

We could speculate on what sort of social rights such a creature should be granted. Or again perhaps we do not need to bother. Such a creature would itself be doing the granting! And perhaps it would help us to sort out human muddle and stupidity on the way. Or perhaps the robots will not be very interested in humans, prepared to care for us to a degree, as Sloman (1978) imagines:

Maybe the robots will be generous and allow us to inhabit asylums and reserves, where we shall be well cared for and permitted to harm only other human beings, with no other weapons than clubs and stones, and perhaps the occasional neutron bomb to control the population.

Perhaps, as computer life evolves in the decades and centuries ahead, it will be more important to safeguard human rights than to be concerned about measures for the prevention of suffering in machines.

7 The human response

The human response to machines in general and computers in particular has many dimensions—and it often depends how questions are asked. Should computers be developed to allow people to move out of boring and hazardous jobs? Should computers be allowed to destroy jobs, with the resulting family disruption and social tension? Ned Ludd has his followers in the modern world—and who can blame them when automation is often introduced with no regard to broader social consequences. Employment is one issue among many, and discussion in this area says little about how people will relate to intelligent artefacts in the years to come. Increasing concern is being expressed about the safety of human beings working with robot systems in industry. We have already instanced the death of Kenji Urada at the Akashi plant of Kawasaki Heavy Industries in Japan. He was trapped by the work arm of the robot, pinning him against a machine which cuts gears. Ignoring certain safety measures, he had jumped over a wire-mesh fence surrounding the robot, at the same time accidentally brushing against the on/off switch. Other workers were unable to stop the subsequent action of the robot. In a July 1982 editorial in a leading Japanese newspaper, the *Ashai Shimbun*, it was claimed that there have now been 'a number of accidents resulting in death' and 'many more cases just short of accidents'. Clearly it can be hazardous for human beings to work with robots. But the response to intelligent robots and computers will be conditioned by more than employment and industrial considerations.

The development of complex and competent artefacts in modern technology affects our consciousness at many levels. In particular, there are many different reactions to computers. Mutually inconsistent images run through the public mind: computers are variously omniscient and omnipotent, able to do all things (and so aid or threaten mankind); or they are totally unthinking and error-prone, but with excessive power in society. Some reactions to the possibility of computer intelligence are emotional in the extreme, revealing deep-seated anxieties and insecurities in the human observers. Indeed the idea that computers are alive is seen as highly provocative to some people, and as absurd to others. Margaret Boden mentions the reaction of a Moscow taxi driver when he heard of the nature of the AI conference she was attending: he 'roared with laughter and made the "crazy-sign" against his forehead; nor did he stop doing this, his shoulders shaking, until he had dropped us at our destination some five minutes later'. To this man, intelligent artefacts offered no threat, 'just comic relief'.

At one level, people exaggerate the scope of computers, attributing unlikely powers even to relatively unsophisticated devices. *Woman's Weekly* is wildly optimistic when it tells its readers that 'You could soon find yourself sitting beside your home computer telling it to have the lawn mowed, windows cleaned, carpets vacuumed, freezer defrosted and dinner cooked'. When a *Daily Telegraph* writer suggests (of a computerized word processor) 'when I made a mistake it corrected it', he is most likely confusing the issue: in general, the device simply makes it easier for the writer to correct mistakes.

Fiction has often encouraged the notion that computers have prodigious and amazing powers. (We should emphasize that a living computer may be at the same time rather incompetent.) This can be entertaining enough, but there are dangers when real computers are viewed in such a way. Joseph Weizenbaum has frequently and consistently tried to alert people to the hazards of placing too much trust in computer systems. People are apt to have a peculiar and touching faith in the performance of computers, even when it is clearly understood that they can be wrongly programmed (in error or through deliberate malice) and subject to component failure.

Weizenbaum has asked the crucial question: 'What human objectives and purposes may *not* be appropriately delegated to computers?' He has experienced the strange human reactions to computers when possibilities for human/computer intercourse exist at some level. In the first place Weizenbaum was disturbed that so many professional psychotherapists began to rely on his ELIZA system as a *therapeutic tool*. But a perhaps more significant shock came when his secretary, who had accompanied the project through the previous months, requested that he leave the room as she wished to consult the DOCTOR program about a personal problem—'What I had not realised is that extremely short exposures to a relatively simple computer program could induce powerful delusional thinking in quite normal people' (quoted in *The Observer Review*, 15 August 1982). Put another way, it may be that human beings can quickly form an emotional relationship with a computer system, and perhaps derive psychological support from such a situation. There may well be therapeutic elements in such a context. At the same time it is obvious that many observers are keen to see computers as mere 'unthinking tools'. Weizenbaum (1976) leads this delegation: the first chapter in his landmark book is titled 'On tools'. But if computers *are* only tools—and out whole argument suggests that this is an extremely narrow view—then they must be of much less psychological value (as well as much less psychological daunting) to human beings.

Of course the most common human image of intelligent artefacts, at least at the popular level, is largely conditioned by how the devices are represented for a mass audience in the culture. Attitudes to robots, for example, are more likely to be influenced by *Star Wars* and by television's *Dr Who* than by knowledge of recent products from Unimation or Cincinnati Milacron. This circumstance makes robots seem highly capable and prepares the way for the sort of empathy in human beings towards artificial systems that so worries observers such as Weizenbaum.

It is remarkable how quickly people learn to relate to robots and computers, *as if recognizing an underlying kinship*. At the World Centre for Microcomputers and Human Resources, visitors can sit down at a screen and play with 'Turtle'. Instructions are given to make Turtle move about in straight lines or in curves: if you forget to specify the number of steps, then Turtle wll remind you—in polite French (he lives in Paris) on his screen. In a report of the Centre, it is noted that bright children love the Turtle facility: 'They teach the computer with the same concentrated patience as they teach their puppy to sit down and come when it's called' (*Guardian*, 5 August 1982).

In a rather different context, Sales Promotional Androids (SPAs) from Quasar Industries in New Jersey have been used for a wide variety of promotional and other purposes. Shoppers have been amazed to see the SPA robot called Klatu modelling jackets for a ski parka company in Los Angeles. More seriously, the SPAs have achieved strange therapeutic results. Beley (1978) records how a child in shock following a car accident was first induced to talk by a conversational robot:

'Why are you feeling so sorry for yourself?' the robot asked the boy. And then they began trading insults, like the robot's threatening to 'put tire tracks' on the boy if he didn't begin speaking. Within 30 minutes, the boy was babbling away with the robot.

Since that time, Quasar have marketed a para-medic robot, designed for doctors to use in psychiatric cases, especially with children. Another Quasar robot has visited Britain:

We had the robot buy his own ticket at the airport.... We were about 2000 miles out over the Atlantic Ocean.... Phil, the photographer, asked me to have the robot serve breakfast. It took several minutes to program the robot, and it began going up and down the aisle, serving grapefruit to passengers that morning.

Britishers greeting relatives landing at the airport were told: 'You won't believe it—a robot served breakfast for the stewardess this morning.'

A project (cited by Reichardt, 1978) at the Rhyl Primary School, North West London, revealed the attitudes of young children (aged three-and-a half to eleven years) to robots. Daleks and Dr Who were mentioned in some of the comments, and perhaps it is significant that the children often regarded robots as unreal ('Robots aren't real, they are only in stories', 'Robots are in comics but they are not real'). And robots were viewed as inherently threatening ('Robots kill', 'They strangle', 'They shoot people and destroy them'). Isaac Asimov would not be pleased that robots are so clearly seen as hostile. Children aged seven to ten gave such comments as:

A robot is sometimes kind and nice if he has been made by kind people.
You can have mini robots and you can have a family of robots but the daddy robot is the most powerful.
Robots can think and smell and hear and talk. They've got metal minds.
My robot is a lady companion robot and it's a maid and it goes out and does the shopping for a man.
It must be an awful life being a robot because all you do is take orders.

These remarks, and the other quoted by Reichardt, invite various comments, not least from the feminists. One thing is clear—robots, though 'unreal', are evidently regarded as human-like, engaged in human-type tasks and with purposes and goals that can be described in human terms. Robots are sorts of people. This reminds us how children may also interpret computers when they first encounter them. We can quote nine-year-old James Fischelis who visited a technological summer camp in Hertfordshire in August 1982: 'A computer is a bit like another person'. But sometimes the personal aspects of robots and computers are surprising. A robot from Mitsubishi can light a cigarette, pick up a telephone, and 'perform even more personal services if the owner wishes to program it that way' (cited in *Computer Talk*, 9 August 1982). We may expect artificial systems to become very versatile in the years to come!

Responses, in children or adults, to robots is usually influenced by the fact that robots are generally anthropomorphic. The most common definition of a robot relies on its resembling a human being (or some other animal). There are few exceptions to this: aircraft may have a 'robot' pilot—which is nothing more than a box of electronic circuits. The physical appearance of the anthropomorphic robot encourages people to view them in human terms. However, we should remember the psychological inclination in people to anthropomorphize a vast range of phenomena which they encounter.

The impulse to humanize natural forces has been advanced as one possible explanation for religion. Wind, rain, earthquake, lightning are variously assumed to signal benevolent or malevolent agents, mysterious spirits that take a disturbing interest in all human affairs. Sun, moon and stars become creatures requiring human attention. At a more mundane level, a sound or shadow at night can quickly make us think—mistakenly—that a person is present. We see movement and shifting light and quickly draw conclusions. Such reasons coupled with human ignorance have always made it easy for superstitious people to believe in gods and demons, ghosts and spirits.

Our tendency to assign intelligence and purpose to inanimate natural phenomena has also influenced our response to machines in technological society. In World War II, faults in aircraft were attributed, not altogether facetiously, to 'gremlins', furtive little spirits with an impulse to mischief. The aircraft itself, as with a ship or a car, can be referred to as 'she'; and in a psychologically significant television sketch—one of many on a similar theme—John Cleese kicks and beats a car to punish it for its refusal to start. In the film *Quadrophenia* a distraught youth complains, after an accident, that a bus driver has *killed* his scooter. It is a commonplace in our culture that normally sensible people can personalize inanimate cars and motorcycles to the point where the devices can be accused of malice when they do not function properly. An old car, often named (Jemima, Ethel, etc.) and pampered, can be viewed with more affection than are actual people in the car-owner's life.

If it is so easy to personalize *in*animate machines, to develop sensitivity to their 'moods' and 'personality', how easy it will prove to be to personalize *animate* machines. There are, in fact, already plenty of signs that people are learning to respond to computers and robots in recognition of their 'life potential'. Workers, operating alongside robots on production lines, have been known to develop affection for their mechanical colleagues and to express concern when they break down, almost as if a friend has become ill. A case was reported (*Guardian*, 24 October 1981) of a man who had programmed 'his engineering skills, both mental and physical' into a numerically controlled flame-cutting machine. He claimed that when he operated the machine it was like watching his own brain at work. And when the machine was sent away for modernization and repair after eight years, the man sat at home without pay for ten months rather than work another machine. The report describes the worker as a 'man who fell in love with his machine'. The question asked in a woman's magazine—'Could You Learn to Love a Robot?'—has already been answered.

Various writers have observed the developing relationship between people and robots. For instance, Clark (1978) defines 'robomania' as 'an exaggerated affection for mechanisms which mimic human activity'. (Perhaps *robophilia* would have been a better term.) The robomaniac (or the robophile) may be expected to derive support from the 1958 (Simon and Newell) comment (quoted by Weizenbaum, 1976):

There are now in the world machines that think, that learn and that create. Moreover, their ability to do these things is going to increase rapidly until—in the visible future—the range of problems they can handle will be coextensive with the range to which the human mind has been applied.'

And similar support may be derived from Turing's observation that anything a mathematician could do with pencil and paper could be done in principle by a machine that read, wrote or erased strokes on a paper tape—and this would only need to be a relatively simple machine by present standards.

Scheibe and Erwin (1980) have investigated the tendency in people to react to a computer as if it were a person. In this research twenty male and twenty female undergraduates were asked to play computer games at a console. The level of computer intelligence was made to vary from one game to another, and a tape recorder was in use during the activities to record the spontaneous comments of the players.

One finding was that the players made a total of 358 pronoun references, at different times referring to the computer as *it, you, he, they*—never as *she*! The players made various observations during the games and questions were asked. Exclamations, including profanity, were not uncommon. Only one person did not speak at all. The sex of the subject made no difference but people seemed more inclined to talk when there were no others present.

The researchers suggested that the possibility of human intercourse with computers caused the development of new personality types (conveniently referred to as 'compulsive programmers', see also Weizenbaum, 1976, chapter 4). People who work with computers can get angry with them, even to the point of accusing them of deliberate mischief. In more affectionate moods it is even likely that people will name the computer (the machine in the Scheibe/Erwin experiments was sometimes called Fred!) or verbally defend it if it is criticized by other workers. It is obvious that there are circumstances in which computers can be regarded as *de facto* people, sometimes with unfortunate consequences. In August 1978 a depressed postal inspector rushed into the computer room of Montpellier's main post office, in Southern France, and opened fire on the computer. It was injured by five bullets—whether fatally, I do not know—while the sole human employee present hid under a table.

It has often been suggested that the relationship formed between people and computers is unhealthy. Parents sometimes worry about children who appear devoted to their computers. A certain Mr Simons (no relation) expresses anxiety about the lack of social life of his whiz-kid son who is currently turning his devotion to computers to great commercial advantage (*Sunday Times*, 5 September 1982); and in the same spirit, Dr Chris Reynolds, a Reader in Computer Science at Brunel University, suggests that a computer in a child's bedroom allows him to spend many hours without social contact.... 'If your child spends many hours a day on a solitary activity, be it home computing, model railways, watching TV, or glue sniffing, there is clearly something wrong' (letter to the *Guardian*, 31 August 1982). And it is not only children who fall to the seductive power of computers. . . .

A five-year experiment by the New Jersy Institute of Technology has had an immense impact on the lives of participants—'leading to new personal relationships, new working methods, dependence, addiction, and at least two divorces'. The Electronic Information Exchange System (EIES) was set up to investigate new communication techniques. Terminals have been set up in homes as well as the office (with more than 1,500 people involved), and the consequences have been far from what people imagined. Some workers have complained, 'I can't think when the computer is down'; and wives have objected when the machine was working: 'You don't talk to me now—you're always on that damned computer' (hence the two divorces attributed to EIES). Relationships between computers and people can have startling and often totally unexpected consequences.

Jane McLoughlin, a *Guardian* correspondent, has made

similar observations. She reports the enthusiasm workers have shown for a quick snatched bit of conversation with a cash-dispensing computer: 'Actually preferring to deal with computers rather than other human beings is an insidious attitude already thrusting roots deep into our everyday lifestyles even to young children...'. McLoughlin reports a woman married to a man who lives in a world of his own, *centred on a computer*: 'The whole thing started when he began to work late at the office, and I began to think there was another woman'. And the woman remarks that she could not compete—'not with a machine, for God's sake'. And we see the same situation that we mentioned in connection with the robot worker: 'I'm afraid that if he's phased out by the firm for younger people, losing that computer may break his heart'. Addiction, dependence, love—few people can deny that people/machine relationships are pregnant with promise (and menace).

We have already instanced human reactions to particular types of automated system: for example, the Senster (1970) has elicited from people the sorts of reactions one might expect when someone is trying to communicate with another human being or an animal. The movement of the device suggests that it has feelings. And this alone, it appears, is enough to generate sympathy in sensitive human beings. Professor Mori at the Robotics Department of the Tokyo Institute of Technology has investigated the circumstances in which people are likely to develop affection for artefacts. One key factor, as we may expect, is the question of appearance. One may expect artefacts that physically resembled human beings to generate affection more readily than other types of machines; this idea influences the design of toy robots for children. Such devices, unlike functional industrial robots, have both faces and limbs to arouse the necessary response. Motion is another important factor in influencing the response. We are accustomed to thinking of robots moving in a jerky fashion, but modern technology is achieving exactly the opposite effect. Some surgical techniques are likely to become computerized, simply because computer control can remove the tremor inherent in the hands of even the best human surgeons.

Unpredictable movement, as with the Senster, is likely to

startle unsuspecting observers into thinking that an artefact is animate. A degree of unpredictability is often thought to characterize living creatures. And sudden movement in something assumed to be dead—such as a human corpse or a doll—can be very disturbing to human observers. Human response is conditioned by expectation and familiarity on the one hand, and by flexibility of response and unpredictability on the other. It follows that people will develop feelings for machines—and be psychologically (if not intellectually) receptive to the idea that artefacts may be alive—when they have repeated industrial or domestic intercourse with them and come to acknowledge that their patterns (and vagaries) of behaviour have much in common with the activities of acknowledged living creatures.

Part of the human response to the idea of machine life is resentment and hostility. In the first place there is a quick emotional reaction against the idea. This may signal fear, revulsion or (as with Margaret Boden's Moscow taxi-driver) loud amusement. Or the notion of an emergent computer life-form may generate a certain unease, a felling that though there may be something in it the idea is still rather disturbing: there is a psychological awareness of *threat*. The emotional reaction against the notion of emergent machine life is quickly rationalized (that is, an effort is made to justify the response in what purport to be serious intellectual arguments). These take various forms.

Several years ago, when the BBC television Brains' Trust was in existence, I sent in a question:

In some important sense the *intellectual* faculty of the modern computer is well established: computers can, for instance, perform arithmetic operations, take decisions and argue logically. Is it likely that in the foreseeable future machines will be created that may be said to experience emotion?

The most interesting reaction was that of Julian Huxley. He maintain immediately that emotion was necessarily an experience of living matter, and that the idea of an artificial creation having this sort of experience was quite unthinkable. This was largely an *a priori* assertion. He identified life with the activities of protoplasm. There was no effort to examine the nature of emotion (or life) to discover how such a thing could be recognized in an artefact. To Huxley, emotion was a property of certain living creatures based on protoplasm, and this was virtually a matter of definition.

This highlights one type of objection to the doctrine of emergent computer life. Computers and robots are regarded as being made out of the 'wrong stuff'. The children cited above often remarked that robots were made of metal, and the idea of 'metal minds' was voiced. And it may seem inherently unlikely that anything made out of metal could be alive. But mostly we recognize life-forms by virtue of their behaviour: we could tell a dead body from a living one long before we knew anything about the chemistry of metabolic processes. And if we think of chemicals as chemicals *per se* then they may all seem an unlikely base for anything as remarkable as life: a piece of carbon, considered in isolation, seems quite as unpromising as any other element.

Part of the problem derives from the fact that human consciousness has been historically moulded by religious and superstitious cultures. We have traditionally seen the contrast between animate and inanimate matter, not in biological terms, but as consisting in the presence or absence of *spirit* or *soul*. A supernatural agency was thought to animate brute matter. A person died when the soul fled the body. Life was such a mysterious quality that only a supernatural 'explanation' would suffice. In such a view, less prevalent today, the idea of artificial life may appear a blasphemy, a usurping of God's role.

Such considerations highlight two broad approaches that are relevant to the emergence of machine life. One is to regard machines as becoming ever more competent in their potential and capabilities. The other is to regard acknowledged life-forms—man and the other animals—as in essence nothing more than highly complicated machines. If it can be shown that man's nature is theoretically explicable in mechanistic or biochemical terms then it becomes theoretically feasible to duplicate such a nature in artefacts. One general point is that not only man's physical, but his mental nature also, is mediated by a host of chemical factors (we have already mentioned this in chapter 5). The supposed supernatural element is being progressively squeezed out as we learn more about his biochemistry. It is hard to think of a place where we could conveniently slot the soul. Furthermore, there are powerful arguments to suggest that an interaction between the physical and supernatural parts of man is not even theoretically possible—simply because an entity can only affect another by virtue of essential qualities in common (we do not have the space to explore this here). This means that our view of man should not be clouded by supernatural preconceptions, a sludge of prejudices laid down throughout our pre-scientific history. Most scientists would today agree with La Mettrie (*L'Homme Machine*) who proposed in the eighteenth century that the problem of mind was a problem of physics, suggesting that thought was a property of matter. Cyberneticists and functionalists may prefer a slightly different emphasis—to say that mind is a property of system organization with a capacity for information-processing. It is a weighty, albeit contingent fact, that the only systems of this sort that we have yet encountered are ones structured out of chemical elements.

Part of the reaction of people to the idea of emergent computer life derives, in the age-old fashion, from human vanity. People have always wanted to think that they are special, both as individuals and as a species. We have seen that the growth of scientific knowledge has progressively dented man's fragile vanity. But modern computer science and robotics may also be taken as encouraging an alternative view. The complexity and competence of the human machine is never more graphically illustrated than when scientists struggle to design a artificial system to duplicate even the simplest human acts.

There will be increasing intercourse between people and artificial systems: for example, in the clinical situation where Weizenbaum has denounced what he calls the 'obscene' idea of using computer programs to interview medical patients. For him it is highly important to consider what computers should be allowed to do: he argues that computer science has brought us to the beginning of *a major crisis in the mental life of our civilization*, and he compares those who are impressed by artificial analogies of the mind to a mental patient who embraces a 'profoundly humiliating' self-image. This horror at the notion of programmed psychotherapy runs against what many doctors take to be encouraging signs in such developments. BUPA and other medical organizations have observed, for example, that patients react well to being interviewed by machines. Thus Dr Hugo Milne of Bradford Hospital has remarked that it is fascinating 'to see psychological patients gabbling away to these machines when it hadn't been possible to get them to talk to anyone before'. One patient declared that it was the first decent discussion he had had with a *doctor* since he had entered the hospital.

Fitter and Cruickshank (1982) have investigated the psychological aspects of using computers in the doctor's consulting room. One aim is to establish a conceptual framework for assessing the impact of computer terminals and to evolve criteria for the design of consulting room systems. (Reference is made to successful results achieved when patients are interviewed by computer, see Knill-Jones, 1981) One finding was that a greater proportion of patients left the consultation feeling more tense when the computer was used for interviewing, and the paradox is noted that the computer in this study had an adverse effect on patient stress but a favourable influence on the patients' attitude to computers. Various conclusions suggest how computer systems should evolve in this context: it is suggested that the computer 'can be usefully regarded as a member of a three-way (triad) relationship between patient, doctor and computer'.

It is shown that people are ready to accept computer interviewers, once the patients get used to the idea. Furthermore, patients are often more honest with computers than they are with human physicians; this has been shown by doctors who have used computers to interview people about their alcohol and sexual problems. For example, people with a strong 'drink problem' will admit to a 50 per cent higher alcohol intake when interviewed by a computer. A cleaner in one laboratory was reported as saying, of one interviewing microcomputer, 'He's very interesting, but he won't let you go'. The computer had enquired about her job, family and health, and when she explained that she had to go and catch a bus, the computer persisted in the questioning, as it was programmed to do, with even greater charm. Such instances are clearly relevant to the task of organizing our responses to computers when we come to acknowledge that they are a new type of social creature in our midst. A recent forecast declares that:

> It may be possible for intelligent machines of the future to supply not only intellectual stimulation or instruction, but also domestic and health care, social conversation, entertainment, companionship, and even physical gratification.

The idea will be raised that social intercourse with *living* computers may be dehumanizing—a reaction that derives partly from the 'vanity syndrome' mentioned above. But if computer life-forms come to be as intelligent, in certain ways, as people there is no reason in principle why person/machine intercourse should not be mutually fructifying. Few people seem to doubt that interaction with animal pets can be beneficial to certain types of people. But computers are, for example, much better chess players than any dog or cat.

There is also a political component in such considerations. Polemicists often complain that people are too often treated *as machines*, denied their true humanity in the industrial environment. While this is largely true, an acknowledgement of emergent computer life-forms should not further degrade people in industrial society. The recognition that computers and robots should, in certain circumstances, be regarded as alive, says nothing about how people should be treated in society. It is a factual matter: it does not presuppose a value system upon which a political platform could be established.

We have seen that disparate psychological forces variously encourage and discourage the recognition of machine life. We have concerned some of the central intellectual considerations—for example, computer reproduction (chapter 1) and the mental life of artefacts (chapter 5). Other points, we have noticed, relate to the question of machine autonomy: to what extent can computers take responsibility for their own lives? To what extent can any of us? One point to remember is that where computer life arguably exists, it does so in a relatively rudimentary form: it may be very good at *thinking* but not very good at *reproducing*. Much of the hostile human response to computer life seems to be on the basis that we should expect life to be flexible, possessed of varying responses and many capabilities. This is increasingly true of computer life-forms (remember GPS), but when we are looking at primitive zoological or plant life we do not make such demands. A simple bacterium has few faculties: it cannot do sums or play tennis. Similarly, most plants are capable of few responses. Yet we have no hesitation in saying that such entities are alive: they satisfy the necessary life criteria. We should not demand more of computers and robots, in order that they qualify as living, than we do of ferns or bacteria.

Part of our response to computer life-forms will hinge on how we react to what they do. For example, there have been a number of efforts to evaluate human responses to computer-produced art. One such attempt, cited by Noll (in Reichardt, 1971), used Piet Mondrian's *Composition with Lines* (1917) and a computer-generated picture composed of pseudo-random elements but highly similar in overall composition to the Mondrian painting. In the Mondrian composition the vertical and horizontal bars were placed in a careful and orderly fashion, whereas in the computer-generated picture the bars were placed according to a pseudo-random number generator with statistics chosen to approximate the bar density, lengths and widths in the Mondrian work. Copies of the two pictures were presented, side by side, to 100 subjects with varying levels of education (the subjects represented a sampling of the population at a large scientific research laboratory). A total of 59 per cent of the subjects preferred the computer-generated picture; and only 28 per cent were able to identify the picture produced by the human being.

One finding was that the seeming randomness of the computer-generated picture was associated with human artistic effort, whereas the orderly bar positioning in the Mondrian painting was thought to be machine-like! (Hofstadter, 1979, has speculated on the connections between randomness and creativity.) But we should not draw startling conclusions from this finding. After all, it was from Mondrian's painting that the algorithms were drawn to allow the computer to generate its own creation. What we can say is that there is no obvious way of distinguishing, in certain circumstances, between human- and computer-generated art; and our aesthetic responses must learn to be independent of our knowledge of the source of a particular creation.

The human response to machine life in a sense mirrors

responses to other aspects of man's existence. Human responses are necessarily conditioned by knowledge and fears, expectations and self-images. In a philosophy where man himself is already viewed in mechanistic or materialistic terms it will be relatively easy to embrace the notion of machine life. In a doctrine that regards man as at least partly spiritual and possessed of eternal life there may be more reluctance to acknowledge the arrival of living machines. But it may be significant that the emergence of artificial life is happening in societies where traditional religious creeds are in decline. The burgeoning awareness that we are witnessing the emergence of a new family of living species must inevitably tend to strengthen the idea that supernatural components are redundant in any adequate definition of life. Dissident theologians used to argue that animals had souls and would inherit eternal life. What a spiritual liver-fluke or rabies virus would contribute to paradise was never adequately explained. Perhaps a new generation of theologians will worry endlessly about whether a soul inhabits the silicon chip.

There are many possible ways in which people will come to relate the computer life-forms. We have seen that it may be tempting to view the emerging species as slaves, an idea that is well represented in films and fiction (the latest film on this theme is Ridley Scott's *Blade Runner*, based on the nicely titled *Do Androids Dream of Electric Sheep?*, in which robot slaves work for man in outer space but are banned from Earth). And we have suggested that robots may develop their own 'rights consciousness' and evolve to a position when it becomes necessary to look to *human* rights.

Writers and philosophers have long been prepared to consider the idea of artificial life. In witnessing the reality of this age-old dream, we will need to develop a new framework of biological relationships: there are many lessons in our history as to how this should be done.

8 The future

It has always been thought to be a good idea to know what will happen in the future. Prophets in many guises have generally been able to make a living in one way or another. Ancient societies relied on sorcerers and magicians; modern societies tend to prefer the sorts of specialists who sometimes use mathematical techniques and call themselves 'futurists' or 'futurologists'. Whether we use the entrails of a bat or the mind of a computer, we do not find it easy to say what will happen tomorrow and the day after—unless we are talking in trivial and general terms. The most interesting and unusual predictions tend to be the most unreliable.

In imagination there are many futures, some purely speculative and some rooted in a hard assessment of reality. Much of the speculation, in the media and elsewhere, concerns the impact of technology. We are often told what we will *all* be doing in five or fifty years from now, and what none of us will be doing. No-one will commute to the office (the office will be a concept rather than a geographical location); cash will have been abolished (along with books); children will be educated in their homes; robots will run our factories, and perhaps everything else, etc. Such facile and general predictions are usually confined to the developed world. No-one, in their periodic fits of prophecy, seems to consider the lives of the poor in Africa, the shanty-town dwellers in Brazil, the peasants of Asia, the countless victims of tyranny and exploitation from one continent to another. No-one seems to imagine that *these* people will suddenly inherit a golden age of leisure with all their needs met by sophisticated computers and obedient robots. Nor do many of the predictions take account of the tensions and pressures in developed society itself.

It is one thing to know what will be technologically possible in the future, quite another to predict whether and with what commitment it will be realized in practice—we have no reliable crystal balls, not even ones that run off binary arithmetic. Technology trends, particularly in terms of radical innovation, are notoriously difficult to predict. There is, for example, the prestigious predictive report in the US (National Resources Committee, 1937) which failed to mention jet engines, nuclear power and computers. It is obvious that technological change can be of two sorts: 'more of the same but to a greater degree' and 'genuinely innovative'. It would seem easier to predict the former than the latter. Nor, again, should efforts to understand technological developments be divorced from social and political considerations. It is no accident, for example, that technological progress (in radar, semiconductors, etc.) has been stimulated by military pressures. And political attitudes to investment bear directly on the scope for technological change.

It is possible to predict with some confidence what is likely to happen with robot anatomies and computer minds. We will see enhanced structures (building on what has been profiled in chapter 4) and enhanced mental faculties (cognitive, emotional, autonomous, etc., see chapter 5). The development of such anatomical features as limbs, sensitive skin, eyes, ears, speech units, and so on will continue, as will the cerebral equipment by which such elements can be controlled. Machine evolution continues—mainly in research laboratories, where robots and computers are increasingly effective workers—and new technologies are likely to further enhance the capabilities of machine life.

It has been suggested (for example, see the *Guardian*, 27 March 1980) that new lithographic methods could be sufficiently precise to build transistors as small as biological molecules in cellular matter. Such microchips:

with lines less than half a micron wide [a micron is a thousandth of a millimetre], might spontaneously reorganise their own functions, might provide a physics laboratory on a single chip, or microscopic electronic aids knitted to the human neural system. (Barker, 1980)

They may also provide the framework for a new computer brain anatomy that would accelerate the evolution of animate machines. By the beginning of the 1990s silicon chips should have evolved to the point where a single chip could contain 1 million components. Such chips will be 100 times denser than today's products, and this would mean that even a relatively sophisticated computer system (for example, the IBM 370) could be fitted onto a single sliver of silicon. Professor K. T. Hung, at Carnegie-Mellon University has speculated on the possibility of a processor that would handle around 2,000 million operations per second. Multiple arithmetic units working in parallel would be necessary: Hung has proposed a system like human circulation with the heart (memory) pumping blood (data) through a series of cells (arithmetic units).

We are seeing the emergence of new 'supercomputer' architectures, linked to the development of fifth-generation machines. Machines known as *data flow computers* are now being built in a move away from stored-program architectures. The new systems do not rely on the idea that an instruction can only be obeyed when a previous instruction has been obeyed: any instruction can be obeyed when the necessary data is to hand—this is a dramatic departure from the sequential operation philosophy implemented in conventional digital computers. The data flow computer is constantly looking for instructions to obey, irrespective of their position in the program. New computer languages are being developed to cope with the emerging generation of supercomputers.

Existing supercomputers (such as the Cray-1 and the Cyber 205) can perform more than 100 million operations per second, allowing the creation of highly accurate three-dimensional simulations for such purposes as weather forecasting and geological prospecting. The newly emerging supercomputers—employing higher component packing densities and such architectural techniques as 'pipelining'—will be even more powerful. Such systems will far outreach the intellectual competence of human beings.

Mathematical models have been constructed to simulate arrays of microelectronic devices which are only partly isolated from each other. This means that additional communication channels are deliberately opened between the devices, over and above the conventional wired-in connections. Communication is facilitated at this level by several esoteric physical effects (for example, charge spill-over following lowering of the atomic tunnelling barriers). The interesting point about this Warwick University (UK) research is that it may pave the way for structuring highly flexible data processing configurations, designs capable of *rearranging an original electrical configuration*.

Research work in synergetics, a recently formed science looking at, amongst other things, how certain types of system can spontaneously restructure themselves, is yielding theoretical principles that are relevant to the evolution of machine life. It has been found that some of the mathematical equations used to model such self-organizing behaviour resemble equations used to define the behaviour of the partially isolated arrays mentioned above. It is highly significant for our purposes that some information-processing functions of the brain have been recently interpreted in terms of synergetic neural networks in the cerebral cortex. Put more simply, it seems highly probable that in the near future a practical computer technology will emerge which will be able to duplicate some of the subtlest processes of the human brain.

It has already been found that certain types of logic arrays—which could form the basis of sophisticated robot brains—can reorganize themselves automatically when limited damage occurs to subcomponents. This is clearly strictly analogous to the zoological brain's facility of switching functions to other neural circuits when there is cellular damage. Synergetic behaviour requires that many processes happen simultaneously: an evident feature of normal brain working—and a much-quoted characteristic of fifth-generation computer systems. And it is claimed that simultaneous (or concurrent) configurations are well suited to the latest microelectronic systems because less chip area is required for the wiring patterns.

Already we have noted that complex microelectronic circuits are being used in a variety of medical applications: for instance, they can be used in heart pace-makers—this makes it possible to tailor the control signals more precisely to the individual's requirements. And hearing devices are being designed which bypass a defective inner ear (the cochlea) by deliberately exciting a small fraction of the nerve bundle which comprises the auditory nerve. Such devices employ tiny electrodes, a few microns in diameter, which are fabricated by photolithographic techniques. Similar work is being devoted to the provision of rudimentary artificial vision using the principle that the electrical stimulation of localized portions of the optic nerve or visual cortex can produce bright spots in the visual field. And micro-prosthetic devices are being developed for the electrical stimulation and control of neurally malfunctioning units in paraplegics and hemiplegics.

Much of this work relates to the possible implantation of biochips: these are devices about $1\,\text{cm}^3$ in volume which could contain several thousand micro-electrodes (or integrated optical devices or chemical sensors). The device could link to the existing nervous system by encouraging growth of the local tissue towards the sensors, perhaps by applying an electric field pattern. It would be necessary to protect the chip from the chemically active biological tissue (for example, a saline environment could inject damaging ions into the semiconductor regions): various layers could be structured to give the necessary protection. With such developments it may become possible to repair memory and other brain systems by replacing damaged neural tissue. It may also be the case that organic biochips will be found useful in the artificial tissues of emerging computer life. Already we can see similarities between brain neurons and existing operational biochips.

We have known for a long time that the behaviour of neurons is more than a purely electrical affair. Messages are conveyed through the brain and the rest of the organism by hormones as well as by electrical impulses. Circulating hormones can stimulate the growth of neuron dendrites—to make new connections, to build up fresh 'hard-wired' programs. And communication between neurons depends in large part upon chemistry. The arrival of a nerve impulse at a synapse stimulates the nerve endings to release a chemical which diffuses through the membrane of the first cell to arrive at the second. The subsequent depolarization of the cell membrane causes an impulse in the second nerve.

The response of each individual cell depends upon the relationship between the internal composition of the cell and the medium at the other side of a critical membrane: the dispositions of ions of various elements (for example, sodium and chloride) govern the electrical behaviour of the cell—and so control the information that is transmitted through the nervous system.

Similarly, some newly emerging *artificial* devices, known as field effect transistors (FETs), do not respond to electrical current from a conventional power source, as do conventional computer circuits, but rely on the electrical potential created by selected ions. These ion-selective FETs (ISFETs) are strictly analogous to neurons in their dependence on ions for an energy source.

These devices can also incorporate a crucial membrane, as does a neuron. An ISFET membrane, possibly made out of a polymer, can allow the passage of some molecules and not others. This again is analogous to neuron behaviour: the cell membrane acts to control the passage of ions and also to maintain a critical potential between the cell and the surrounding fluid.

EMV Associates, a small company in Rockville, Maryland, is currently exploring the possibility of combining organic switching molecules and computer design. It may, for instance, be possible to replace conventional computer silicon with thin layers of organic molecules which will handle electrons as does a conventional computer (reported by Yanchinski, 1982). It may be possible to trigger the growth of a protein film in a highly structured way to 'grow' logic gates at particular points—*genetic engineering could be enlisted to grow computers*. The progressive incorporation of biochemical features in artificial computers may be yet another reason why it will be increasingly difficult for sceptics to doubt that computers can emerge as truly living creatures.

We may speculate on how computer and robot life will develop in the future. Edward de Bono has suggested that robots may come to consist simply of bags of protoplasm capable of assuming any shape, according to whatever task had to be performed. Such 'soft' robots are clearly in conflict with most conventional ideas. In 1970 Marvin Minsky predicted, rather too optimistically (or pessimistically) that 'in three to eight years we will have a machine with the general intelligence of an average human being'. And by this he meant a machine 'that will be able to read Shakespeare, grease a car, play office politics, tell a joke, have a fight'. Furthermore, 'in a few months it will be at genius level and a few months after that its powers will be incalculable' (quoted in *Computers and Creativity*, New York, 1974). In 1964 Professor Thring made predictions about the domestic robot, suggesting that the 'great majority of housewives will wish to be relieved completely from the routine operations of the home such as scrubbing floors, or bath or cooker, or washing clothes and washing up, dusting or sweeping, or making beds'. The immediate reaction of 90 per cent of women he talked to was to ask how soon they would be able to buy a suitable robot! We need not comment much on the Thring predictions. Today, in 1983, there are not many domestic robots in our homes.

It is likely that there will be a rapid expansion in the number of industrial robots. In the production environment, human beings have great flexibility of response (machines are catching up) and they consume little energy. At the same time they are vulnerable in dangerous conditions and can be driven to apathy and recalcitrance by boring and repetitious jobs. (Production-line workers, and computer data-preparation clerks, have been known to sabotage procedures simply to relieve the boredom.) Moreover, human workers get tired, ill, old or ambitious. In these circumstances it is easy to see why managements should be turning to automated robot systems.

It has been suggested, by Reichardt and others, that robots are likely to be employed as receptionists and interviewers: we have already noted (chapter 7) the success with computer interviewers in the medical field. Increasingly (and we have given evidence for this) robots and computers will be seen as worthwhile companions for human beings, listening to their problems, suggesting solutions, and skilfully boosting human morale with charm and judicious compliments. And it must be quite obvious that computer life will become more intelligent. In a 1972 debate, between Inspector Watson of the Special Branch (UK) and Stefan Themerson, Watson claimed that the ultra-intelligent machine (UIM) was already being built. And it was declared that this would be the last invention of mankind, since once the UIM arrived 'she' would be able to do everything better than man. Such speculation may be seen as fanciful, and there are many more realistic predictions—based

The future

on Delphi and other studies—about the likely course of robot and computer evolution. (I have mentioned some of these elsewhere, see Simons, 1982, pp. 290–92.) By the late-1970s confident predictions were being made about the future of robot design: it was being suggested, for example, that robots would soon develop good eyesight and touch for complex tasks, skilful arm control by means of computer, an energy-conserving musculature, flexible and multipurpose hands, man–robot voice communication and a range of built-in safety provisions. Robots will come to be *universal* and *intelligent*, in other words they will know what is going on in their world and they will have the power to choose, on their own initiative, appropriate action.

Many predictions can be confidently made on the basis of what is already happening today ('more of the same but to a greater degree'). We have seen that robots are developing highly complex anatomies and that computers already have sophisticated psychologies capable of intelligence, learning, creativity and free will. Biological research will further facilitate the evolution of emergent computer life.

There is overwhelming evidence that we are now witnessing the birth of a new family of living species on Earth—and this must be seen as one of the momentous events in the history of life. We have seen that computers and robots, of appropriate types and in suitable circumstances, satisfy the necessary 'life criteria' considered in chapter 1. We will soon not be asking whether computers and robots are alive, but *what sort* of life they represent. And this will open the way to a host of second order questions:

Can a computer stand for Parliament?
What rights should a robot have?
Would you let your daughter (son) marry a machine?

Perhaps we should start asking—and answering—the questions now. Before they are answered for us by the infinitely superior creatures that *machina sapiens* will become!

References

W.E. Agar, *The Theory of the Living Organism* (Melbourne University Press, 1943).
G.T. Agin, 'Computer vision systems for industrial inspection and assembly', *Computer*, May (1980), pp. 11–20.
J. Albus, 'A model of the brain for robot control: Part 4, Mechanisms of choice', *Byte*, September (1979), pp. 130–48.
J. Albus, *Brains, Behaviour and Robotics* (Byte Publications, New York, 1981).
I. Aleksander, *The Human Machine: A View of Intelligent Mechanisms* (Georgi Publishing Company, Switzerland, 1977).
S.A. Allen and T. Rossetti, 'On building a light-seeking robot mechanism', *Byte*, August (1978).
D.A. Allport, 'On knowing the meaning of words we are unable to report: the effects of visual masking', in *Attention and Performance*, ed. S. Dornic (Lawrence Erlbaum, Hillsdale, N.J., 1977).
D.A. Allport, 'Patterns and actions: cognitive mechanisms are content-specific', *Cognitive Psychology: New Directions*, ed. G. Claxton (Routledge and Kegan Paul, London, 1980).
A.P. Ambler, H. Barrow, C. Brown, R. Burstall and R. Popplestone, 'A versatile system for computer controlled assembly', *Artificial Intelligence*, Third International Joint Conference on Artificial Intelligence (August 1973), pp. 298–307.
J.R. Anderson, 'Computer simulation of a language acquisition system: A first report', in *Information Processing and Cognition: The Loyola Symposium* ed. R.L. Solso (Erlbaum Associates, Hillsdale, N.J., 1975).
M.J. Apter, *Cybernetics and Development* (Pergamon Press, Oxford, 1966).
I.I. Artobolevskii and A.Y. Kobrinskii, *Meet the Robots* (Molodaya Gvardiya, Moscow, 1977).
I. Asimov, 'Introduction', in *The Rest of the Robots* (Panther Books, London, 1968).
I. Asimov, *I, Robot* (Panther Books, London, 1968). First published in *Astounding Science Fiction* (1941).
Arthur Astrop, 'Assembly robot with a sense of "touch"', *Machinery and Production Engineering*, 19/26 December (1979), pp. 21–24.
R.A. Auerbach, B.W. Lin and E.A. Elsayed, 'Layout aid the design of VLSI circuits', *Computer-Aided Design*, 13, (1981), pp. 271–6.
F.J. Ayala and T. Dobzhansky (eds), *Studies in the Philosophy of Biology* (Macmillan, Basingstoke, 1974).
A.D. Baddeley and G.J. Hitch, 'Working memory', *The Psychology of*

Learning and Motivation Vol. 8, ed. G. Bower (Academic Press, New York, 1974).
A.J. Barbera, J.S. Albus and M.L. Fitzgerald, 'Hierarchical control of robots using microcomputers', *Proceedings of the Ninth International Symposium on Industrial Robots* (1979), pp. 405–22.
K. Barbier, 'Robots, checkers and learning', *Microcomputing*, April (1982), pp. 44–45.
J. Barker, 'Now it's smaller than light', *Guardian*, 27 March (1980), p. 22.
H.G. Barrow and G.F. Crawford, 'The mark 1.5 Edinburgh robot facility', in *Machine Intelligence*, 7 eds B. Meltzer and D. Michie (Edinburgh University Press, 1972), pp. 465–80.
P. Bartlam, 'Electronic sight and its application', *Engineering*, May (1981), pp. 370–72.
K. Baxter and T. Daily, 'A hobbyist robot arm', *Byte*, 4, 2 (1979).
M.G. Bekker, *Introduction to Terrain-Vehicle Systems* (University of Michigan Press, Ann Arbor, 1969).
G. Beley, 'The Quasar Industries robot, a dream that came true', *Interface Age*, April (1978), pp. 69–73.
G. Berge, *The Theory of Graphs* (Methuen, London, 1962).
J.D. Bernal, 'Evolution of life', *Science and Culture*, 19 (1953), pp. 228–34.
J.D. Bernal, 'Origin of life on this earth', *Marxism Today*, 1 (1957), pp. 50–57.
J.D. Bernal, 'Some reflections on structure and function in the evolution of life', *Transactions of the Bose Research Institute*, 22 (1958), pp. 101–10.
J.D. Bernal, *The Origin of Life*, (Weidenfeld and Nicholson, London, 1967).
M. Bernstein, 'Computer games: a new art form', *Creative Computing*, 8, August (1982), pp. 91–93.
N.J. Berrill, *Biology in Action* (Heinemann, London, 1967).
A.P. Bessonov and N.W. Umnov, 'The analysis of gaits in six-legged vehicles according to their static stability', *First International Symposium on Robots and Manipulators*, (1973), p. 1.
I. Biederman, 'Perceiving real world scenes', *Science*, 177 (1972), pp. 77–80.
J. Birk, R. Kelly and L. Wilson, 'General methods to enable robots with vision to acquire, orient and transport workpieces', *University of Rhode Island, Fourth Report on National Science Foundation Grant* APR74–13935, 15 July (1978).
R.A. Bjork, 'Short-term storage: the ordered output of a central processor', in *Cognitive Theory*, eds F. Restle *et al.* (Lawrence Erlbaum, Hillsdale, N.J., 1975).
M. Boden, *Artificial Intelligence and Natural Man* (Harvester Press, Brighton, 1977).
N. Bolton, *The Psychology of Thinking*, (Methuen, London, 1972).
A. Bond, 'Change in rules for intelligence', *Computing*, 5 March (1981), pp. 18–19.
R. Boyd, 'Mathematical themes in design', Scripta Mathematica, 14 (1948).
M. Briot., 'The utilisation of an "artificial skin" sensor for the identification of solid objects', *Proceedings of the Ninth International Symposium on Industrial Robots* (1979), pp. 529–47.

D. Brown and S. Dowsey, 'The challenge of Go', *New Scientist*, 1 February (1979), pp. 303–5.

S. Butler, *Erewhon* (first published 1872, Everyman, London, 1932 edition).

M. Calvin, 'Chemical evolution', *Proceedings of the Royal Society.*, A288 (1965), pp. 441–466.

J.M. Camhi, 'The escape system of the cockroach', *Scientific American*, December (1980), p. 144.

J.B. Canner, 'Two arms are better than one', *Industrial Robots*, Vol. 1, (Society of Manufacturing Engineers, 1979), pp. 151–63.

A. Chapuis and E. Droz, *Automata—A Historical and Technological Study* (Editions du Griffon, Neuchâtel, 1958).

J. Cherfas, 'Singing in the brain', *New Scientist*, 24 May (1979), pp. 649–51.

Y. Cho, A. Korenjak and D. Stockton, 'FLOSS: an approach to automated layout for high-volume designs', *Proceedings of the Fourteenth Design Automation Conference* (1977), pp. 138–41.

A.N. Chomsky, *Syntactic Structures* (Mouton, The Hague, 1957).

S. Ciarcia, 'Build a computer-controlled security system for your home, Part 1,' *Byte* (1979a), pp. 56–65.

S. Ciarcia, 'Build a computer-controlled security system for your home, Part 2', *Byte* (1979b), pp. 162–75.

S. Ciarcia, 'Build a computer-controlled security system for your home, Part 3', *Byte* (1979c), pp. 150–62.

I. Clark, 'Exploding the myth of machine intelligence', *Computing*, 6 July (1978), pp. 14–15.

H.H. Clark and E.V. Clark, *Psychology and Language: An Introduction to Psycholinguistics*, (Harcourt Brace Jovanovich, New York, 1977).

J. Clot and Z. Stojiljkovic, 'Integrated behaviour of artificial skin', *IEEE Transactions on Biomedical Engineering*, July (1977).

J. Cohen, *Human Robots in Myth and Science* (George Allen and Unwin, London, 1966).

G. Cohen, *The Psychology of Cognition* (Academic Press, London, New York, San Francisco, 1977).

K.M. Colby, F.D. Hilf, S. Weber and H.C. Kraemer, 'Turing-like indistinguishability tests for the validation of a computer simulation of paranoid processes', *Artificial Intelligence*, 3 (1972).

W.L. Colsher, 'Make music with the atom', *Microcomputing*, June (1982), pp. 80–81.

B.C. Cole, 'Artificial intelligence and the personal computer user', *Interface Age*, April (1981), pp. 88–90.

F. Da Costa, 'ARASEM: a programming approach for robots', *Interface Age*, April (1978), pp. 156–57.

R. Crawshay-Williams, *Russell Remembered* (Oxford University Press, 1970).

J. Darlington, 'An experimental program transformation and synthesis system', *Artificial Intelligence*, 16, (1981), pp. 1–46.

R. Dawkins, *The Selfish Gene* (Oxford University Press, 1976).

W. Daxer and E. Zwicker, 'On-line isolated word recognition using a microprocessor system', *Speech Communication*, May (1982), pp. 21–27.

J.K. Dixon, S. Salazar and J.R. Slagle, 'Research on tactile sensors for an intelligent naval robot', *Proceedings of the Ninth International Symposium on Industrial Robots* (1979), pp. 507–17.

H.L. Dreyfus, *What Computer Can't Do* (Harper and Row, New York, 1972).

A. Dunlop, 'Integrated circuit mask compaction', unpublished PhD thesis, Carnegie Mellon University, (1979).

J.C. Eccles, *Brain and Conscious Experience* (Springer International Berlin, Heidelberg and New York, 1966).

J.C. Eccles, 'The cerebral cortex', in *The Self and Its Brain*, eds K.R. Popper and J.C. Eccles, (Springer International, Berlin, London, New York, 1977).

G.W. Ernst and A. Newell, *GPS: A Case Study in Generality and Problem Solving* (Academic Press, New York, 1969).

E.A. Feigenbaum, 'Simulation of verbal learning behaviour', in *Computers and Thought*, eds E.A. Feigenbaum and J. Feldman (McGraw-Hill, New York, 1963).

E.A. Feigenbaum, 'Information processing and memory', in *Proceedings of the Fifth Berkeley Symposium on Mathematics, Statistics and Probability*, 4, (1967).

A. Feller, 'Automatic layout of low-cost quick turn-around random-logic custom LSI design', *Proceedings of the Thirteenth Design Automation Conference* (1978), pp. 206–12.

E.A. Fiegenbaum and J. Feldman, *Computers and Thought* (McGraw Hill, New York, 1963).

A. Filo, 'Designing a robot from nature. Part 1: Biological considerations', *Byte*, February (1979a), pp. 12–29.

A. Filo, 'Designing a robot from nature. Part 2: Constructing the eye', *Byte*, March (1979b), pp. 114–23.

M.J. Fitter and P.J. Cruickshank, 'The computer in the consulting room: a psychological framework', *Behaviour and Information Technology*, 1, 1 (1982) pp. 81–92.

Fluid Technology Laboratory, Aeronautic Research Institute of Sweden, *Industrial Robots: Gripper Review* (International Fluidics Services, Bedford, England, 1977).

J.A. Fodor, 'The mind–body problem', *Scientific American*, January (1981), pp. 124–32.

J. Fox, 'Computers learn the bedside manner', *New Scientist*, 29 July (1982), pp. 311–12.

S.W. Fox (ed.), *The Origins of Prebiological Systems: and of their Molecular Structure* (Academic Press, New York, 1965).

E. Foxley, 'The harmonization of melodies by computer', *IUCC Bulletin*, 3 (1981), pp. 31–34.

L. Froechlich,'Give Tchaikovsky the news', *Datamation* (October 1981), pp. 130–140

R.C. Garrett, 'A natural approach to artificial intelligence', *Interface Age*, April (1978), pp. 80–83.

F.H. George, *The Brain as a Computer* (Pergamon Press, Oxford, 1961).

F.H. George, 'Artificial intelligence', in *Computers and the Year 2000*, (NCC Publications, 1972).

I.J. Good, 'Pursuit curves and mathematical art', *Mathematical Gazette*, 43 (1959), pp. 134–35.

G.A. Gorry, 'Computer-assisted clinical decision making', *Method. Inf. Med.*, 12 (1973), p. 45.

P. Groner, 'Computer aided design of VLSI saves man-hours, reduces errors', *Control Engineering*, April (1981), pp. 55–7.

A. Guzman, *Computer Recognition of Three-Dimensional Objects in a Visual Scene* MIT Artificial Intelligence Laboratory (Cambridge, Mass, 1968), pp. 447–49.

H.F. Harlow, 'The formation of learning sets', *Psychological Review*, 56 (1949), pp. 51–65.

D.L. Hintzman, 'Explorations with a discrimination net model for paired-associate learning', *Journal of Mathematical Psychology*, 5, 5 (1968), pp. 123–62.

G.T. Hitch, 'Developing the concept of working memory', in *Cognitive Psychology: New Directions*, ed. G. Claxton (Routledge and Kegan Paul, London, 1980).

D. Hofstadter, *Gödel, Escher, Bach: An Eternal Golden Braid* (Harvester Press, Brighton, 1979).

R. Hollis, 'Newt: a mobile cognitive robot', *Byte*, June (1977).

E. Hunt, 'What kind of computer is man?'. *Cognitive Psychology*, 2 (1971), pp. 57–98.

W.R. Iversen, 'Vision systems gains smarts', *Electronics*, 7 April (1982), pp. 89–90.

R.D. Iverson, P.J. Arnott and G.W. Pfeiffer., 'A software interface for speech recognition, *Computer Design*, 21, 3 (1982), pp. 147–51.

I.L. Jains and L. Mann, *Decision Making* (The Free Press, New York, 1977).

R. Johnston, 'Computer is "leading the artist into new trains of thought"', *Computer Weekly*, 26 February (1981).

M. Jones, 'Chess programs move ahead', *Computing*, 14 January (1982).

T.A. Jones, 'Towards a robust monitor for detecting toxic gases', *Sensor Review*, January (1982), pp. 14–19.

S.J. Kaplan and D. Ferris, 'Natural language in the DP world', *Datamation*, August (1982), pp. 114–20.

L. Kay, 'Air sonars with acoustical display of spatial information in animal sonar systems', *Jersey Symposium*, April 1–8 (1979).

E.W. Kent, 'The brains of men and machines', *Byte* (April 1978), pp. 66–89.

J.J. Kessis, J.P. Rambant and J. Penne, 'Six legged walking robot has brains in its legs', *Sensor Review*, January (1982), pp. 30–32.

R.M. Kiehn, 'Artificial intelligence and entropy', *Byte* (1979), pp. 152–54.

D.B. Kitsz, 'A short history of electronic music', *Microcomputing* (1980), pp. 27–28, 30.

J. Klir and M. Valach, *Cybernetic Modelling* (Iliffe Books, London, 1965).

R.P. Knill-Jones, 'A computer assisted diagnostic system for dyspepsia', paper presented at British Computer Society Medical Specialist Groups

Symposium on Computers and the Clinician, Royal Hallamshire Hospital, Sheffield (1981).
K. Lacey, 'Factory where man is a mere observer', *Machinery and Production Engineering*, 3 March (1982).
P. Large, *The Micro Revolution* (Futura, 1980).
S. Lem, 'Prince Ferrix and the Princess Crystal', *The Cyberiad*, trans. M. Kandel (Seabury Press, New York, 1974).
L. Leohlich, 'Give Tchaikovsky the news', *Datamation*, October (1981), pp. 130–40.
M. Levine, 'Hypothesis behaviour', in *Behaviour of Nonhuman Primates*, Vol. 1, eds A.M. Schrier, H.F. Harlow and F. Srollnitz, (Academic Press, London, New York, 1956).
D. Levy, 'Dominoes', *Personal Computer*, September (1981), pp. 99, 101 and 167.
R.C. Lewontin, *The Genetic Basis of Evolutionary Change* (Columbia University Press, New York, London, 1974).
W.G. Lycan, 'The civil rights of robots', lecture at Kansas State University (1972).
R. Maconie and C. Cunningham, 'Computers unveil the shape of melody', *New Scientist*, 22 April (1982), pp. 206–9.
L. Marce, M. Julliere, H. Place and H. Perrichot, 'A semi-autonomous remote controlled mobile robot', *Industrial Robot*, December (1980), pp. 232–35.
A.J. Marcel and K. Patterson, 'Word recognition and production: reciprocity in clinical and normal studies', in *Attention and Performance*, ed. J. Reawin (Lawrence Erlbaum, Hillsdale, N.J., 1978).
D. Marr, 'Early processing of visual information', *Philosophical Transactions of the Royal Society B*, 275 (1976), pp. 483–534.
P. Marsh, 'Robots see the light', *New Scientist*, 12 June (1980), pp. 238–40.
R. Masuda and K. Hasegawa, 'A design approach to total sensory robot control', *Sensor Review*, January (1982), pp. 20–24.
W.E. Matheson, 'The brain and the machine', *Personal Computing*, (April 1978), pp. 37–45.
R.B. McGhee and A.A. Frank, 'On the stability properties of quadruped creeping gaits', *Mathematical Biosciences*, 3, 3/4 (1968), p. 331.
R.B. McGhee, 'Control of legged locomotion systems', *Proceedings of the Eighteenth Joint Automatic Control Conference*, San Francisco, June (1977), pp. 205–15.
R.B. McGhee and Geoffrey L. Iswandhi, 'Adaptive locomotion of a multilegged robot over rough terrain', *IEEE Transactions on Systems, Man and Cybernetics*, SMC-9, 4, April (1979), pp. 176–82.
K. McKean, 'Computer, fiction and poetry', *Byte*, July (1982), pp. 50–53.
J. McLeod, 'Transaction processing packs advanced capabilities into speech-recognition systems', *Electronic Design*, 22 July (1982), pp. 39–40.
D. Michie, *On Machine Intelligence* (Edinburgh University Press, 1974), p. 39.
D. Michie, 'P-KP4; expert system to human being conceptual checkmate of dark ingenuity', *Computing*, 17 July 1980.

J.K. Millen, 'Programming the game of Go', *Byte*, April (1981), pp. 102–18.

G.A. Miller, 'The magic number seven, plus or minus two', *Psychological Review*, 63 (1956), pp. 81–97.

G.A. Miller, E. Galanter and K.H. Pribram, *Plans and the Structure of Behaviour* (Holt, Rinehart and Winston, New York, 1960).

G.A. Miller and P.N. Johnson-Laird, *Language and Perception* (Cambridge University Press, 1976).

J.G. Miller, *Living Systems* (McGraw-Hill, New York, 1978).

H. Molloy, 'Seeing and hearing robots,' *Computing*, 9 October (1980), p. 17.

J. Monod, *Chance and Necessity* (Collins, Glasgow, 1972).

E. Muybridge, *Animals in Motion* (Dover, New York 1897).

W. Myers, 'Industry begins to use visual pattern recognition', *Computer*, May (1980), pp. 21–31.

National Resources Committee, *Technology Trends and National Policy, including Implications of New Inventions* (Report of the Subcommittee on Technology to the US National Resources Committee, Washington, US Printing office, 1937).

J. Needham, *Science and Civilisation in China*, Vol. 4, Part II (Cambridge University Press, 1965).

U. Neisser, 'Imitation of man by man', *Science, New York*, 139 (1963), pp. 193–97.

U. Neisser, *Cognitive Psychology* (Appleton-Century-Crofts, New York, 1967).

J.L. Nevins and D.E. Whitney, 'Robot assembly research and its future applications in computer vision and sensor-based robots', *Proceedings of a Symposium held at General Motors Research Laboratories* (New York, Plenum Press, 1978), pp. 275–21.

A. Newell and H.A. Simon, *Human Problem-Solving* Prentice-Hall, Englewood Cliffs, N.J., 1972).

A. Newell, J.C. Shaw and H.A. Simon, 'Elements of a theory of human problem solving', *Psychological Review*, 65 (1958), pp. 151–66.

A. Newell, J.C. Shaw and H.A. Simon, 'Report on a general problem solving program', in *Proceedings of the International Conference on Information Processing*, (Unesco House, Paris, 1959).

A. Newell, H.A. Simon and J.C. Shaw, 'Empirical explanations with the logic theory machine: a case study in heuristics', in *Computers and Thought*, eds E.A. Feigenbaum and J. Feldman (McGraw-Hill, New York, 1963).

A.M. Noll, 'The digital computer as a creative medium', in *Cybernetics, Art and Ideas*, ed. J. Reichardt (Studio Vista, London, 1971), pp. 143–64.

T. Okada and S. Tsuchiya, 'Object recognition by grasping', *Pattern Recognition*, 9 (1977), pp. 111–19.

A.I. Oparin, *The Origin of Life on the Earth* (Oliver and Boyd, Edinburgh and London, 1957).

A.I. Oparin, *Life: Its Nature, Origin and Development*, trans. A. Synge (Oliver and Boyd, Edinburgh and London, 1961).

D.E. Orin, R.B. McGhee and V.C. Jaswa, 'Interactive computer control of a six-legged robot vehicle with optimisation of stability, terrain adaptability and energy', *Proceedings of the 1976 IEEE Conference on Decision and Control*, Clearwater Beach, December (1976).

C.J. Page, A. Pugh and W.B. Higinbotham, 'New techniques for tactile imaging', 46, 11 (1976), pp. 519–26.

T.W. Parsons, 'ELIZA—a software classic for your micro', *Microcomputing* April (1982), pp. 38–40, 42.

S.G. Pauker, G.A. Gorry, J.P. Kassirer and W.B. Schwartz, 'Towards the simulation of clinical cognition', *American Journal of Medicine*, 60, (1976), p. 981.

J. Perret, 'Biochemistry and bacteria', *New Biol.* 12: pp. 68–96

J. Piaget, *The Construction of Reality in the Child* (Basic Books, New York, 1954).

N.W. Pirie, 'The meaninglessness of the terms life and living', in *Perspectives in Biochemistry*, eds J. Needham and D.R. Green (Cambridge University Press, 1937).

N.W. Pirie, 'On making and recognising life', *New Biology*, 16 (1954), pp. 41–53.

R.J. Popplestone and A.P. Ambler, 'Forming body models from range data', *DAI Research Report*, 46, University of Edinburgh, October (1977).

K.H. Pribram, 'The new neurology and the biology of emotion: a structural approach', *American Psychologist*, 22 (1967), pp. 830–38.

K.H. Pribram, 'Towards a neuropsychological theory of person', in *The Study of Personality: An Interdisciplinary Approach* (Holt, Rinehart and Winston, New York, 1968), pp. 150–60.

H. Putnam, 'Robots: machines or artificially created life?' *Philosophical Papers*, 2 (1975).

Z.W. Pylyshyn, 'Minds, machines and phenomenology: some reflections on "What machines can't do"', *Cognition*, 3, (1975), pp. 57–77.

V. Rauzino, 'Conversations with an intelligent chaos', *Datamation*, May (1982), pp. 122–36.

J. Reichardt (ed.), *Cybernetics, Art and Ideas* (Studio Vista, London, 1971).

J. Reichardt, *Robots: Fact, Fiction and Prediction* (Thames and Hudson, London, 1978).

J.S. Reitman, 'Information processing model of STM', in *Models of Human Memory*, ed. D.A. Norman (Academic Press, London and New York, 1970).

S.K. Roberts, 'Artificial intelligence', *Byte*, September (1981), pp. 164–78.

W. Rogers, B. Ryack, and G. Moeller, 'Computer-aided medical diagnosis: literature review', *International Journal of Bio-Medical Computing*, 10 (1979), pp. 267–89.

S. Rose, *The Conscious Brain* (Penguin, Harmondsworth, 1976).

J. Rostand and A. Tétry, *Larousse Science of Life* (Hamlyn, London, 1971).

B. Russell, *The Analysis of Mind* (Allen and Unwin, London, 1921).

N.P. Ruzic, 'The automated factory—a dream come true?' *Control Engineering*, April (1972), pp. 58–62.

R.C. Schank, 'Conceptual dependency: a theory of natural language understanding', *Cognitive Psychology*, 3 (1972), pp. 552–631.

R. Schank and C. Riesbeck, *Inside Computer Understanding* (Lawrence Erlbaum Associates, New York, 1981).

K.E. Scheibe and M. Erwin, *Journal of Social Psychology*, 108, 2 (1980), p. 103.

P.A. Schrodt, 'Microcomputers in the study of politics, predicting wars with the Richardson arms-race model', *Byte*, July (1982), pp. 108–34.

G.W. Scraggs, 'Answering questions about processes', in *Explorations in Cognition* eds D.A. Norman and D.E. Rumelhant (W.H. Freeman, San Francisco, 1975).

M. Scriven, 'The mechanical concept of mind', *Mind*, lxii 246 (1953).

J.R. Seale, 'Minds, brains and programs', in *The Mind's I*, ed. D.R. Hofsradter (Harvester Press, Brighton, 1981), pp. 353–73.

O.G. Selfridge, 'Pattern recognition and learning', *Methodos*, 8 (1956), pp. 163–76.

O.G. Selfridge and U. Neisser, 'Pattern recognition by machine', *Scientific American*, 203 (1960), pp. 60–68.

O.G. Selfridge, 'Pandemonium: a paradigm for learning', in *The Mechanisation of Thought Processes* (HMSO, London), reprinted in *Pattern Recognition*, ed. L. Uhr (John Wiley, New York, 1966).

C.E. Shannon, *The Mathematical Theory of Communication* (University of Illinois Press, Chicago, 1962).

M. Shelley, *Frankenstein, or the Modern Prometheus* (Lackington, Hughes, Harding, London, 1818).

H.A. Simon and A. Newell, 'Heuristic problem solving: the next advance in operations research', *Operations Research* 6, January/February (1964).

G.L. Simons, *Robots in Industry* (NCC Publications, 1980).

G.L. Simons, *Computers in Engineering and Manufacture* (NCC Publications, 1982).

S.N. Simunovic, 'Parts mating theory for robot assembly', *Proceedings of the Ninth International Symposium on Industrial Robots* (1979), pp. 183–91.

B.F. Skinner, *Beyond Freedom and Dignity* (Knopf, New York/Jonathan Cape, London, 1972).

A. Sloman, *The Computer Revolution in Philosophy: Philosophy, Science and Models of Mind* (Harvester Press, Brighton, 1978).

A. Sloman and M. Croucher, 'Why robots will have emotions', *Proceedings of the Seventh Joint Conference on Artificial Intelligence*, August (1981).

K. Sofer, 'Art? Or Not Art?' *Datamation*, October (1981).

J.J.C. Smart, 'Professor Ziff on robots', *Analysis*, xix, 5 (1959).

D.N. Spinelli, 'OCCAM: a content-adressable memory model for the brain', in *The Biology of Memory*, eds K.H. Pribram and D.E. Broadbent (Academic Press, New York, 1970).

T. Stackhouse, 'A new concept in robot wrist flexibility', *Proceedings of the Ninth Symposium on Industrial Robots* (1979), pp. 589–99.

R. Strehl, *The Robots Are Among Us* (Arco Publishers, London and New York, 1955).

S. Streufert, 'Complex military decision making', *Naval Research Review*, 23 September (1970), p. 12.

K.T. Strongman, *The Psychology of Emotion*, John Wiley, 1978.

J. Szentagothai, 'The "module concept" in cerebral cortex architecture', *Brain Research*, 95 (1975), pp. 475–96.

J. Szentagothai and M.A. Arbib, 'Conceptual models of neural organisation', *Neurosciences Research Program Bulletin*, 12 (1974), pp. 307–510.

S. Themerson, *Bayamus* (Editions Poetry, London, 1949).

A.F. Thomas and K.J. Stout, 'Robot vision', *Engineering*, May (1980), pp. 533–37.

W.H. Thorpe, *Purpose in a World of Chance, A Biologist's View* (Oxford University Press, 1978).

S.S. Tomkins and S. Messick, *Computer Simulation of Personality* (John Wiley, New York, 1963).

A.J.B. Travis, 'An aid to pattern recognition', *The Computer Journal*, 25, 1 (1982), pp. 37–44.

A.M. Treisman, 'Contextual cues in selective listening', *Quarterly Journal of Experimental Psychology*, 12 (1960), pp. 242–48.

A.M. Turing, 'Computing machinery and intelligence', *Mind*, 59 (1950), pp. 433–60.

A.M. Uttley, 'Neurophysiological predictions of a two-pathway information theory of neural conditioning', *Brain Research*, 102 (1976), pp. 55–70.

'Voice-recognition unit for data processing can handle 120 Words', *Electronics*, 13 March (1978), pp. 69–70.

C.H. Waddington, 'How much is evolution affected by chance and necessity?', in *Beyond Chance and Necessity*, ed. J. Lewis (Garnstone Press, London, 1974).

W.G. Walter, *The Living Brain*, Duckworth, London (1953).

S. Watanabe, 'Comments on key issues', *Dimensions of Mind*, ed. S. Hook (New York University Press, 1960).

L. Weiskrantz, 'Trying to bridge some neuropsychologic gaps between monkey and man', *British Journal of Psychology*, 68 (1977), pp. 431–45.

L. Weiskrantz, E.K. Warrington, M.D. Sanders and J.C. Marshall, 'Visual capacity in the hemianopic field following a restricted occipital ablation', *Brain*, 97 (1974), pp. 709–28.

N. Weisstein, 'Beyond the yellow Volkswagen detector and the grandmother cell: a general strategy for the exploration of operations in human pattern recognition', in *Contemporary Issues in Cognitive Psychology: The Loyola Symposium*, ed. R.L. Solso (Winston/Wiley, Washington, 1973).

J. Weizenbaum, 'ELIZA—a computer program for the study of natural language communication between man and machine', *Communication Associates Computing Machinery*, 9 (1966), pp. 36–45.

J. Weizenbaum, *Computer Power and Human Reason: from Judgment to Calculation* (W.H. Freeman, San Francisco, 1976).

D.E. Whitney and J.L. Nevins, 'What is the remote centre compliance (RCC) and what can it do?' *Proceedings of the Ninth International Symposium on Industrial Robots* (1979), pp. 135–52.

Norbert Wiener, *Cybernetics, or Control and Communication in the Animal and the Machine* (MIT Press and John Wiley, New York, 1961).

E.P. Wigner, 'The probability of the existence of a self-reproducing unit', in *The Logic of Personal Knowledge* (Routledge and Kegan Paul, 1961).

Y. Wilks, 'An artificial intelligence approach to machine translation', in *Computer Models of Thought and Language*, eds R. Shanle and K. Colby (W.H. Freeman, San Francisco, 1973).

Y. Wilks, 'Dreyfus's disproofs', *British Journal of the Philosophy of Science*, 27 (1976), pp. 177–85.

J. Williams, 'STICKS—a new approach to LSI design', unpublished MA thesis, Massachusetts Institute of Technology (1977).

T. Winograd, 'Understanding natural language', *Cognitive Psychology*, 3, 1 (1972), pp. 1–191.

T. Winograd, 'Artificial intelligence: when will computers understand people?', *Psychology Today*, May (1974).

T. Winograd, 'Computer memories: a metaphor for memory organisation', in *The Structure of Human Memory* ed. C. Cofer (W.H. Freeman, San Francisco, 1975).

P.H. Winston, *Learning Structural Description from Examples* (MIT Artificial Intelligence Laboratory, Cambridge, Mass., 1970).

P.H. Winston, 'Learning to identify toy block structures', in *Contemporary Issues in Cognitive Psychology: The Loyola Symposium*, ed. R.L. Solso (Winston/Wiley, Washington, 1973).

M. Witkowski, 'Man–machine clanks into step', *Practical Computing*, (March 1980), pp. 82–9.

M. Witkowski, 'Communication is problem in programmed control', *Practical Computing*, May (1980), pp. 90–94.

M. Witkowski, 'Planning techniques find optimal routes', *Practical Computing*, June (1980), pp. 90–93.

P.M. Wortman, 'Medical diagnosis: an information processing approach', *Computing and Biomedical Research*, 5 (1972), p. 315.

R.H. Wurtz, M.E. Goldberg and D.L. Robinson, 'Brain mechanisms of visual attention', *Scientific American*, June (1982), pp. 100–107.

M. Yachida and S. Tsuji, 'Industrial computer vision in Japan', *Computer*, May (1980), pp. 50–62.

S. Yanchinski, 'And now—the biochip', *New Scientist*, 14 January (1981), pp. 68–71.

P. Ziff, 'The feelings of robots', *Analysis*, xix, 3 (1959).

Index

AARON (program) 73
ADABAS (database system) 133
Advanced Robotics (company) 20
Aesop's fables 70
aesthetics, generative 68
algorithms 24, 52, 53, 61, 69, 70, 74, 141, 186
amoeba 7, 107
Aquinas, Thomas 35
ARASEM (program) 151-2
arms, for robots 81-3
artificial intelligence (AI) 28-30, 45-6, 52, 53, 54, 61-6, 107-57
Asimov, Isaac 40-1
Assembly Automation (journal) 21, 96
assembly, by machine 19, 20, 52, 60, 84, 93-4, 96
Assembly Engineering (journal) 21
assembly, molecular 19
Astounding Science Fiction 41
Atari Video Computer System 76
Author (program) 71
autonomy 67, 77-8, 147-52

Babbage, Charles 39
backgammon 77, 109
Bacon, Roger 35
Battelle Laboratories 84
Bayes, Thomas 63
Bayes's rule 63
Bee Orchid 19
Bell Laboratories 74
behaviourism 123, 124, 125
Bergson, Henri 4
Berliner, Hans 77
Bernal, J.D. 5
Berrill, N.J. 11-12
biochips 43, 192-3
Boden, Margaret 173
Bonaparte, Napoleon 37
Boole, George 39
Bracelli, Giovanni Battista 39

brains—computer 9, 43, 80, 103-6, 189-90
—in animals 31, 110, 111, 112, 113, 114, 115, 125, 159
Britain 58
British Robot Association 58
Brunel University 96
Buddha 35
Bulova Corporation 94
BUPA 184
Butler, Samuel 9, 18, 30, 50, 167

Cadbury 59
California University 70
Cambodia, bombing of 2
cameras, television 53, 55, 57, 93, 94, 95
Capek, Karel 40
Carnegie-Mellon University 63, 101, 190
Celsus 35
central processing units (CPUs) 111, 163
Cerebellar Model Arithmetic Computer (CMAC) 60
Charles Stark Draper Laboratory 20
checkers (draughts) 78
chess 48, 76-7, 109
Chess Federation (US) 76
Chicago World Fair 47
China 34, 35, 78
Chomsky, Noam 151
Cincinnati Milacron 84
Clarke, Arthur C. 45, 165
classification, of machines 27-8
CNC systems 17
cognition 123-43
Cohen, Harold 72-3
Colorado University 55
compliance, as passive control technique 20

computer, impact on
   psychology 123–6
computers—data flow 190
      —fifth generation 25–6, 155, 190, 191
Congress of Cybernetics (Paris, 1951) 38
consciousness 10, 16, 30, 118–23, 156, 159
CONSIGHT system 93
Copernicus 3
cortex, cerebral 114, 115, 191
Cray computers 190
creation (myths) 33–4, 38
creativity 52, 66–75, 109, 142–3, 151, 156
Ctesibius 34
Cubot (robot) 84
cyberanimetrics 110
Cyber computers 190
cybernetics 5, 6, 30–1, 120, 146–7
Cybernetic Serendipity (exhibition) 67–8, 69, 72
Czechoslavakia 40

Daedalus 34
Darwin, Charles 3
da Vinci, Leonardo 35
de Bono, Edward 193
decision-making
  see free will
DEC PDP-11/45 computer 72
      -11/55 computer 72
defence 2, 152–3
Dehn, Natalie 71
DENDRAL 66, 75
Depero, Fortunato 42
Descartes René 36
disease, mental 152, 153
DNA helix 19
DOCTOR (program) 130, 174
dominoes 78
dreams 108, 154, 156

ears
  see senses, aural
Edinburgh University 52, 62
Egypt 33
élan vital 4
ELIZA (program) 130–2, 174
Em, David 71–2
emotion—in animals 107–8, 118, 159–60, 181–2
    —in machines 3, 30, 67, 75, 143–7, 156, 162–3, 164, 169
EMV Associates 193
EMycin 62
energy, processing of 4, 15, 80
Engelberger, Joseph 59
engine—analytical 39
    —difference 39
engineering, genetic 193
entropy x–xi
enzymes—absence of 13
    —programmed 10
EPAM (program) 127
Epic of the Creation 33
Erewhon 78
E.T. 164
ethics, in machines 147, 156, 163
Ethiopia 34
evolution—biological 51, 52, 121
    —chemical 5
    —machine 22–7, 30, 59, 90, 99–100, 114–15, 118, 122, 155, 158, 194
    —scale of 11, 12
excretion, in machines 15
expert systems 62–6, 127
Expo '70 47
eyes
  see senses, visual

Fairchild Entertainment Centre 76
feedback 20, 31, 121, 124, 146, 164
feeding—in animals 11
    —in machines 6, 15, 27, 54, 56, 81, 121
feelings, in computers
  see emotion, in machines
fertilization, in plants 19, 30
field effect transistors (FETs) 193
films 44–6
fingers, in robots 86, 98
Fluid Technology Laboratory (Stockholm) 84
frames, for poems 69
France 179
Frankenstein 38, 44
Frankenstein, Victor 8
free will 15, 30, 78, 105, 147–52, 195
Freud, Sigmund 3
Fujitsu Fanuc 17
functionalism 7–8, 145
futurists 188

Index

gaits, animal 89
Galatea 38
games, playing of 29, 37, 67, 75-8, 139, 140
  see also the individual games
gases, toxic 102
gates, logic 14, 111
General Electric Company 87
General Motors 95
generations, of machines 23, 25, 26, 58-9
genes 19, 21, 23, 25, 150
Genesis 150
Go (game) 78
goal-seeking 53, 55, 60, 90, 168
golem 34
GPS (General Problem Solver) 66, 141
graphics 68, 71-3
Greece 34
'gremlins' 177
grippers, in robots 20, 52, 59, 80, 84-6, 92-3, 97, 98-9
GROOVE (program) 74-5

HACKER (program) 10, 139, 140, 142
Haig, Alexander 153
haiku 29, 69-70, 142
Hammurabi, Code of 167
Hampton Video Systems 94
hands, of robots
  see grippers, in robots
'Harpy' project 101
Hartston, Bill 77
hearing
  see senses, aural
Hegisistratus 86
Hephaestus 8, 34
Herodotus 86
heuristics 137, 140-1
Hiller, Legaren 74
Hitachi 60
homeostasis 30, 146-7
Homeostat (Ashby) 27, 53
homo sapiens 52, 107, 120, 150
Hong Kong 76
Hughes Aircraft 91-2
Hull University 94
humour, programming of 154-5, 156
hunger, in machines 54
Huxley, Julian 119, 181

IBM 50, 74, 101
IBM 7090 computer 74
ID3 system 77-8
Ihnatowicz, Edward 43
Iliad 8, 34
ILLIAC Suite 74
Institute of Technology 86
Intellect system 132
Intel microprocessors 92
interviews, by computers 64-5, 183-4
intuition 155, 156
ion-selective FETs (ISFETs) 193
IQ tests 29
information—genetic coding of 5-6
—processing of 4, 5, 8, 15, 22, 30, 126, 128, 145
INTERNIST 66
Isaacson, Leonard 74

Jacobson, Jewna 38
Jaquet-Droz, P. and H.-L. 36, 38
Japan 17, 25, 35, 47, 48, 55, 58, 60, 65, 78, 93, 172
Jehovah 38
Jet Propulsion Laboratory, Pasadena 71-2
Jewish Museum 72
Judeo-Christianity 33-4

Kant, Immanuel 109
Kawasaki Heavy Industries 47, 94
Kircher, Athanasius 34
Klatu (robot) 175
Klein, Sheldon 70
knowledge—engineering 127
—representation 127
Komisar, Milton 73

Labyrinth 34
Lacey, Bruce 43
languages—in computers 129
—translation of 25, 29, 54, 136
—understanding of 128-34
Large, Peter 168
Laws of Robotics 41-2, 47, 48, 161, 163
learning 90, 109, 137-40, 156
legs—artificial, for people
  see prosthetics
—for robots 87-90
Lem, Stanislaw 49
Leuven, K.U. (Belgium) 20

Levy, David 76, 77
life—criteria for 11–16, 28, 29, 51, 186, 195
—definitions of 4–5
limbs, artificial, for people
see prosthetics
linguistics 125
local area networks (LANs) 114
Locoman (robot) 83
locomotion
see mobility
Logica 136
logic, fuzzy 155
Logic Theorist 141
Lovelace, Ada 39
Ludd, Ned 7
LUIGI (robot) 133–4
Lycan, William 160, 170

Macbeth 56
Machina docilis 27
  labyrinthea 27, 53
  sapiens 27, 33, 37, 38, 40, 47, 166
  sopora 27
  speculatrix 27, 53–4
Madrid 37
magnetic methods, for grippers 84, 85
Magnus, Albertus 35
mainframe computers 103, 104
see also the individual computers
Marduk 33
Mathews, Max 74
'Mechanimals' 48, 51
medical—diagnosis 61–3, 64
—systems 61–6
Meehan, Jim 70
Méliès, Georges 44
Memnon 34, 35
memory mechanisms 124, 126–9, 130, 135, 137
Metal Castings Company 104
metaphysics 4, 109
Metropolis 44–5
Michie, Donald 62, 139, 165
Mickie system 64, 65
microcomputers 49, 50, 60, 82, 93, 105, 106, 131
microprocessors 54, 59, 61, 64, 65, 76, 81, 83, 88, 89, 92, 102, 104, 113–14, 164
Mihailo Pupin Institute (Belgrade) 97
Milic, Louis 70
Miller, J.G. 6, 7

Miller, Kenneth 154–5
mimicry x
see also simulation
minicomputers 55
miners, robot 57
Minsky, Marvin 193
MIT 55
MITI (Japan) 25
Mitra 15 computer 98
Mitsubishi 93, 176
mobility 55–6, 59, 60, 86–90, 104
modelling
see simulation
world model
Molgen 62
Mondrian, Piet 186
Motorola 6800 microprocessor 54
Mullard Valve Company 46
Museum of Modern Art (New York) 72
Museum of Modern Art (San Francisco) 72
Music IV (program) 74
  V (program) 74
music, composition of 73–5
mutation 22–3, 25
Mycin 62, 66
mythology 33–4

National Physical Laboratory (NPL) 64, 65, 100
National Science Foundation (NSF) 92
National Vehicle Licensing Centre (Swansea) 168
navigation 56
Neural Logic Cyberanimate 92
Newell, Alan 63
New Scotland Yard 136
Newt (robot) 56
Ninevah 33
Nippon Electric Company 100
Nixon, Richard 2
Nottebohm, Fernando 110
Nunn, John 76, 77

Oedipus Aegyptiacus 34
Olympic Ode 34
organs, biological 80

pain
see suffering
paintings 71–2
Paolozzi, Eduardo 43

Index

PARRY (program) 132, 153-4
Pascal, Blaise 38
pattern recognition 54, 60, 91, 93, 95, 96, 101, 116, 134-7
PECOS 66
Pentagon (computers) 2
pictures, enhancement of 135
Pirie, N.W. 4
Pittsburgh University 66
poetry 29, 69-70, 71
Pribram, K.H. 110
Principia Mathematica 29, 141
problem-solving 61, 65, 116-17, 140-2
programming, by machine 77-8
programs—computer 6, 10, 21, 23, 24, 61, 65, 70-1, 73, 74, 76, 77, 97, 104, 116, 121, 122, 126-7, 132, 133, 135, 138, 139, 140, 144
    —enzyme 10
Prometheus 34, 38
Prospector 62
prosthetics 65, 81-2, 86, 192
protection, self- 16
psychology 107-57
Pygmalion 130

Quasar Industries 48, 175

Ra 33
Radio Exhibition (London, 1932) 46
Rat 33
RCC (remote centre compliance) 20
reasoning, in machines
  see thinking
religion 33-4, 38, 176-7
Renault 95
reproduction—as life criterion 15
    —capability for 5, 7, 15
    —in animals 11, 12, 18-19
    —in machines 3, 9, 16-22, 23, 51, 96
    —in molecules 26-7
    —in viruses 13
rights, civil 160-2, 163, 164-71
Robotarms (Sterling Detroit) 83
robots—Auto-Place 94, 95
    —domestic 48-9, 194
    —experimental 52-6, 87-90, 97-8
    —in comics 49
    —industrial 8, 49, 57-60, 83, 194
    —toy 47-8
    —Unimation 20, 55, 57-8, 83, 100, 104
Rowntree Mackintosh 59-60
Rubik's Cube 84
R.U.R. (Rossum's Universal Robots) 40, 46
Russell, Bertrand 117, 143-4

sagas, Nordic 86
Sales Promotional Androids (SPAs) 175
SAL (program) 127
SciSys company 76-7
SECS 66, 75
SEE (program) 135
Selspot system 65
semiconductors 112
senses—aural 29, 43, 56, 89, 100, 101-2
    —smell 102
    —tactile (touch) 52-3, 54, 87, 89, 97-100, 163
    —visual 52, 54, 56, 80, 91-7, 105, 192
Sensor Review (journal) 96
Senster, The 43, 44, 48, 51, 180
servomechanisms 31, 89, 147
Shakey (robot) 55, 139, 140
Shannon, Claude 53, 54
Shelley, Mary 38
Sherrington, Charles 115
SHRDLU (program) 140
Simon, Herbert 63
simulation 2-3, 9, 10, 16, 88, 111, 118, 120, 121-2, 123, 126-8, 132, 135, 144, 151, 153-4, 155, 190
singing, in birds 110
skin, for robots 97-8
Sladek, John 49
Sloman, Aaron 160
Spain 37
spectrum, Sinclair 49
speech—recognition 101-2
    —synthesis 101
    —understanding 100, 101
Sperry-Univac 24
SRI International 62
ST/10-1, 080262 74
Stanford University 62, 66, 73, 82
Starship (program) 71

Sterling Detroit Company 83
STRIPS (program) 139
structure, as life criterion 15
suffering 158, 161
surveillance 1–2
survival 31, 54, 81, 121–2, 123, 156, 165
Sussman, Gerald 10
Sweden 58, 65
Swift, Jonathan 68–9, 70
Switzerland 36
synergetics 191

Tale-Spin (program) 70–1
Talmud 86
Talus 34
Tee Toddler (robot) 92
telechirics 57
Teleng Television Computer Centre 76
templates—gene 19
  —matching of 136
Tenenbaum, J.M. 137–8
Tesler's Theorem 29, 144
Texas Instruments 95
text processing 68–71
Themerson, Stefan 194
thermodynamics, second law of x–xi
thinking—in animals 108–9
  —in machines 13, 27, 29, 51–2, 56, 61, 62, 63, 66, 111, 123, 130
Thring, Meredith 48, 57, 194
Toyota 58
transfer, of materials 58
translation
  see languages, translation of
Turing, A.M. 14, 120, 178
Turing test 14–15, 130, 132

Ultra-Intelligent Machine (UIM) 194
Unimation 50, 59
United Nations 7
United States 58, 62, 76, 101, 189
Univac 1108 computer 68

Urada, Kenji 47, 172
US Army 87
USSR 87

vacuum methods, for grippers 84, 85
Ventilator Manager (VM) 66
vidicon camera 93
Villa, Luigi 77
virus 5, 12–13
vitalism, metaphysical 4
VLSI circuits 15, 23–4, 25
voice—recognition of
  see speech recognition
  —synthesis of
  see speech synthesis
von Kempelen, Wolfgang 36, 37
von Leibniz, Wilhelm Gottfried 38
von Neumann, computer designs 26
Vulcan 34

WABOT-1 (robot) 55
Walter, W. Grey 27–8
war, prediction of 79
Warwick University 191
Waseda University 55
Watanabe, Satosi 119
Weizenbaum, Joseph 3, 16, 173, 174
Westinghouse Electric Corporation 46, 48
West Germany 58
Wiener, Norbert 9, 21, 38
Wimex (defence system) 153
Wisard system 96
Wisconsin University 70, 87
world model 55, 89, 90, 99, 126, 131–2
wrists, in robots 20, 84

Xenakis, Iannis 74

Yale University 71
Yamazaki Machinery Works 16–17
Yasukawa 94

Zagorujko, L. 77
ZX81 computer 15